DIPLOMATIC ASYLUM

DIPLOMATIC ASYLUM

LEGAL NORMS AND POLITICAL REALITY IN

LATIN AMERICAN RELATIONS

by

C. NEALE RONNING

Tulane University, New Orleans

MARTINUS NIJHOFF / THE HAGUE / 1965

PRINTED IN THE NETHERLANDS

TABLE OF CONTENTS

PART I

INTRODUCTION

The legal status of the institution of diplomatic asylum really presents two separate questions. (1) Is there evidence that states have regarded the practice of granting such asylum to political refugees as sanctioned by a rule of international law? (2) Assuming this to be the case, does the available evidence make it possible to define a "political refugee" and to determine which party to a dispute has the right to decide upon this question?

While in many cases the two questions are not clearly separated in the discussions between the parties involved, they will be treated separately in the following pages. Part one will attempt to answer this question: *Assuming* the political nature of an offence can be established, is there evidence that states have regarded the practice of granting diplomatic asylum as sanctioned by a rule of international law? Obviously, the two questions cannot be separated entirely but it seems advisable to try to isolate them as much as possible.

CHAPTER I

NATURE AND SCOPE OF THE PROBLEM

The term "asylum" is used to identify such a variety of phenomena that the following distinctions must be made before the problem can be properly discussed

1. *Between diplomatic and territorial asylum.* The importance of this distinction was pointed out by the International Court of Justice in the *Colombian-Peruvian Asylum Case*,[1] often referred to as the *Haya de la Torre Case.*

In the case of extradition, the refugee is within the territory of the State of refuge. A decision with regard to extradition implies only the normal exercise of territorial sovereignty. The refugee is outside the territory of the State where the offence was committed, and a decision to grant him asylum in no way derogates from the sovereignty of that State.

In the case of diplomatic asylum the refugee is within the territory of the State where the offence was committed. A decision to grant diplomatic asylum involves a derogation from the sovereignty of that State. It withdraws the offender from the jurisdiction of the territorial State and constitutes an intervention in matters which are exclusively within the competence of that State. Such a derogation from territorial sovereignty cannot be recognized unless a legal basis is established in each particular case.

For these reasons, it is not possible to deduce from the provisions of agreements concerning extradition any conclusions which would apply to the question now under consideration.[2]

It is interesting to note that the government of Chile drew the same distinction in connection with a case in 1851.

The Law of Nations establishes a great difference between asylum which a nation concedes in its own territory and that which a diplomatic minister accords in some cases, in virtue of the immunities which his house affords ... Asylum which a nation grants on its own soil is more ample, may be conceded in a

---

[1] *Colombian-Peruvian Asylum Case, Judgment of November 20th, 1950:*I.C.J. *Reports* 1950, p. 266.

[2] *Ibid.*, pp. 274-275.

greater number of cases and is, for that reason, more effective. The criminal who takes refuge on foreign soil ceases to exist in the country whose laws he has transgressed.[1]

This of course raises the question of exterritoriality of the diplomatic premises. Exterritoriality, however, is at most a fiction used to explain the inviolability of such establishments and, as a doctrine, it is almost universally rejected in modern international law. The large number of writers and cases cited by Oppenheim, Briggs, and Morgenstern are in support of this.[2] By way of illustration it may be noted that the Sub-Committee on Diplomatic Privileges and Immunities of the League of Nations Committee of Experts for the Progressive Codification of International Law reported the same conclusion:

> It is perfectly clear that ex-territoriality is a fiction which has no foundation either in law or in fact .... The mere employment of this unfortunate expression is liable to lead to legal consequences which are absolutely inadmissible.[3]

A circular sent to American diplomatic officers in Latin America in 1930, dealt with the question of diplomatic immunities in relation to asylum as follows.

---

[1] Veras, Minister of Foreign Relations of Chile, to the Minister from the U. S., May 15 1851, Chile, Ministerio de Relaciones Exteriores, *Jurisprudencia de la cancillería chilena, hasta 1865, año de la muerte de Don Andrés Bello*, por Alberto Cuchaga Ossa (Santiago de Chile: Imprenta Chile, 1935), p. 260. (My translation). Hereafter cited as Chile, *Jurisprudencia de la cancillería chilena*.

This view is widely held among publicists. "It is almost unnecessary to point out the difference between protection afforded by a state to a refugee by granting him an asylum in or upon its diplomatic or consular buildings or public ships within the territory of the State that 'wants' him, and the protection which a refugee obtains by escaping to, or, running upon, the territory of a State other than the State that 'wants' him ..." Lord McNair, *International Law Opinions: Selected and Annotated* (Cambridge: the University Press, 1956), p. 67.

[2] L. Oppenheim, *International Law: A Treatise* (7th ed. by H. Lauterpacht; New York: Longmans, Green and Co., 1955), p. 793n. For similar expressions of policy in numerous diplomatic exchanges see Felice Morgenstern, "Extra-Territorial Asylum," *The British Yearbook of International Law*, XXV (1948), pp. 236-240. For decisions to this effect by French, German, and Afghan courts see Herbert W. Briggs, *The Law of Nations* (2d ed.; New York: Appleton-Century-Crofts, 1952), pp. 790-791.

[3] Doc. C. 196. M. 70 (1927), V, p. 79. The report of the full committee stated that it did not consider that the conception of ex-territoriality, whether regarded as a fiction or given as a literal interpretation, furnishes a satisfactory basis for practical conclusions." Thus, so far as asylum was concerned, the Sub-Committee on Diplomatic Immunities said there was no need to pronounce upon the question since "all that is not connected at any rate directly, with diplomatic prerogatives." *Ibid.*, pp. 76, 80,

The comment on Article 6, of the Draft Convention on Diplomatic Immunities of the Research in International Law, Harvard Law School, says: "With the rejection of exterritoriality as an explanation for the 'inviolability' of the premises of the mission, it becomes apparent that this inviolability can have no influence upon the personal status of the individuals upon the premises, or upon the law applicable to an offense occurring there." *American Journal of International Law*, Supplement, XXVI (1932), p. 64.

Immunity from local jurisdiction is granted foreign embassies and legations to enable the foreign representatives and their suites to enjoy the fullest opportunity to represent the interests of their states. The fundamental principle of legation is that it should yield entire respect to the exclusive jurisdiction of the territorial government in all matters not within the purposes of the mission. The affording of asylum is not within the purposes of the diplomatic mission.[1]

The Soviet delegate to the United Nations took the same position in the Third Committee of the United Nations General Assembly in connection with the Bolivian and Uruguayan proposals to include the right of diplomatic asylum in the Draft Declaration of Human Rights. He opposed such a provision on the grounds that the "sole purpose of embassies and legations was to permit governments to transact business with one another." [2] Similarly, the Regulations Concerning Diplomatic Missions ... of Foreign States in the Territory of the Union of Soviet Socialist Republics of January 14, 1927, clearly assert that no right of asylum can be deduced from these immunities:

The premises occupied by diplomatic missions as well as the premises inhabited by persons mentioned in Article 2, and their families are inviolable ... Nevertheless, the inviolability of these premises gives no right to retain anyone there by force or to give asylum to persons against whom orders of arrest have been delivered by competent organs of the U.S.S.R. or of the Federated Republics.[3]

This means that a right of asylum cannot be deduced from the position of diplomatic premises in international law. It also means that rules applicable in the practice of *territorial asylum* cannot on these grounds be made applicable to the practice of *diplomatic asylum*.

As discussed here, the term will be applied only to refuge granted to persons in places enjoying diplomatic immunity from local jurisdiction. In other words, protection granted to the subject of a state *within the territory of that state* by the resident representative of a foreign state. This will limit the discussion primarily to protection granted in legations and embassies. The practice is often extended to consulates and public (and occasionally private) vessels but such cases will be considered only where it is clear that it is regarded as falling within the scope of diplomatic asylum. The term "exterritorial asylum"

---

[1] Diplomatic Serial 998, Oct. 2, 1930, MS. Dept. of State, file 311.0022/10, quoted in Green H. Hackworth, *Digest of International Law*, II (Washington: U.S. Govt. Printing Office, 1941), p. 623.

[2] Doc. A/C.3/SR.122, p. 3.

[3] Quoted in Herbert W. Briggs, *The Law of Nations* (2d ed.; New York: Appleton-Century-Crofts, 1952), p. 768.

is sometimes used to encompass all of these premises [1] but this tends to confuse an already difficult problem inasmuch as there is by no means unanimous agreement as to whether the same rule may be applied in each case. This writer feels that it is preferable to concentrate first on the form concerning which there is at least the greatest agreement and then assess the extent to which asylum granted in consulates and vessels is regarded as being subject to the same rule.

Various terms are used to distinguish between the parties involved in cases of diplomatic asylum. Two fairly standard and seemingly satisfactory terms will be employed here. The designation "territorial" will be used for the state in whose territory the embassy or legation granting asylum is located. This, then, will be the state from whose jurisdiction the refugee is removed. The designation "state of refuge" will be used for the state whose embassy or legation grants the asylum.

2. *Between "temporary" and what, for want of any agreed term, may be called "definitive" asylum.* "Temporary" asylum would be protection afforded against mob action and general lawlessness. In such cases the refugee would be surrendered on the demand of qualified officers of the government in power. Inasmuch as this does not actually withdraw the individual from the jurisdiction of the territorial state, such cases generally provoke no real controversy and will not be of major concern in this discussion. "Definitive" asylum involves the withdrawal of the refugee from the jurisdiction of the territorial state. He may, at the time of the grant of asylum, be pursued by officers of the government, by arbitrary and lawless action, or anticipate either or both of these. The significant difference between this and "temporary" asylum is that in this case (definitive), the state of refuge refuses to surrender the refugee to the jurisdiction of the territorial state. In such cases the state of refuge is willing to terminate the protection afforded only upon suitable guarantees that the refugee will not be prosecuted for the existing or anticipated charges or, more likely, only upon a guarantee of safe conduct out of the territorial state. The United States has at times asserted that it would protect the refugee until tribunals affording adequate standards of justice were available, but the discussion in chapter six will show that this does not really solve the problem.

3. *Between political offences and common crimes.* No state is known to claim or to admit a right of asylum for common criminals. The

---

[1] Morgenstern, *op. cit.*, p. 236.

problem arises in determining what is a "common criminal" and to whom it shall pertain to qualify the nature of the offence in question. It will be clear from the cases which follow that asylum is assumed to be "asylum for political offenders."

Moore points out that the practice of granting asylum in various places arose from conditions wherein punishment was a matter of private vengeance. "The slayer was pursued by the avenger of blood, and if overtaken, was summarily killed." [1] Thus it served as a means of mitigating the effects of arbitrary and indiscriminating violence. As the administration of justice improved and as private vengeance was replaced by regulated operations of tribunals of justice the practice has disappeared.

It is important to remember also that the practice arose at a time when the idea of the absolute jurisdiction of the state within its own territory had not yet fully developed.[2] In this respect, Moore asserts, that it is probably no mere coincidence that in France, where national authority was first and most completely established, evidence of "freedom of quarter" is lacking.[3]

Whether the granting of diplomatic asylum, even when the practice was most widespread, was claimed as a *legal right* by the state of refuge and admitted as such by the territorial state is perhaps of no great consequence at this point. Text writers generally assert that it was "recognized." But recognized as what? Typical of such assertions is that of John W. Foster.

The right of asylum which at one time was generally recognized in Europe has long since been abandoned there, and it is now held that the immunity of the mission premises from local jurisdiction extends only to the minister, his suite and household.[4]

But it should be noted that even at this time, although claimed and often respected, it would be difficult to show that asylum was universally recognized as a practice sanctioned by a rule of law.

---

[1] *A Digest of International Law*, II (Washington: Government Printing Office, 1906), p. 756.

[2] Maine, *Ancient Law*, p. 103, quoted in Moore, *op. cit.*, p. 761.

[3] *Ibid.*, p. 762. This is Moore's translation of *franchise des quartiers*. While it will be observed below that *franchise des quartiers* is not the same as diplomatic asylum, the principle remains the same, i.e., both practices were largely the result of the imperfect establishment of state authority.

[4] John W. Foster, *The Practice of Diplomacy as Illustrated in the Foreign Relations of the United States* (New York: Houghton, Mifflin and Co., 1906), p. 165.

Satow cites a case dated as early as 1540 where the Venetian government refused to recognize such a right and forcibly entered the house of the French ambassador in order to apprehend political criminals.[1] The Venetian government's flat denial of a right of asylum for persons accused of high treason had been supported by two cannons placed outside the French ambassador's palace. The French King was sufficiently incensed over the matter to refuse for two months an audience to the Venetian ambassador, but the audience which was finally given is of interest. The King reportedly asked the Venetian ambassador what he would do if he had been treated as the French ambassador had been treated. To this the Venetian ambassador replied: "if subjects who rebelled against Your Majesty dared take refuge in my house, I myself would deliver them to the judges; and if I would have done otherwise, I should have been rigorously punished by the Republic." [2] According to de Martens, "this sage answer succeeded in calming the monarch." [3]

The controversy between Pope Innocent XI and Louis XIV is often cited but really sheds little light on diplomatic asylum as it is conceived today and as it is treated in this discussion. The Pope had resolved to abolish the privilege then known as the *franchise du quartier*. The English, Polish, and Spanish ambassadors gave up the privilege, but in 1687, when the Pope gave notice to the French court, Louis XIV declared that he would be deprived of none of his rights and sent a force of seven hundred men along with his new ambassador in order to maintain the privilege. The Pope's answer was a bull of excommunication and the result was a quarrel which continued until 1693, when a compromise was finally reached.[4] But for purposes of this discussion the question is obscured by the fact that it is not clear whether objections were based upon the exercise of the *franchise du quartier* or the exercise of diplomatic asylum. The former, according to Satow, covered two privileges: "namely, the right to prevent the arrest of persons dwelling in the vicinity of their embassy houses, and

---

[1] Sir Ernest Satow, *A Guide to Diplomatic Practice* (2d ed., revised; New York: Longmans, Green and Co., 1922), I, p. 310. The account in M. de Flassan, *Histoire générale et raisonnée de la diplomatie française* ... (Paris: Treuttel et Würtz, 1811), II, pp. 6-8 suggests that this was a denial of a right of asylum generally, i.e., it was not a question whether or not this particular refugee could be granted asylum under a generally recognized practice. But this, like most accounts is very sketchy. See also Abraham de Wicquefort, *L'ambassadeur et ses fonctions* (Amsterdam, 1730), p. 414.

[2] Charles de Martens, *Causes célèbres du droit des gens* (deuxième édition; Leipzig: F.A. Brockhaus, 1858), I, p. 328. (Translation by Charles Ruas).

[3] *Ibid.*

[4] Satow, *op. cit.*, p. 323.

the exemption from octroi-tax supplies brought in, nominally for their use." [1] While it was clearly the first of these privileges which was at stake here, it is also clear that this involves something more than the practice of diplomatic asylum as it is conceived today. The *franchise du quartier* extended the immunity generally attached to the minister's house to the quarter of the city in which the house was situated.[2] In the specific case out of which this whole controversy arose it appears that it was the *extension* of the privilege to an area beyond the house to which the Pope objected and not the exercise of the right of asylum within the minister's house itself. It also appears that it was the former privilege only which the French King agreed to abandon,[3] but it would be difficult to draw any positive conclusions as to what the attitudes were toward the practice of diplomatic asylum as contrasted with the *franchise du quartier*.

In 1702 the French ambassador at Copenhagen granted asylum to Count de Schlieben who had been arrested "on a charge of embezzling money for recruiting a regiment for the Danish service." We are only told that a controversy developed and that the French ambassador "was recalled shortly afterwards, and a secretary was left in charge of the French embassy." [4] There can be little doubt, however, that the Danish government refused to concede any right of asylum for what would today be called "political refugees."

> ... The protection which you are granting to a criminal of state [is] equally out of conformity with the dignity of a representative, and with the just sentiments assured him by our most Christian King. In conclusion, I must tell Your Excellency that the King is no longer in any humor to suffer in his kingdom the interference of interrupting the course of justice and of exercising acts of sovereignty, having had until now enough complacency to show the world that it is the only consideration for the person of His Very Christian Majesty ...[5]

The French ambassador answered with a long and rather insulting note in which he explained his conduct. Among other things. he said:

---

[1] *Ibid.*, p. 315.

[2] See also Moore, *op. cit.*, p. 759; Raoul Genet, *Traité de diplomatie et de droit diplomatique* (Paris: Librairie de la Cour d'Appel et de l'Ordre des Avocats, 1931), p. 557; P. Pradier-Fodéré, *Cours de droit diplomatique* (Paris: Librairie de la Cour d'Appel et de l'Ordre des Avocats, 1899), II, p. 107.

[3] Satow, *op. cit.*, pp. 316, 323; Pradier-Fodéré, *op. cit.*, pp. 107-111; Genet, *op. cit.*, pp. 558-559.

[4] Satow, *op. cit.*, p. 310.

[5] Note addressed to Count de Chamilli (no date), quoted in M. de Flassan, *op. cit.*, IV, p. 234. (Translation by Charles Ruas).

... I don't understand how one can blame me for exercising "the right of asylum," established with all ambassadors of the christian world several centuries before I was born, and which will not suffer any extension by the use made for the Count de Schlieben ...[1]

Nevertheless, M. de Flassan concludes, this letter "did not succeed, and the Count de Chamilli [the French ambassador] was soon after recalled by his court, leaving only a legation secretary at Copenhagen.[2]

In 1714 a merchant (a native of Russia, domiciled in Sweden) was convicted of high treason in Sweden. He escaped from prison and took refuge in the house of the English ambassador. The Swedish government surrounded the house and the ambassador surrendered the refugee under protest. The English government instructed its ambassador to demand redress, but such demands were of no avail. The ambassador was then recalled from London and diplomatic relations were for a time suspended.[3]

In 1726, the Duke of Ripperda, who was accused of high treason, took refuge in the residence of the British ambassador in Madrid. When the British ambassador refused to surrender the fugitive the latter was arrested and removed. The Council of Castile had ruled that such asylum would "operate to the subversion and utter ruin [of sovereigns] if persons who had been intrusted with the finances, the power and the secrets of the state, were, when guilty of violating the duties of their office, allowed to take shelter *under a privilege which had been granted to the houses of ambassadors in favor of only ordinary offenders."* [4]

Satow asserts that "the Spanish Court ... began to regret that it had not from the first accused Ripperda of some common crime, in which case Stanhope would not have given him asylum." [5] This is a little difficult to reconcile with his observation that "it appears from the Spanish Circular of May 25th, [Sept. 27th] 1726, that the privilege of asylum at foreign embassies covered common-law crimes (délits communs) in Spain, at least, though not in all countries, but was not held to extend to political offences." [6] Whatever may have been the practice regarding common crimes, it is clear that the Council of Castile regognized no right of asylum for what would today be called

[1] Note of July 1, 1702, *ibid.*, p. 236. (Translation by Charles Ruas).
[2] *Ibid.*, p. 238. See also Abraham de Wicquefort, *op. cit.*, p. 414.
[3] Moore, *op. cit.*, p. 766.
[4] *Ibid.*, p. 765.
[5] *Op. cit.*, p. 312.
[6] *Ibid.*, p. 313n, citing de Martens, i, p. 195.

"political offenders." De Martens observes that they "recognized the duke's offence as a crime of *lèse majesté* in the highest degree" and that "criminals of this type can have no asylum, without excepting even that of the church." [1]

It is equally clear that the British government claimed no right of asylum in this case.

> ... I must begin by pointing out to you that His Majesty does not claim [ne prétend] that public ministers can protect persons who are in the service of the Princes with whom they [the public ministers] reside, or persons accused of crimes against them: and His Majesty has remarked with pleasure, that his ambassador has never had such a thought, as it evidently appears from the conduct of Mr. Stanhope towards the Duke of Ripperda ... [2]

The note then pointed out that the duke had assured the British ambassador that he was no longer in the service of the Spanish King and that there were no charges against him. In order to convince the minister of this a letter from the King was produced. The minister was told by the duke that he only feared certain enemies including "the rage and furor of the populace." [3]

The ambassador was apparently still in doubt and had an audience with the Spanish King where he was informed that the duke was not in disgrace but that the King wished to have him held in the house of the ambassador pending disposition of certain papers in the hands of the duke.[4] It seems clear that the British objection was based solely upon the violation of the immunity of the ambassador's house.

> But what surprised my King even more, which renders the treatment given to his ambassador even more censurable, is that it does not seem that before using force, after all that had happened, that proper demands were made that his ambassador give up the duke, or make him leave the building; not even after the resolution taken by the Council of Castile, by which he was declared guilty of the crime of *lèse majesté*. Even this very resolution, or what it contained, was not communicated to him until that moment that an officer of justice, accompanied by a military officer and sixty guards, having entered His Excellency's house, with orders to take him by force, remitted to him a letter from the Marquis de la Paz, in which he informed him that this was discharged by orders given by His Catholic Majesty and that his officers had orders to remove the duke from the building ... [5]

---

[1] *Op. cit.*, p. 195. (Translation by Charles Ruas).

[2] The Duke of Newcastle, Secretary of State to His Britannic Majesty, to the Marquis de Pozzo Bueno [Spanish Ambassador to Britain], June 20, 1726, *ibid.*, p. 199.

[3] *Ibid.*, p. 200.

[4] *Ibid.*, p. 201.

[5] *Ibid.*, p. 202

A case cited by Raoul Genet provides an excellent example of the failure of text writers to take note of important details.[1] In attempting to show that the ambassador's carriage enjoys the same immunities as his house, Genet refers to a case involving the French ambassador to Rome in 1750. The latter had granted asylum to some Neapolitan exiles and rebels and attempted to convey them out of Rome in his carriages. The carriages were stopped at the city gates and the refugees removed and imprisoned by the Pope's guards. In answer to the ambassador's complaint the Pope asserted that his sole motive had been that of arresting them. "Since the ambassador took the liberty of harboring villains and affording protection to every criminal in papal territory, he at least, who is the sovereign of the state, should have the right to have them retaken wherever they could be found; as the rights and privileges of the ambassador were not to be carried to any such lengths." [2] The ambassador replied "that he did not find that he had given shelter to subjects of the Pope, but to Neapolitans, to whom he could surely give protection against the Spanish." [3]

Genet merely observes that "the Pope released the prisoners and it was agreed that the nuncio would settle with the King of France upon the reparation due for the offences to the ambassadors carriage." [4] Vattel (whom Genet cites as his source) observes more correctly that, by his answer quoted above, "the minister tacitly conceded that he would not have been authorized to complain of the stoppage of his carriages, if he had employed them for the purpose of favouring the escape of any of the Pope's subjects, and aiding criminals to elude the pursuit of justice." [5]

A favorite of text writers is the case of the Duke of Sotomayor in Spain. The latter, along with a group of conspirators, had stormed the royal palace in Madrid in 1841 and, apparently unsuccessful, had been granted asylum by the Danish *chargé d'affaires*. Five years later, when the party of the conspirators was in power, the Danish *chargé* was given the title of Baron del Asilo.[6] While there is reason to believe

---

[1] *Op. cit.*, pp. 556–557.

[2] *Ibid.*, p. 556. (Translation by Charles Ruas.)

[3] *Ibid.*

[4] *Ibid.*, p. 557.

[5] *The Law of Nations or Principles of the Law of Nature Applied to the Conduct and Affairs of Nations and Sovereigns*, trans. J. Chitty (Philadelphia: T. & J. W. Johnson & Co., 1861), p. 469. But Moore, *op. cit.*, p. 760 quotes Wicquefort, with approval: "all the advantage was on the ambassador's side since the Pope, by surrendering the prisoners, tacitly owned he had done better not to have arrested them, and that he had made a noise for nothing."

[6] Satow, *op. cit.*, p. 302; Moore, *op. cit.*, p. 768.

that this represented a feeling of gratitude on the part of the conspirators the text writers offer little in the way of evidence as to what either party felt was the law in the case. Earlier Spanish and Danish cases cited by these same writers would suggest that *neither* clearly recognized a rule of law on the matter.

Shortly after this the British ambassador granted asylum to a Spanish subject involved in a revolutionary movement and was given his passport for these efforts. Moore observes, however, that it was on grounds of *abuse* of the practice that this was done and not out of an absolute refusal to recognize the practice.[1] The Duke of Sotomayor also ordered the search of the Danish and Belgian legations in an effort to apprehend certain conspirators. It may well be, as Moore observes, that the Duke of Sotomayor *recognized a right of asylum within certain limits*, especially since this was the same duke who had awarded a title in recognition of just such activities, but it is apparent that there was no agreement as to what these limits were.[2] To say that one recognizes asylum "within certain limits" is not a particularly meaningful phrase in the absence of agreement as to what these limits are.

As for the present, there is substantial agreement among foreign offices and writers that "the practice of asylum is not sanctioned by international law" and that "it can be defended only on the ground of the consent of the state within whose jurisdiction it is sought to be maintained." [1] Oppenheim observes that "during the nineteenth

---

[1] *Op. cit.*, p. 769.

[2] *Ibid.*, pp. 769–770: Pradier-Fodéré, *op. cit.*, pp. 92–93, cites several cases which took place toward the end of the 19th century. With the exception of one in Spain (for which no date is given) all of them took place in the Middle East. They are of interest here primarily because they show the extent to which some writers have gone in trying to show that the practice of asylum is widely "recognized." At the 1895 session of the institute of International Law held at Cambridge, an eminent member observed that the cases of asylum were very rare and that "a diplomatic agent will never admit a refugee into his house." On this matter Pradier-Fodéré observes that this affirmation was from several viewpoints inexact and offers some cases as evidence. He is forced to recognize that these cases were confined to the Middle East but observes that "one makes exceptions for the countries of the Orient; but Constantinople is in Europe and Turkey has been for a long time in the Concert of European States." (My translation.) In 1862 asylum was granted in the British consulates in Greece, and in 1867 in Moldavia and Wallachia but the fact that both Greece and the Danubian principalities were at this time more or less under foreign tutelage leaves their relevance open to question. See Moore, *op. cit.*, pp. 767–768.

[3] Moore, *op. cit.*, p. 779. See also Morgenstern, *op. cit.*, p. 242; Hildebrando Accioly, *Tratado de derecho internacional público*, Tomo II, (Rio de Janeiro: Imprensa Nacional, 1946), p. 344. Simon Planas–Suárez, *El asilo diplomático* (Buenos Aires: Imprenta López, 1953), pp. 15–18; Hackworth, *op. cit.*, p. 622; Sir Robert Phillimore, *Commentaries on International Law*, II (2d ed.; London: Butterworths, 1871), pp. 234–236; Amos S. Hershey, *The Essentials of International Law* (New York: Macmillan, 1921), p. 271; John Westlake, *International Law*, I (Cambridge: The University Press, 1910), p. 283; Wm. E. Hall, *A Treatise on International Law* (8th ed. by A. Pearce Higgins; Oxford: Clarendon Press, 1924), p. 233.

century the remains of this so-called right of asylum vanished, and when in 1867 the French envoy in Lima claimed it the Peruvian Government refused to concede it." [1]

But the diplomatic notes exchanged in connection with this case suggest that France claimed this as a right *based upon Latin American practice* and not as a right under general international law. Instructions from the French foreign office advised that "we can invoke a constant practice in support of what is called in America the right of asylum." [2]

At this same time, the Peruvian envoy to France and England informed his government in Lima that he had solicited the British view on this matter. After explaining the Peruvian grounds for objecting to asylum to the British Secretary of State for Foreign Affairs he noted:

> Lord Stanley, agreeing with me in these observations, remarked that if any Fenians were to take refuge in an embassy in London, it would be ridiculous to suppose that the British government would have no right to reclaim them. [3]

British policy statements have been remarkably consistent in this respect. The Queen's advocate in 1866 referred to asylum as an "exceptional privilege not in accord with general law." [4] The Law Officers of the Crown offered a statement of their views on diplomatic asylum in general in connection with a grant of asylum by the German consulate in Zanzibar in 1896.

> ...There is, in our opinion no doubt that this right of asylum, *even in the case of ambassador*, can be properly conferred only by the consent of the countries to whom they are accredited. It is in no way necessary for the discharge of an Ambassador's duty that his house should be an asylum for persons charged with crime of any description, and *no such privilege can be asserted by an Ambassador*, still less a Consul. [5]

The idea that asylum could only be justified on the basis of local toleration was again asserted in connection with the British legation

---

[1] *Op. cit.*, p. 794.

[2] DeLesseps, [French *Chargé d'Affaires*], to Pacheco, Peruvian Secretary of Foreign Relations, April 24, 1866, Peru, Secretaría de Relaciones Exteriores, *Correspondencia diplomática relativa a la cuestión sobre asilo, publicado por orden de S. E. el Jefe Supremo Provisorio para ser presentada al Congreso Constituyente* (Lima: Imprenta del Estado por J. Enrique del Campo, 1867), p. 19. (My translation.) Hereafter cited as *Correspondencia diplomática relativa a la cuestión sobre asilo*.

[3] Rivero, Peruvian Minister to France and England, to Osori, Peruvian Minister of Foreign Relations, May 30, 1867, translation (enclosure in Hovey, U. S. Minister to Peru, to Seward, U. S. Secretary of State, July 14, 1867), *For. Rel. of the U. S.* 1876, I, p. 773.

[4] *Reports from the Law Officers of the Crown*, 1866, p. 193, quoted in Morgenstern, *op. cit.* p. 243

[5] 1896, pp. 8–11, *ibid.*; McNair, *op. cit.*, p. 76. (My italics).

in Persia in 1908. Sir Edward Grey, while defending general British policy in that area, said:

There is a custom in Persia that anybody who has a grievance against the Persian Government takes refuge in a foreign Legation. It is a custom peculiar to Persia, and I am most desirous it should not be extended. In fact, it has really become necessary to keep it within bounds in Persia ... The instructions that have been given are these: That refuge is not to be refused to anyone who is in danger of life, but that refuge must not be given to people who use the Legation for political purposes ... Within these bounds we have kept.[1]

Additional case material cited by Morgenstern and McNair leave no doubt that this had been the general pattern of British policy.[2]

In 1885, the Italian legation in Bogota answered a Colombian circular on asylum and diplomatic immunities in the following words.

It is incontrovertible for me that as a general rule foreign ministers lack the faculty of conceding asylum to persons involved in the political conflicts of the country of their residence and I desire and hope that examination of the question which up until now has not been of an urgent character, will not be necessary.[3]

United States policy will be dealt with in a separate chapter but at this point it is worth noting that it has, in fact, been virtually identical to the British policy outlined above.

Nowhere has the confusion and ambiguity of the theory and practice of diplomatic asylum been better demonstrated than in the cases arising out of the Spanish Civil War. According to the Chilean delegate to the League of Nations, fourteen states had afforded protection in the embassies and legations in Madrid. Six of these fourteen were European states – Belgium, Norway, the Netherlands, Poland, Rumania, and Turkey.[4] The Proceedings of the Diplomatic Corps in Madrid in connection with a projected note to the Spanish government demonstrate the confusion and evasiveness so well that they are worth quoting at some length.

The British representative said that he could not become a party to the note on the right of asylum, to be sent to the Spanish Government; he received

---

[1] Great Britain, 193 *Parliamentary Debates*, 1908, CXCIII, pp. 975–978.

[2] Morgenstern, *op. cit.*, pp. 243–246; McNair, *op. cit.*, pp. 74–76.

[3] Segre, Italian Minister to Colombia, to Restrepo, Colombian Minister of Foreign Relations, February 21, 1885, Colombia, [Ministerio de Relaciones Exteriores?], *Anales diplomáticos y consulares de Colombia*, Tomo III, (Edición Oficial por Antionio José Uribe; Bogotá: Imprenta Nacional, 1914), p. 351.

[4] League of Nations, Council, *Official Journal*, minutes of the 96th session, January 25, 1937, p. 96.

instructions from his government not to interfere, in any respect, with the civil struggle in Spain ...

The Ambassador of the U. S. S. R. declared that he would also have to be counted out of the projected note to the government. His point of view was that the right of asylum, as it was understood in Latin America, could not be considered adaptable to Europe. Most of the efforts made in behalf of the right of asylum affected, [sic] only the Latin American States, [sic] and some others that might have a special interest in this right.

The French representative contended that the declarations of the Soviet Ambassador were personal opinions, and could not be taken as the opinion of all the European Missions. The Soviet Ambassador said that what he had expressed was only the point of view of his government ...

The Soviet representative ... observed that in Europe the right asylum was not an international law. If some of the European representatives recognize the Latin American conception of the right, the following problem would arise: some countries would receive Spanish refugees of different categories; the representatives of the United States, England, and the Soviet Union were not interested in this, without being sure of the value of this right ...

The Mexican Ambassador said that the attitude of some missions ... had to be cleared up. Was it the position of the United States, Britain, and Russia, that they did not wish to sign the note ... or was it, simply, that they did not recognize the right of asylum.

The British representative said that he had no intention of denying the right of asylum. The simple fact was that his country was not a signatory to the Montevideo or Havana treaties.

The U. S. representative said that his country held a restricted concept of the right of asylum, and considered it dangerous for American nationals to grant asylum to Spaniards ...

The Austrian representative said there were occasions when everyone was called upon to perform a humanitarian act, but this had nothing to do with the right of asylum ...

The representative of Norway stated that the right of asylum, in actual practice, was a strictly humanitarian question, and that it was impossible to deny it to a person who needed it to save his life ...[1]

At no point in this controversy did the government of Spain admit that it was under any legal obligation to respect the practice of asylum. In July 1937, after months of controversy it insisted that the magnitude of the difficulty was due to the abusive use "of the right which Spain has not recognized and which is completely foreign to the usages and customs of International Law." [2] But, "in order to resolve [the controversy] the Government applied diverse formulas, the first based

---

[1] "Proceedings of the Diplomatic Corps, In Assembly, Session of October 28, 1936, Chilean Embassy," in Henry Helfant, *The Trujillo Doctrine of Humanitarian Diplomatic Asylum* (Mexico, D. F., 1947), pp. 197–200. The author of this treatise was secretary to the Diplomatic Corps in Madrid at this time. His record is in agreement with dispatches from the U. S. envoy to Madrid: Wendlin, Third Secretary of the U. S. Embassy in Spain to the Secretary of State, October 29, 1936, *For. Rel. of the U. S.*, 1936, V, p. 749.

[2] Giral, for the Spanish Ministry of State, to Lynch, Chilean *Chargé d'Affaires*, July 7, 1937, Chile, *Memoria*, p. 263. (My translation.)

upon the greatest liberality and tolerance, when it still did not know the number of persons protected in this way." [1]

Thus, this writer must disagree with Norman J. Padelford's conclusion that "the practice and eventually the right, were accepted by the Madrid government." [2] The practice certainly was accepted for reasons already pointed out by the Spanish government and, more likely, because Spain was hardly in a position to do otherwise. That Spain held out until the bitter end is clearly indicated by an extract from the Chilean *Memoria* for 1938.

> Time was passing in these negotiations until the end of 1938, which saw the fall of Cataluña into the hands of the Nationalists and the flight of the Republican Government to France.
> With these events the activities of the English Commission of Pau were paralyzed and it was clearly seen that the refugees would leave when Madrid fell into the hands of the Nationalist forces, as in fact occurred. [3]

At the same time the Iranian delegate to the League clarified what he considered a misconception with regard to the policy of Iran. The Chilean delegate, as a part of his sweeping but not well-substantiated claims made before the League of Nations, had referred to the existence of the right of asylum in Iran. [4] In response to this, the latter government submitted the following note:

> ... The allusion was obviously to the practice of that right in remote times... I should like to make it clear that the right asylum has not for a long time past existed in Iran. [5]

The United Nations has been the scene of a very brief discussion of diplomatic asylum. This time it was in connection with the Draft International Declaration of Human Rights discussed in the Third Committee of the General Assembly. The Bolivian and Uruguayan delegations proposed amendments which would extend the right of asylum (territorial asylum was then under discussion) to embassies and legations. [6] Not one delegation outside the Latin American group spoke favorably of the amendment. [7] On the contrary, India, Pakistan,

---

[1] *Ibid.*

[2] *International Law and Diplomacy in the Spanish Civil Strife* (New York: Macmillan, 1939), p. 68.

[3] P. 436. (My translation.)

[4] League of Nations, Council, *Official Journal*, 96th sess., 3rd Meeting, Jan 25, 1937, p. 97.

[5] *Ibid.*, January 27, 1937, pp. 109–110.

[6] A/C.3/227; A/C.3/268.

[7] United Nations, General Assembly, 3rd Committee, *Official Records*, 3d sess., part I, 121st and 122d Meetings, November 3–4, 1948, pp. 335–342.

Australia, U. S. S. R., Ukraine and France opposed it.[1] Under these conditions the Bolivian and Uruguayan delegates withdrew their respective amendments. "The Latin American countries considered that right sacred: it was preferable not to submit it to the vote as an adverse vote taken by the Third Committee might create an unfortunate precedent and weaken the principle involved." [2]

Efforts aimed at the codification of international law have resulted in similar conclusions. It has already been noted that the Committee of experts of the League of Nations refused to admit any direct connection between asylum and diplomatic immunities. At the same time, the Subcommittee on the Legal Position and Function of Consuls decided that "this right is a prerogative that need not be discussed; it is quite inadmissible. No State would admit such a privilege and at the present time it ought no longer to exist, in however limited a form, *even in the case of diplomatic agents.*" [3]

The Research in International Law of the Harvard law School was even more explicit. Article 6 of the Draft Convention on Diplomatic Privileges and Immunities provides that:

A sending state shall not permit the premises occupied or used by its mission or by a member of its mission to be used as a place of asylum for fugitives from justice.[4]

The comment on this article points out that it attempts to make no distinction between "political" and "ordinary" crimes "and lays down as a general rule that the exemption of the premises of a foreign mission from the jurisdiction of the receiving state should not defeat the operation of the criminal law of the receiving state as to all fugitives from justice who do not have diplomatic immunities." [5]

---

[1] *Ibid.* The French delegate urged that "no attempt should be made to render universal what was specifically a Latin American tradition. That tradition had on certain conditions not received a purely humanitarian interpretation." The Indian delegate "could not accept the principle of extending the right of asylum to embassies and legations of foreign powers as that would give rise to serious disorders in non-American countries."

[2] *Ibid.*, pp. 345–346.

[3] Reprinted in *A.J.I.L.*, Special Supplement, XXII (January, 1928) p. 108. (My italics.) These conclusions were amended and the final report simply said "Consuls do not possess this prerogative." *Ibid.*, p. 110.

[4] *A.J.I.L.*, Supplement, XXVI (1932), p. 62.

[5] *Ibid.*, p. 65. Arthur Kuhn, commenting on the 1948 Brussels sessions of the Institute of International Law, reported that "wide divergence of opinion was manifested concerning the article treating of asylum accorded in buildings of diplomatic missions and upon battleships and other war constructions. It was found impossible to reconcile differences and accordingly it was determined to postpone further consideration of the subject to the next session of the institute." *A.J.I.L.*, XIII (1948), p. 878.

In spite of statements declaring that it is not sanctioned by international law, asylum continues to be granted sporadically not only in Latin America but in other parts of the world as well. Thus Cabral de Moncada cites thirteen cases granted in Oriental states, since 1900, by England, Germany, Italy, Turkey, Russia, Japan and the Netherlands.[1] Some additional cases will be noted in the chapter on United States practice.

How can such practice be reconciled with the statements of policy quoted above? Morgenstern has concluded that "the fact that asylum is not exercised in the territory of leading states, and is mainly resorted to in the 'backward' countries of the Near and Far [except Japan] East and of Latin America, suggests that it is a practice followed only in states who are not fully civilized in the Western sense of the term, and as such it is a temporary exception to the system of international law which obtains in the community of civilized nations." [2]

Apart from the fact that these states might raise serious objections to being classified as something less than civilized, an important qualification must be added to this statement. Strictly speaking, the practice *is*, in fact, resorted to in other parts of the world although perhaps less frequently. The Argentine *Memoria* for 1948–1949, reports that in the early part of 1948, a Spanish Jesuit Father was granted refuge in the Argentine embassy in Rumania. Following action on the part of the Argentine envoy, safe conduct was granted and the refugee left Rumanian territory.[3]

On November 24, 1956, the *New York Times* quoted the following official announcement of the Budapest Radio.

Former Premier Nagy and some of his colleagues, as is known, found asylum on November 4, in the Yugoslav Embassy in Budapest. Their stay ended November 22. For two weeks Nagy and his companions had sought permission from the Hungarian Government to leave the territory of the Hungarian People's Republic and betake themselves to the territory of another Socialist Country.[4]

---

[1] Hugo Cabral de Moncada, *O asilo interno em direito internacional público* (Coimbra, Brazil: Edição do Autor, 1946), pp. 58–62.

[2] *Op. cit.*, p. 242.

[3] P. 201.

[4] P. 2. On Nov. 13, 1956, the *New York Times*, p. 21, reported that the White House had confirmed the receipt of a letter from Joseph Cardinal Mindszenty, reportedly carried from Hungary by a correspondent of the North American Newspaper Alliance. The letter said, in part: "as a shipwreck of Hungarian liberty I have been taken abroad by your generosity in a refuge of my own country as a guest of your legation. Your hospitality surely saved me from immediate death."

The only generalization which seems at all acceptable is that the practice of states in this regard is not based upon any generally recognized *right of asylum* so far as general international law is concerned. Instead, it is a *de facto* result of the fact that international law accords to the various accredited diplomatic officers certain well-recognized immunities from local jurisdiction, such as immunity of their official residences and offices from invasion by local authorities. Humanitarian, political or other motives may lead to the original grant of asylum but once the refugee is inside the legation the territorial state is faced with an insoluble dilemma. Assuming the state of refuge will not surrender the refugee, the territorial state can apprehend him only by violating the immunity of the diplomatic premises or, possibly, by breaking diplomatic relations. The fact is that such extreme measures are considered too high a price to pay for apprehension of the refugee.[1]

But a right cannot be deduced from the mere fact that the other party has no immediate remedy. Thus there is no alternative but to call it "a temporary exception to the system of international law which obtains in the community of civilized nations." [2] But to limit the operation of this "exception" to any particular part of the world would be dangerous indeed.

It cannot be denied, however, that in some parts of the world the practice is far more widespread than in others. And in no part of the world has this practice been so widespread as in Latin America. The extent of this practice has led to claims. particularly among Latin American writers, that it is sanctioned by American International Law [3] even though it is not sanctioned by general international law.

This paper will attempt to ascertain, on the basis of practice and conventions, whether there exists a rule of law sanctioning the practice of diplomatic asylum in Latin America. This will involve, first of all,

---

[1] The comment on the Draft Convention on Diplomatic Privileges and Immunities of the Harvard Research in International Law says: " In event of the abuse of diplomatic privileges through the granting of asylum, the authorities of the receiving state are nevertheless obliged to respect the immunity of the mission. The sanction of the present article [Article 6, forbidding the grant of asylum to fugitives from justice] can be made effective only through the diplomatic channel." *A.J.I.L.*, Supplement, XXVI (January and April, 1932), p. 65. Thus, in *United States v. Jeffers*, 4 Cranch, Circ. Ct. Rep. 704, the court held that it was a violation of international law for a constable to enter the house of the secretary of the British legation and remove a fugitive slave.

[2] Morgenstern, *op. cit.*, p. 242.

[3] See dissenting opinion of Judge Alvarez in *Colombian-Peruvian Asylum Case, Judgment of November 20th, 1950:* International Court of Justice *Reports* 1950, p. 292.

a consideration of some of the questions relating to the establishment of a regional international law and the possibility of its existence. It will then consider the requirements for the creation of a customary rule of law *as related to the practice of asylum* and, on the basis of this, analyse the extent and nature of that practice.

CHAPTER II

THE HISTORICAL DEVELOPMENT OF
DIPLOMATIC ASYLUM IN LATIN AMERICA

The development of the practice of diplomatic asylum in Latin America seems to be less the result of a conscious application of European patterns than of the fact that history often shows the development of similar institutions as a product of human interaction confronted by similar circumstances in different times and different places. On the other hand, it cannot be denied that in this case the very circumstances and antecedents which gave rise to the practice of diplomatic asylum in Latin America were in large part a product of Spanish culture which was transferred to the New World. Thus, Eduardo Anze Martienzo concludes that, in Latin America, Spain and Italy, religious asylum was defended the longest due to the intense struggle between the civil power and the power of the church. A case in point is the decree of Philip II which abolished the practice of asylum in all his possession but "which was shattered against the resistence of the people and the clergy. Thus it was possible for San Carlos Borromeo to maintain the ecclesiastical privileges against the Spanish government." [1]

Two careful and well-documented studies trace this development in Guatemala and in Chile. Adolfo Molino Orantes points out that when the Spanish conquistadores came to the new world they brought with them the legal system of Spain and, as a part of this, the institution of religious asylum.[2] Attempts to limit and even abolish the practice make up much of the remainder of the story. The unsuc-

---

[1] "Acotaciones sobre el derecho de asilo," *Pan-América: revista de derecho internacional americano*, II (Buenos Aires: febrero de 1947), p. 21. See also Aviles Soriano, "El derecho de asilo, institución religiosa," *Información jurídica*, nums. 62–63 (Madrid: julio-agosto, 1948), pp. 31–35. (My translation.)

[2] "Aspectos históricos del derecho de asilo en Guatemala," *Revista de la asociación guatemalteca de derecho internacional*, N. 1 (Guatemala, Centroamérica, enero de 1954), pp. 106–119.

cessful attempt of Philip II has already been mentioned. Philip III made a more modest attempt in 1681.

> We command and charge the prelates of the churches and monasteries of our Indies not to admit delinquents who might take refuge there in those cases which, according to the law of our Kingdom of Castile, should not enjoy ecclesiastical immunity; nor to impede our justice to exercise their jurisdiction and that those who may and ought to enjoy immunity not consent nor give cause that they remain in the churches and monasteries for a long time.[1]

Up until the eve of the wars of independence repeated attempts were made through royal decrees and papal bulls to limit the offences for which asylum could be granted and the number of churches and monasteries in which it could be granted as well. It appears that the royal authority was particularly frustrated in its attempts to apprehend military delinquents, with the result that a decree of 1787 provided that they might if necessary be removed from the sacred places after certain precautions in order to ascertain whether or not the offence was one which permitted asylum. But it appears that this was to be determined by the officers of the crown.[2] Finally, in 1800, "the century ended with another royal decree which gave the *coup de grâce* to ecclesiastical asylum." [3] Hereafter, asylum could only be a delaying tactic and even in the case of certain offences for which asylum was permitted it had only the effect of placing certain limitations upon the sentence. [4]

The Church persisted in claiming its privileges and as late as 1831 asserted that "no one could be deprived of asylum except in accord with the rules established by the Holy Canons and that violence in a church would be considered as a crime." [5] But by this time "the institution of ecclesiastical asylum was totally uprooted in the public conscience." [6] In 1826 the Vice Chief of State of Guatemala, fearing popular resentment, took refuge in a church, where he was pursued by a most unpleasant mob of women. The priest's attempts to protect him by taking him to the pulpit were of no avail and the refugee was dragged from the church and thrown to the mob outside – apparently

---

[1] *Recopilación de leyes de Indias*, Madrid, 1681, Libro I, título III, Ley II, *ibid.*, 109. (My translation.)

[2] Archivo Nacional de Guatemala, documento A. 1–28. I, 4669, *ibid.*, pp. 116–117.

[3] Domingo Cavalario, *Instituciones de derecho canónico* (Valencia: 1864), p. 241, paraphrase, *ibid.*, 117. (My translation.)

[4] *Ibid.*

[5] Molino Orantes, *op. cit.*, p. 117. (My translation.)

[6] *Ibid.*

made up of caballeros less willing to face the wrath of the Church.[1]

Mario del Valle Muñoz provides a similar account of the development and decline of religious asylum in Chile.[2] Most of the same documents are cited since they applied to the Spanish Indies generally. In addition to the famous *Recopilación* of 1680 and the Royal Decree of 1787, which were a type of codification of many earlier and conflicting regulations, the number of documents cited here serves to emphasize the fact that the practice of asylum was a constantly vexing question for the Spanish crown. Among the more important documents bearing on this question are the following.

Royal Decree 1741
Royal Decree 1746
Pragmática of 1754
Decree of the Governor of Chile 1785
Royal Decree 1764
Royal Decree 1768
Royal Decree 1773
Agreement between the President and the Bishop of
    Santiago 1774
Royal Decree 1794
Royal Decree 1797 [3]

In each case there is an attempt to circumscribe further the authority of the churches and other religious places in the practice of granting asylum. But what seems most significant to this writer is the fact that the practice seems to have received its *coup de grâce* in precisely the same way that it did in Guatemala. The last of seventeen cases related by the author occurred shortly after independence was first proclaimed. Figuero, the leader of an attempt to re-establish Spanish rule, failed to do so and took refuge in the Convent of Santo Domingo. Soldiers searched the convent in vain but later apprehended the refugee in the garden of the padre, after which he (the refugee) was tried and shot.[4]

---

[1] Alejandro Maure, *Bosquejo histórico de las revoluciones de Centro América* (Paris: 1913), p. 159, cited *ibid.*, pp. 177–188.

[2] *El derecho de asilo eclesiástico en el reino de Chile*, Publicaciones de los Seminarios de la Facultad de Ciencias Jurídicas y Sociales de la Universidad Católica de Chile (Santiago: [1925?]).

[3] *Ibid.*, pp. 25–26. (Titles are my translation.)

[4] *Colección de historiadores de la independencia de Chile*, XIX, pp. 235–262, cited *ibid.*, pp. 46–47.

What are the factors responsible for the eventual termination of the practice of religious asylum in Latin America? There can be little doubt that the changed position of the church which came with the establishment of independence had an important effect here just as the rise of the state had its effect at an earlier date in Europe. It was pointed out above that the conflict between religious and secular power continued longer in Spain and Latin America than elsewhere and that this was in part responsible for the longer perpetuation of the practice of religious asylum. While this is essentially correct it should be emphasized that this struggle was of a somewhat different nature here than it had been in Europe. It is perhaps somewhat of an overstatement to say that the struggle was more akin to an interdepartmental struggle within the government, yet in some respects it did resemble just this. C. H. Haring in *The Spanish Empire in America* has described the relationship this way:

> The Church in America was under the direct and immediate control of the crown in all matters except doctrine and religious discipline. And this control was much closer, much stricter, than in any Catholic monarchy in Europe. The patronage of the Church was regarded as the most honorable and most valuable of the crown's attributes ...[1]

Thus it seems quite reasonable that the granting of asylum, while obviously annoying to the crown, presented less of a threat to its power than would have been the case had the relationship been the same as that which existed in Europe.

This relationship took a drastic change with the establishment of independence and with it a decline in the power of the church. J. Lloyd Mecham in *Church and State in Latin America* has shown that the new republics continued to grant the Church its same favored position. But a change soon took place.

> Yet, in a short time opposition to the favored cult appeared and it began to be shorn of its old privileges. In the decades of the 1820's and 1830's the Catholic Church was subjected to attack in many of the republics, particularly in Argentina, Chile, Mexico and the Federation of Central America ...
> The basis of this early opposition to the Roman Catholic organization – not the Roman Catholic religion – was largely political. The abolition of tithes, suppression of religious orders, confiscation of ecclesiastical property, and like measures, were as a rule acts of vengeance wreaked upon the clergy by their political opponents ... The ecclesiastics plunged into politics with greater zeal than ever before, for they felt, quite correctly, that their rights would be endangered in representative republics.[2]

[1] (New York: Oxford University Press, 1947), p. 180.
[2] (Chapel Hill: University of North Carolina Press, 1934), pp. 502–503.

The significance of this is not only the fact that the Church occupied a somewhat weaker position but also the fact that it was one of the factions in the numerous political struggles. It seems quite reasonable, then, that the new governments could hardly afford to let the partisans of one faction take refuge in the immunity of the Church. The cases discussed above suggest that they did not in fact allow this to happen. The rest can only be surmised, but in all probability members of political factions soon found that they could not depend upon such protection and began to look elsewhere. By this time there were representatives of foreign powers with permanent diplomatic missions within the country. The newly-recognized governments did not wish to risk the "prize" of recognition by violating the immunity of these establishments.

There follows a period of about twenty-five years during which it is apparent that the practice of granting asylum in embassies and legations was quite general. The basis upon which the practice was justified during this period is unknown to this writer but it is quite likely that it was never clearly stated by the state granting asylum. By the middle of the century it seems to be suspended in a curious position, being justified on the basis of humanitarian consideration, Latin American practice, and general international law, but it is never entirely clear which of these grounds is claimed.

In the earliest case of which there is any substantial record we find the United States Department of State approving the conduct of the minister to Venezuela in having granted asylum. He was further advised that "the extent ... to which this protection may be justly carried, must be determined by the minister himself, under the exigencies of each particular case, and with reference to the established principles of the law of nations."[1] Nowhere in the note is there any reference to Latin American practice.

Yet only three years later the Department of State advised its minister to Chile that "if there should be any precedents showing that the Chilean government had previously acquiesced in such a proceeding on the part of the diplomatic representative of any foreign nation at Santiago, it could not justly complain of your course." But it cautioned that "inasmuch, ... as the right itself is more than doubtful under the public law, and as a formal demand had been made

---

[1] Buchanan, Secretary of State, to Shields, U. S. *Chargé d'Affaires* at Caracas, March 22, 1848, Wm. R. Manning, *Diplomatic Correspondence of the United States: Inter-American Affairs, 1831–1860* (Washington: Carnegie Endowment for International Peace, 1939), XII, p. 470.

upon you for the offender, if he should still be your guest when this reaches you, it is deemed advisable that you should inform him that your house can no longer screen him from prosecution." [1] In 1859 the same advice was given to the United States minister in connection with a case involving our consulate.

The Department is also informed that the practice on the part of consuls of extending asylum to political refugees is almost generally permitted in the Pacific republics and in none more frequently than in Chile. If this be so, the existence of such an usage, . . . would go far to induce this Government to require the restoration of Mr. Trevitt's exequatur.[2]

In no place in the long exchange of notes growing out of the granting of asylum to certain refugees in the French legation in Venezuela (1848) is there any precise claim by the former as to the legal basis upon which it had acted.[3] At one point the *Chargés d'Affaires* of Britain and France insisted that they had only "complied with a duty to humanity." [4] But they also asked: "have the undersigned done more than exercise an acquired right, consecrated by a constant practice and always respected, particularly by the ex-President and his government?" [5] And it seems clear that this practice was a Latin (South) American practice for they spoke of "the full exercise of the right of asylum *such as is understood and practiced in Spanish America.*" [6] The Venezuelan Foreign Office, while not denying that there had been such a practice in Latin America, insisted that it was not sanctioned by general international law and refused to concede that there should be a separate rule in America. After observing the lack of any basis for the practice in international law the Venezuelan Minister of Foreign Relations observed:

I have here the expression of the European law; which has been practiced in various cases in the same French nation; it is not understood why in America a distinct usage should be followed unless it might be accepted as a source of difference, a proposition inadmissible to Venezuela.[7]

---

[1] Webster, Secretary of State, to Peyton, July 2, 1851, *ibid.*, V, p. 17.

[2] Cass, Secretary of State, to Bigler, U. S. Minister to Chile, June 1859, Moore, *op. cit.*, p. 789.

[3] See notes reprinted in Venezuela, *Cuestión promovida a Venezuela por los agentes de Francia y de la Gran Bretaña* and in Planas-Suárez, *op. cit.*, pp. 399–500.

[4] Levraud and Bingham, French and English *Chargés d'Affaires* in Venezuela, April 15, 1858, *ibid.*, p. 405. (My translation.)

[5] *Ibid.*

[6] *Ibid.*, p. 412. (My italics.)

[7] Toro, Venezuelan Minister of Foreign Relations, to Bingham and Levraud, April 30, 1858. *ibid.*, pp. 465. (My translation.)

Much confusion reigned at the meeting of the diplomatic representatives in Peru in 1867. No one was willing to declare that the practice was sanctioned by international law nor were they willing to assert that a separate rule existed in America. Yet none was willing to agree to abandon the practice except the Peruvian Minister of Foreign Relations and the United States minister. The former asserted that "having carefully studied the subject of asylum, the Peruvian government thought that custom had no precedent foundation in law" and that "there was no necessity to introduce new principles, applicable only to certain nations of America, and unknown to the rest." [1] Mr. Martínez, the Chilean representative, noted that "international law was very vague, and that he was not acquainted with those fixed principles which admitted the right of asylum in case of danger of death." [2] The Brazilian representative observed that although "the practice of asylum exists in Europe, and cases of it occur frequently in duty, what is necessary is to avoid abuses and the best way to obtain this end is to regulate said practice." Nevertheless, "he would not send to the government a letter sustaining the right of asylum." [3] The Bolivian minister noted that "according to the assertions of M. Varnhagan, Cavalchini, and Lesseps, [representatives of Brazil, Italy, and France], the practice of asylum was known in Spain, Portugal and Italy, and that Señor Cavalchini knew besides of a case of temporary asylum in the United States during the recent war." [4] This brought a prompt reply by the United States representative to the effect that no such right was recognized in his country.[5] About all that one can conclude from this is that no one at the conference was quite certain as to the basis upon which a right of asylum could be claimed.

Yet even the Peruvian Minister of Foreign Relations admitted that the practice had been widespread in South America and that it existed here simply because it had been tolerated. In a note to the Peruvian minister to Chile he observed that the foreign minister of the latter country had made the following observation:

Señor Covarrubias states first that the right of asylum naturally appears inadmissible if it is judged according to the soundest doctrines of international law, expressed by the majority of publicists, but he adds that it cannot be denied that the practice of nations, *especially those of America*, has not always

---

[1] "Translation of Protocol," [January 29, 1867], *For. Rel. of the U. S.*, 1867, II, p. 740.
[2] *Ibid.*
[3] *Ibid.*, pp. 740, 741.
[4] *Ibid.*, pp. 741.
[5] *Ibid.*

reasserted the legitimate prescriptions of the law of nations, but on the contrary, has displayed a tolerance . . .[1]

The Peruvian Minister of Foreign Relations agreed with these observations and noted that the practice prevailed in America simply because these nations had tolerated it. As to the Chilean proposal that the practice be limited to political refugees he observed that this expressed "only the principles which practice has introduced in America, in the matter of asylum." The only solution which would "restore to the American governments their respectability so many times impaired, . . . [would be] the frank and open adoption of the common principles of the law of nations, such as is practiced today in the rest of the countries of Europe and America." [2]

The immediate source of this particular controversy had been the granting of asylum in the French legation. It is by no means clear on what grounds the French legation justified its action. At one point it relied on an established practice in America. It asserted that "the practice of asylum constitutes in America an immunity universally admitted in diplomatic usages, provided always that it is confined within the limits which prudence and loyalty naturally prescribe to foreign agents." It also pointed out that "we can invoke a constant practice in support of what is called in America the right of asylum." [3]

The cases which occur between this period and the turn of the century offer little help. The practice of asylum is supported and objected to but it is never clear whether it is supported as a regional practice (though at this point it could hardly be supported as anything else), whether objections are raised because of the fact that the practice has been confined to this region alone, because it has been merely tolerated without thereby creating any legal obligation, or whether it was merely the nature of the particular refugee which determined the attitude. In the case of the United States and Britain,

[1] Pacheco, Peruvian Minister of Foreign Relations, to the Peruvian Minister to Chile, July 23, 1866, Perú, Secretario de Relaciones Exteriores *Correspondencia diplomática relativa a la cuestión sobre asilo*, publicado por orden de S. E. el Jefe Supremo Provisorio para ser presentada al Congreso Constituyente (Lima: Imprenta del Estado por Enrique del Campo, 1867), p. 25. (My translation and italics.) Hereafter cited as *Correspondencia diplomática relativa a la cuestión sobre asilo*.

[2] *Ibid.*, pp. 25–26.

[3] This note apparently was addressed to the Peruvian Foreign Office since it is published by the latter. It is signed by E. de Lesseps and came from the French Legation in Peru, see *ibid.*, pp. 19–20. Although de Lesseps' title is not given it appears that he was then French *Chargé d'Affaires*, see *For. Rel. of the U. S.*, 1867, II, p. 740; Satow, *op. cit.*, p. 303. The second quotation given here is a *paraphrase* of instructions received from the French Foreign Office.

however, there can be no doubt that asylum was justified solely on the grounds of local toleration.[1]

In the present century it has clearly been regarded as an American practice. The report of the sub-committee presented to the Committee on International Public Law at the Sixth International Conference of American States held at Havana in 1928 observed that:

> The incorporation of the article relating to the right of asylum [in] to the project of codification of International Public Law is sufficient proof that a large majority of the nations of America has not considered proper the application of strict or unbending rules to such special cases as those which originate in the asylum, and that humane sentiments should be taken into consideration. .
>
> As if this were not enough, the practice of the majority of the American nations may be invoked, a practice which consecrates the right of asylum, as has been proved in the frequent cases, which is not necessary to mention because they can surely be easily recalled by the members of the Honorable Committee.[2]

Considerable editorial and official opinion was expressed in connection with the *Colombian-Peruvian Asylum Case*. In support of its position before the Court, the Colombian government published a document containing some of the more favorable responses. While it was unable to offer many official opinions, it is significant here that all of them discussed the case in terms of the status of asylum in American practice rather than in general international practice.[3]

The Foreign Office of Ecuador called attention to the necessity of "re-affirming the Right of Asylum, which signifies an irrenounceable attainment in America" and took "the greatest pleasure in advocating every measure or means which defends and facilitates this American principle." [4] The final judgment of the International Court of Justice would be "of transcendental importance for the development of the juridical norms established and consecrated in American International Law" according to the Guatemalan reply.[5] The outcome of this problem was of primary importance "for the definitive consecration or loss of one of the most precious attainments of the Inter-American System," said the government of El Salvador.[3] This attainment, the

---

[1] *Infra*, ch. VI, On British practice see McNair, *op. cit.*, pp. 74–75.

[2] International Conference of American States, Sixth, 1928, *Minutes and Reports of the Committees*, Part I (Havana, 1928), various pagings. (Binder's title.)

[3] Only five governments replied; see Colombia, Ministerio de Relaciones Exteriores, *La opinión americana y el derecho de asilo* (Bogotá: Imprenta Nacional, 1951).

[4] Ponce, Minister of Foreign Relations of Ecuador, to Canessa, Minister of Foreign Relations of El Savador, December 8, 1950, *ibid.*, p. 9. (My translation).

[5] "Note sent to the Court by the Chancellery of Guatemala," November 16, 1950, *ibid.*, p. 12. (My translation.)

[6] Canessa, Minister of Foreign Relations of El Salvador, to the International Court of Justice, November 17, 1950, *ibid.*, p. 9. (My translation.)

latter continued, has been incorporated into various inter-American conventions and "what is even more significant, in the customary law which has happily regulated the relations of the American countries."[1]

The Cuban statement was particularly emphatic:

This humanitarian tradition, inspired by broad liberal principles, was incorporated in the juridical life of America through practice and custom, being initially recognized as customary law and submitted, later, to the American international organizations, which determined its juridical structure.

In this way, a juridical and humanitarian tradition concerning asylum has existed for many years in America, based upon certain principles which ought to be considered fundamental and immutable, which have always been practiced and sustained by Cuba and the Majority of the countries of America ...[2]

Following a revolution in Bolivia in 1946, the members of the diplomatic corps met in the residence of the Venezuelan ambassador, dean of the corps, and by unanimous agreement, empowered him to present a list of refugees in the various legations and "to solicit for all of them ... the respective safe-conduct ... in conformity with international law and *customary American law*."[3] In reply to this memorandum, the Bolivian government said that it fully shared "with the rest of America the criteria by which diplomatic asylum has been and is ample and generous when dealing with those pursued for political reasons."[4] This, however, would not apply to common criminals "according to the spirit and the letter of international agreements in force and the practice of Latin American Customary Law."[5]

The concept of a regional practice was recognized in a note from the Argentine Ministry of Foreign Relations which accompanied its *Project of Convention on the Right of Asylum* in 1937. After referring to cases in Europe and Asia, the note emphasized "that the continent of America is that in which the right of asylum has been respected in practice and codified expressly in international agreements."[6]

In the *Colombia-Peruvian Asylum Case*, the government of Peru raised the question whether there was an American International

[1] *Ibid.*

[2] "Statement Presented before the International Court of Justice by the Government of the Republic of Cuba," February 15, 1951, in Perú, Ministerio de Relaciones Exteriores, *Proceso sobre asilo entre el Perú y Colombia ante La Corte Internacional de Justicia*, segunda parte (Lima, 1952), p. 70. (My translation.) Hereafter cited as *Proceso*, II.

[3] "Memorandum," July 30, 1946, in Chile, *Memoria*, 1946, p. 51. (My translation).

[4] "Memorandum," August 4, 1946, *ibid.*, p. 52. (My translation).

[5] *Ibid.*

[6] "Notes of the Argentine Ministry to the Foreign Diplomatic Representatives," July 27, 1937, Argentine Republic, Ministry of Foreign Affairs and Worship, *Project of Convention on the Right of Asylum* (Buenos Aires, 1937), p. 9.

Law and pointed out that such a concept had been rejected in some quarters. This point was not labored, however, and the Peruvian arguments proceeded under the assumption that if a Latin American practice, accepted as legally binding, were clearly established, this would be evidence of a rule of law binding on both parties.[1] Indeed, the written and oral arguments of both parties tried to show what American custom *is* or *is not* rather than whether or not such a custom, if established, would be binding.[2]

Peru made it clear that her arguments did not reject the idea of the existence of separate or modified versions of particular norms as applied to Latin America or that these norms might, under proper conditions, be regarded as binding upon nations of this area. She insisted, instead, that Colombia must prove that a particular rule, which the latter said was evidenced by practice, had been accepted as law by the states who supposedly adhered to said practice. Thus the Peruvian argument:

> We agree, nevertheless, that it would be excessive to interpret the text of Article 38 literally and demand, for the validity of every customary norm, a general or universal acceptance. We admit that it is possible to have particular customs, especially regional customs, on condition that they contain the two former elements [constant usage and *opinio juris sive necessitatis*].[3]

Reference has already been made to the Bolivian and Ecuadorean proposals to include diplomatic asylum in the Draft Declaration on Human Rights. In the discussions before the Third Comittee of the General Assembly, the Brazilian delegate referred to this as a Latin American practice.[4] The Chilean delegate "hoped that the great Latin American tradition would soon be adopted by the rest of the world.[5]

On the other hand, it must be admitted that Latin American practice has not always been consistent in the assertion that the practice of diplomatic asylum has a special status in this region. In the discussion of asylum during the Spanish Civil war it will be seen that some Latin American states made virtually the same claims in support of their

---

[1] Perú, Ministerio de Relaciones Exteriores, *Proceso sobre asilo entre el Perú y Colombia ante la Corte Internacional de Justicia: documentación pertinente al desarrollo del juicio sentencia del 20 de noviembre de 1950* (Lima, 1951), p. 256. (My translation.) Hereafter cited as *Proceso*.

[2] *Ibid.*, pp. 78–199, *passim*.

[3] *Ibid.*, p. 147. (My translation.)

[4] General Assembly, 3d committee, *Official Records*, 3d sess., part 1, 121st Meeting, December 3, 1948, p. 340.

[5] *Ibid.*, 122d Meeting, December 4, 1948, p. 347.

practice in Madrid as has been the case in Lima, Santiago, or Caracas.[1]

But this discussion is not so much concerned with the existence of such a *practice* in Latin America. This is too well known to need further elaboration. The primary concern here is with the legal status of this practice. The fact that this is a practice confined primarily to one particular region of the world and the fact that the practice is itself in derogation of a well established rule of international law (territorial jurisdiction) leads to certain complications.

The practice of Latin American states sheds little light on this question. Nowhere in the documentation of the cases cited in chapters V, XI, and X is there any evidence that objections were raised concerning a particular case of asylum (after the middle of the last century) because of the fact that the practice is no longer recognized in general international law. Chapter V will show that a number of Latin American states, while admitting that they have respected the practice, assert that they have done so only as a toleration or a humanitarian measure. For the most part there simply is no indication whether or not the fact that the practice has been limited to this region of the world has in any way influenced this attitude.

If one assumes, as does Lauterpacht, that "International Law is based on the assumption that there exists an international community embracing all independent states and constituting a legally organized society," and that "from this assumption there necessarily follows the acknowledgement of a body of rules of a fundamental character universally binding upon all the members of that society," [2] this need not necessarily present any difficulties so far as a regional rule of law is concerned *so long as no conflict arises between the two.* Lauterpacht also notes that "diversities between states may render necessary developments and adjustments on the basis of a regional community of interests, but such particular International Law between two or more States presupposes the existence and must be interpreted in the light of principles of International law binding on all states." [3]

So far as establishing the existence of a regional community, in this case one seems to be on safe ground. The numerous International Conferences of American States (under various titles) which have produced treaties and conventions regulating innumerable matters of regional concern, the Inter-American organizations which have sprung

[1] *Infra*, ch. V.
[2] *Op. cit.*, p. 51.
[3] *Ibid.*

from these conferences and the countless declarations and resolutions testify to this. A common historical, ethnic and social background within an isolated geographic setting should be noted also.[1]

But what happens when a "regional rule of law" is in conflict with a general international rule? This would certainly be the case with a right of asylum which derogates from a generally accepted rule regarding territorial jurisdiction.

It would seem that a part of the difficulty arises from the assumption with which Lauterpacht begins, namely, that of a world community. Percy Corbett raises this objection to Lauterpacht's thesis.

> The objection, as I see it, is the extent to which it distorts the world of fact...
> The disparity begins with the assumption of international community ...
> [But] to classify the congeries of States as one community or society is to rob those terms of the most of their content ...
> If we nevertheless posit an international community or society with a common law, we must logically ... go on to accept the primacy of that law over the legal systems of the State members ... Their acts, which, it will probably be agreed, are for substantial purposes more important than their words, constantly negative such subordination of the State to any society.[2]

It is interesting to note that Alejandro Alvarez, the leading proponent of an American international law, also bases the existence of a legal system upon the prior existence of a community. Here is his explanation of the basis for an American international law:

> By American international law one ought to understand the aggregate of institutions, principles, rules, doctrines, conventions, customs and practices which are characteristic of the American republics in the domain of international relations.
> The existence of law is due to the geographic, economic and political conditions of the American continent, to the way in which the new republics were formed and entered into the international community, as well as to the solidarity which exists among them.
> American international law understood in this way does not tend in any way to create a system of international law which has for an object the separation of the republics of this hemisphere from the concert of the other nations of the world.[3]

Particular attention is called to his observation *that these are not different rules of law* and, presumably, *not in derogation of general international*

---

[1] See bibliography, *ibid.*, p. 185, n. 2. See also C. G. Fenwick, *The Inter-American Regional System* (New York: The Declan X. McMullen Co., 1949), pp. 33-61.

[2] *Law and Society in the Relations of States* (New York: Harcourt, Brace and Company, 1951), pp. 75-76.

[3] Alejandro Alvarez, *Después de la guerra* (Buenos Aires, Imprenta de la Universidad, 1943), pp. 182-183. Translation provided in H.B. Jacobini, *A Study of the Philosophy of International Law as seen in Works of Latin American Writers* (The Hague: Martinus Nijhoff, 1954), p. 127.

law. But note now how he deals with "apparent" conflicts between the two systems in his dissenting opinion in the *Colombian-Peruvian Asylum Case*.

> If certain precepts, which are held to be universal, are not accepted by the countries of the American continent, it is obvious that they no longer have that character; and if American precepts are not recognized by the countries of other continents, they must be applied only in the new world.[1]

In other words, what he seems to be suggesting is that perhaps the rule concerning territorial jurisdiction is not quite as absolute as it has been held to be. If Latin American practice shows that it has been subject to certain qualifications then the old rule obviously no longer has a universal character. But this seems to be getting much closer to the view that law is law simply because it can be shown that states have regarded it as such.

Hildebrando Accioly takes a position which is perhaps closer to that of Lauterpacht:

> We also judge as defective the denomination of European international law, American international law, Asian international law. If in this or that continent, the state of development of positive international law or the utility of any order [o las conveniencias de cualquier orden] might not yet permit the adoption of certain international juridical principles already admitted in another or in others, this does not mean that there exists an international law for Europe, another for America, another for Asia, another for Africa. If this should be, we might also admit the existence of an international law even more particular, applicable to small groups of countries on the same continent and even to a single state . . .[2]

Presumably, then, there can be "international rules" which are not presently applicable in certain regions. But it would also seem that they are replaced by some other "rule" of conduct although it is nowhere clear precisely what status this "rule" has.

Something which might be called a middle position is taken by Daniel Antokoletz.

> ..It would be inadmissible to speak of an Asian or American international law: but such a designation would be fitting and would be adjusted to the circumstances when there might have developed in the common civilization of the

---

[1] Dissenting opinion by Judge Alvarez, *Colombian-Peruvian Asylum Case, Judgment of November 20th, 1950;* I. C. J. *Reports 1950,* p. 293. The Colombian Government argued in the *Colombian-Peruvian Asylum Case* that "American International Law, such as we conceive of it, is not contrary to universal international law. On the contrary, it is an extension and complement of the latter." Perú, *Proceso,* p. 348. (My translation.)

[2] *Op. cit.,* I, p. 3. (My translation.)

Asian or American states a system of juridical rules, of international relations, different from the system admitted in the European states.[1]

Although it is by no means clear, the implication seems to be that certain rules which have been generally regarded as "international rules" would still be regarded as such but would be replaced in certain areas by other rules. Again, this could take place only with the development of regional juridical communities although it is not clear precisely how one goes about establishing the existence of such a community. He does not at the present time, however, see any justification for assuming the existence of such a juridical community in America.[2]

After discussing the conflicting views of Latin American writers on this subject, H. B. Jacobini concludes that the position defended is largely a matter of the premise from which one begins. The writers associated with Alvarez, who contend that there is an American International Law, generally base this contention upon the existence of a sentiment of continental solidarity and community consciousness. Law is something which flows from the actual existence of such a community.[3]

The opposite school holds that the existence of law depends primarily upon the social acceptance of a particular juristic view rather than upon the social data *per se*. Admitting that the social acceptance of a particular juristic view itself may have in large part resulted from the *influence* of juristic theories based upon the idea of continental solidarity, they insist that it is the social acceptance which gives it the force of law. It follows that legal force does not attach to a mere *de facto* practice which has not been given *de jure* recognition.[4]

---

[1] *Tratado de derecho internacional público en tiempo de paz* (Buenos Aires: Juan Roldan y Cía., 1924), I. 256. Quoting F. de Holtzendorf, *Introduction au droit des gens* (My translation.)

[2] *Ibid.*, pp. 256–260.

[3] *Op. cit.*, pp. 121–136.

[4] *Ibid.* In support of the thesis that there exists an American International Law, see Alejandro Alvarez, *Le droit international américain* (Paris: A. Pedone, 1910), pp. 259–261; Alvarez, *La reconstrucción del derecho de gentes: el nuevo orden y la renovación social* (Santiago de Chile, 1944) and, by the same author, "Latin America and International Law," *A.J.I.L.*, III (1909),pp. 269–353. For a similar but cautious American view, see C. H. Fenwick, "The Juridical Nature of the Organization of American States," *Cursos Monográficos*, IV, publication of the Academia Interamericana de Derecho Comparado y Internacional (La Habana, Cuba: Editorial Lex, 1954), pp. 255–261. For an excellent discussion of the development of rules governing inter-American intercourse, see C. G. Fenwick, *The Inter-American Regional System* (New York: the Declan X. McMullen Company, 1949), pp. 33–61. For a different view see V. Savelberg, *Le problème du droit international américain*, étudié spécialement à la lumière des conventions panaméricaines de La Havane (The Hague: Stols, 1946).

If it can be clearly shown that a particular group of nations accepts a given practice as legally binding and acts accordingly, then it would indeed be difficult to say that it is not law simply because it does not square with a general international rule which has been traditionally accepted as law. And even assuming that one accepts the idea of the primacy of international law over regional law it does not rule out the possibility that either can be subject to change. Thus there is some validity in Alvarez's assertion that "if certain precepts, which are held to be universal, are not accepted by the countries of the American continent, it is obvious that they no longer have that character; and if American precepts are not recognized by the countries of other continents, they must be applied only in the new world." This of course leaves open the possibility that the existence of an international rule of law can be denied on the grounds that it is not accepted by certain "regions" which may become smaller and smaller.

Alvarez's method of resolving the conflict seems, in one sense, much more at home with the theory which holds that law flows from the social acceptance of it as such. If it is clear that the states of a certain region accept a practice as law then it is obvious that a rule conflicting with this cannot be considered international law. But in this case one really destroys the theoretical basis upon which it can be said that all the states in the region are legally obliged to follow the rule.

If, on the other hand, one posits the primacy of the international community this simply does not correspond with the facts. If one attempts to resolve this difficulty by pointing out that if the facts show that smaller communities do not abide by these rules this merely means that those rules are no longer universal, then one is in fact opening up the possibility that any group of nations can change the international rules and the whole idea of law flowing from the existence of a community seems to be considerably damaged.[1]

As to the attitude of the International Court of Justice toward this controversy, I cannot agree with Lauterpacht's assertion that in the *Haya de la Torre Case* it "showed no disposition to attach decisive importance to some of the apparent consequences of the institution of asylum which ... acquired a certain prominence among Latin American countries." [2]

---

[1] Perhaps it should be no more difficult to ascertain at what point a group of nations can no longer claim certain rules as applicable among themselves and in derogation of general international rules of law than it is to ascertain at what point a given practice has been accepted as legally binding *by a sufficient number of states* in order to term it a rule of law.

[2] *Op. cit.*, p. 53.

In its judgment, the Court noted that Colombia had invoked "American international law in general" and that, in addition to rules arising from agreements, it had "relied on an alleged regional or local custom peculiar to Latin American States." [1] To this argument the Court said:

> The Party which relies on a Custom of this kind must prove that this custom is established in such a manner that it has become binding on the other Party. The Colombian Government must prove that the rule invoked by it is in accordance with a constant and uniform usage practiced *by the States in question*, and that this usage is the expression of a right appertaining to the State granting asylum and a duty incumbent on the territorial State. [2]

This suggests that the Court rejected the Colombian arguments not so much because it rejected the idea of a rule limited in its application to a particular region but because Colombia had failed to "prove that the rule invoked by it is in accordance with a constant and uniform usage *practiced by the States in question* and that this usage is the expression of a right appertaining to the State granting asylum and a duty incumbent on the territorial State." [3] Furthermore, since the entire Colombian case was based upon Latin American practice (as evidence of law) the court could have disposed of the case immediately had it not recognized the possibility of a regional rule (which in this case was in conflict with a generally accepted rule of international law.) This writer is aware of the claims made that the Court was primarily concerned with the interpretation of the treaty of Havana. But the interpretation of the treaty itself was in large part a matter of showing what customary law was. No one questioned the fact that the Havana convention did not state explicitly which party should qualify the nature of the offence. The real question was whether or not *customary law* held that the state granting asylum should have the right of unilateral qualification and this Colombia attempted to prove by reference to *Latin American* practice. If the Court objected to the Colombian case *on these grounds* it certainly made no effort to point this out.

---

[1] *Colombian-Peruvian Asylum Case, Judgment of November 20th, 1950:* International Court of Justice *Reports* 1950, p. 276.

[2] *Ibid.*, pp. 276–277. (My italics.)

[3] The Court does not appear to have been particularly concerned over the precise interpretation of Article 38, paragraph 1, clause b, of the Statute of the International Court of Justice which provides that the Court shall apply "international custom, as evidence of a general practice accepted as law." In other words, can "international custom" mean "regional custom" and can "general practice accepted as law" mean "regional practice accepted as law."? See *Colombian-Peruvian Asylum Case, Judgment of November 20th, 1950:* I. C. J. *Reports 1950,* pp. 276–277.

Since it was concluded in the last chapter that no general rule of international law sanctioned a right of asylum it is obvious that this discussion, at least tentatively, admits the possibility of a regional rule of law in derogation of a generally accepted (presumed) rule of international law. To do otherwise would be to destroy the necessity of the inquiry.

CHAPTER III

OPINIO JURIS SIVE NECESSITATIS AND THE PRACTICE OF DIPLOMATIC ASYLUM

Repeated claims are put forth that a customary rule of law has grown out of the practice of diplomatic asylum in Latin America.[1] In view of the undeniable frequency of the practice in this region,[2] the matter would be simple enough if practice alone were an agreed source of law. On this score, however, there is by no means unanimous agreement.

But if there is not unanimous agreement, at least the dominant view seems to be that expressed by Oppenheim:

Custom must not be confused with usage. In everyday life and language both terms are used synonymously, but in the language of the international jurist they have two distinctly different meanings. International jurists speak of a *custom* when a clear and continuous habit of doing certain actions has grown up under the aegis of the conviction that these actions are, according to international law, obligatory or right. On the other hand, international jurists speak of a *usage* when a habit of doing certain actions has grown up without there being the conviction that these actions are according to International Law, obligatory, or right ... Certain conduct of States concerning their international relations may therefore be usual without being the outcome of customary International Law.[3]

---

[1] Camilo Barcia Trelles, "El derecho de asilo diplomático," *Revista de derecho internacional*, LIX (Habana, 1951), p. 177. See also the dissenting opinion of Judge Alvarez in *Colombian-Peruvian Asylum Case, Judgment of November 20th, 1950:* I.C.J. *Reports 1950*, p. 292. But there is by no means unanimous agreement even among Latin American writers: see Lucio M. Moreno Quintana, *Derecho de asilo* (Buenos Aires: Imprenta de la Universidad, 1952), pp. 48–49; Planas-Suárez, *op. cit.*, pp. 95–117.

[2] See numerous cases cited in Perú, *Proceso*, pp. 377–384; Cabral de Moncado, *op. cit.*, pp. 34–48; Moreno Quintana, *op. cit.*, pp. 41-48. Morgenstern, *op. cit.*, p. 241n, has found about thirty instances of asylum, mostly in Haiti, in the British Foreign Office Correspondence of the Years 1865–1902. *For. Rel. of the U. S.* lists about thirty instances of asylum given in Latin America by diplomatic and consular officers of the United States but this writer apparently uses a moɪe restricted criterion as to what constitutes a "case of asylum" than does Morgenstern inasmuch as the latter lists fifty such cases in general U.S. practice, *ibid.*, p. 241; whereas I would list but forty-one. In any event the number is probably considerably greater than this since all cases are not reported in *For. Rel. of the U. S.*

[3] *Op. cit.*, p. 26. See also, C. F. von Martens, *The Law of Nations*, trans. Wm. Cobbett (4th ed.; London: Wm. Cobbett, 1829), pp. 59–60. Jackson H. Ralston, "The Value of Au-

Reference has already been made to the fact that the International Court of Justice was unwilling to accept mere usage as evidence of law in the *Colombian-Peruvian Asylum Case*. Referring to the Colombian arguments, the Court said:

... The Colombian Government has referred to a large number of particular cases on which diplomatic asylum was in fact granted and respected. But it has not shown if the alleged rule of unilateral and definitive qualification was invoked or – if in some cases it was invoked – that it was, apart from conventional stipulations, exercised by the States granting asylum as a right appertaining to them and respected by the territorial States as a duty incumbent on them and not merely for reasons of political expediency.[1]

This is in accordance with the practice of both the Permanent Court of Arbitration and the Permanent Court of International Justice. In the *North Atlantic Coast Fisheries Case* (1910) decided by the Permanent Court of Arbitration, the issue concerned the interpretation of treaty provisions between the United States and Great Britain which excluded American fishermen from certain "bays, creeks, or harbors of His Britanic Majesty's dominions in America" not specifically listed in said treaty.[2] The United States contended that long usage wherein American fishermen had in fact had access, since the signing of the treaty, to certain bodies of water now in question, showed that these could not be considered as "bays" within the meaning of the treaty.[3]

The Court would not accept this argument. While "established usage" might serve as the basis for claiming certain historic bays as territorial, it was not willing to apply this *a contrario* so that mere toleration on the part of Britain would be grounds for removing them from this category for purposes of the treaty.

---

thorities in International Law," *Proceedings of the American Society of International Law*, An Address before the Fifth Annual Meeting of the American Society of International Law (Washington, 1911), p. 302. P. E. Corbett, "The Consent of States and the Sources of the Law of Nations," *British Yearbook of International Law*, XVI (1925), pp. 26–27; Ernest Nys, "The Codification of International Law," *American Journal of International Law*, V (1911), pp. 872–874. Marcellus D. A. R. von Redlich, *The Law of Nations* (2d ed.; U. S. A.: World League for Permanent Peace, 1937), p. 9. Georg Schwarzenberger, *International Law*, I (London: Stevens and Sons Ltd., 1945), p. 13. Hall, *op. cit.*, pp. 5–13. For a different view see L. Kopelmanas, "Custom as a Means of the Creation of International Law," *British Yearbook of International Law*, XVIII (1937), pp. 127–157.

[1] *Op. cit.*, p. 277. See excellent editorial comment by Herbert W. Briggs, *The American Journal of International Law*, XLV (1951), pp. 728–731.

[2] James Brown Scott (ed.), *The Hague Court Reports* (New York: Oxford University Press, 1916), p. 145.

[3] *Ibid.*, p. 185.

Because neither should such relaxations of this claim, as are in evidence, be construed as renunciation of it; nor should omissions to enforce the claim in regard to bays as to which no controversy arose, be so construed. Such a construction by this tribunal would not only be intrinsically inequitable, but intrinsically injurious; in that it would discourage conciliatory diplomatic transactions and encourage the assertion of claims in their fullest extent.[1]

In the *Lotus* [2] case the agent for the French government argued that there was a customary rule conferring exclusive jurisdiction in maritime collision cases upon the country of the ship's flag, as regards incidents on the ship. It was argued that, in collision cases, questions of jurisdiction frequently arise before civil courts but are rarely encountered in the practice of criminal courts. From this it was deduced that "prosecutions only occur before the courts of the state whose flag is flown and that the circumstance is proof of a tacit consent on the part of states and, consequently, shows what positive international law is in collision cases." [3]

The Court ruled that mere practice was not necessarily evidence of law.

Even if the rarity of the judicial decisions to be found among the reported cases were sufficient to prove in point of fact the circumstance alleged by the Agent of the French Government, it would merely show that States had often in practice abstained from instituting criminal proceedings, and not that they recognized themselves as being obliged to do so; for only if such abstention were based on their being conscious of having a duty to abstain would it be possible to speak of an international custom.[4]

While the decision was not as clear in the case of the *Jurisdiction of the European Commission of the Danube*,[5] the Court at least declared that it *was not* basing a rule of law on mere practice.

In this connection the Court wishes to record that, in the course of the arguments submitted on behalf of Roumania, it has been more than once admitted that the European Commission may have exercised certain powers in the contested sector; but that, at the same time, it has been contended that such exercise was based on mere toleration by the territorial State and that toleration could not serve as a basis for the creation of legal rights.

In this respect it will suffice to observe that, under the construction of Article 6 of the Definitive Statute adopted by the Court, *even if before the war, an actual exercise of certain powers by the Commission ... was based on mere toleration, the practice has now been converted into a right by Article 6 of the Definitive Statute.* It is therefore not necessary to examine whether, in international law, the

---

[1] *Ibid.*, pp. 185-186.
[2] Permanent Court of International Justice (1927), *Series A*, No. 10.
[3] *Ibid.*, p. 27.
[4] *Ibid.*, p. 28.
[5] Permanent Court of International Justice (1927), *Series B*, No. 14.

continued exercise of certain powers might not have converted into a legal right even a situation considered by Roumania as mere toleration.[1]

A careful study of the circumstances surrounding asylum cases reveals strong evidence in support of the requirement of *opinio juris sive necessitatis*. The dictum of the Permanent Court of Arbitration that failure to recognize this "would discourage conciliatory diplomatic transactions and encourage the assertion of extreme claims in their fullest extent" seems particularly applicable here. Six categories of cases may be distinguished in order to show how mere practice, which may be only toleration in the absence of *opinio juris sive necessitatis*, would present serious complications if used as the basis for a rule of law.

I. *Cases where the territorial state has no charges against the "refugee" and raises no objections to his leaving the country or returning to his home in safety.* An excellent example of a case in this category is shown in the diplomatic exchanges involving the grant of asylum to the entire González family in the United States legation in Costa Rica in 1917.

...At five o'clock, Domingo González, six sons and three daughters, most of the former office holders under Alfredo, sought refuge here saying that they are in danger of immediate arrest in view of virtual martial law and execution in case of intervention, Conditional asylum only granted dependent on instruction from Department.[2]

Nevertheless, the U. S. representative informed the State Department the next day that he did not think they were in danger of arrest, the Costa Rican Minister of Foreign Relations having volunteered this information.[3]

While the Costa Rican government was willing to grant safe conduct

---

[1] *Ibid.*, pp. 36–37. (My italics.) In his dissenting opinion, Judge Negulesco insisted that the Court was, in fact, basing a rule of law upon mere toleration on the part of Rumania. See *ibid.*, pp. 105–106.

The relevant cases in national courts have been less precise in this respect. In *West Rand Central Gold Mining Co. v. Rex* (1905), 2 K.B. 391, p. 407, the Court said that the evidence must prove that the alleged rule " is of such a nature, and has been so widely and generally accepted, that it can hardly be supposed that any civilized state would repudiate it." In *The Paquete Habana* and *The Lola* (1900) 175 U.S. 677, the United States Supreme Court said "the period of a hundred years which has since elapsed is amply sufficient to enable what originally may have rested in custom or comity, courtesy or concession, to grow, by general assert of civilized nations, into a settled rule of international law ..." See excellent discussion of cases in editor's note in Herbert W. Briggs, *The Law of Nations* (2d ed.; New York: Appleton-Century-Crofts, 1952), pp. 46–48.

[2] Hale, U. S. Minister to Costa Rica, to the Secretary of State, tel., May 17, 1917, MS. Dept. State, file 818.00/151.

[3] Johnson [positionunknown] to the Secretary of State, tel., May 18, 1917, MS. Dept. of State, file 818.00/152.

to the aged parents and the sisters, it was not immediately prepared
to do so in the case of the González brothers.

The Costa Rican Government in refusing to permit the departure of the
González brothers, based its action on its knowledge that they were involved in
the revolutionary plans which González and Castro Quesada are maturing.
Concerning these plans the Government has much information, but has preferred
to take no repressive measures so long as the peace of the country is in no real
danger.[1]

After further investigation, however, the Costa Rican government
decided it had nothing to fear from the "refugees" and was willing
to permit their departure from the country.

Lara [Minister of Foreign Relations of Costa Rica] said to me and asked me
to repeat to the Department that having received assurance from Chamorro
that Tinocco [Costa Rican Chief Executive] had nothing to fear from him, all
cause for alarm has disappeared and the González family including all sons can
leave the country if they desire. They will decide today.[2]

   2. *Cases where the "refugee" leaves the legation after a very short time
when it appears that his person is no longer in danger.*[3] In many cases

---

[1] Guardia, Costa Rican Representative to the United States to Lansing, U. S. Secretary
of State, MS Dept. of State file 818.00/153.

[2] Johnson to the Secretary of State, tel., May 21, 1917, MS Dept. of State file 818.00/155.
For a case in this same category see exchanges dealing with asylum granted to Vice Presi-
dent Roberto Leguía of Peru; Angoli, Italian Minister at Lima to Tudela, Peruvian Minister
of Foreign Relations, trans. July 25, 1913 (enclosure in Howard, U. S. Minister at Lima to
the Secretary of State, August 19, 1919, MS Dept. of State file 823.00/113), and Tudela to
Agnoli, trans. July 29, 1913, *ibid.* For such a case involving asylum granted to General
Ubico in the U. S. legation in Guatemala see McCafferty, U. S. *Chargé* in Guatemala to the
Secretary of State, tel., Dec. 12, 1930, Dept. of State file 314.0022/1 in *For. Rel. of the U. S.,*
1930, III, p. 173. For a case involving asylum granted to a Venezuelan student in the Colombian legation in Caracas see Itriago Chacín, Venezuelan Minister of Foreign Relations to
Zuleta, Colombian Minister to Venezuela, April 18, 1928, in Venezuela, *Libro Amarillo*
1929, pp. 202–204. For a case involving asylum granted to Haitian government officials
in the U. S. legation and against whom no charges were preferred see Ferere, Haitian
Minister of Foreign Relations to Powell, U. S. Minister to Haiti, trans., June 13, 1905, (inclosure no. 2 in Powell to the Secretary of State, June 14, 1905), *For. Rel. of the U. S.,*
1905, p. 552. See also Jones, U. S. Minister to Honduras, to the Secretary of State, July 21,
1919, Dept. of State file 815.00/1919; Jones to the Secretary of State, tel., July 19, 1919,
MS Dept. of State file 815.00/1890; Jones to the Secretary of State, tel., July 28, 1919, MS
Dept. of State file 815.00/1912. For an interesting case involving a U. S. subject who had
participated in an unsuccessful revolution in Nicaragua see exchange of notes printed in
For. Rel. of the U. S., 1914, pp. 940–943.

[3] For such a case involving asylum granted in the U.S. legation in Ecuador to an ex-
Minister of War and his family see Olney, U. S. Secretary of State to Tillman, U. S. Minister
to Ecuador, Sept. 25, 1895, *For. Rel. of the U. S.,* 1895, I, p. 245. See case of asylum granted
to the two small sons and nurse of Mrs. Plaza (wife of the President) in the U. S. legation in
Ecuador: Hartman, U. S. Minister to Ecuador, to the Secretary of State, tel., Feb. 26, 1914,
Dept. of State file 822.00/363. See also Dawson, U. S. *Chargé* in Ecuador, to Castle, Acting
Secretary of State, tel., Aug. 24, 1931, Dept. of State file 822.00/792, *For. Rel. of the U. S.,*
1931, II, p. 138.

the stay is only a matter of hours and evidence suggests that the case may not even have been reported to the government of the territorial state or, if so, it was reported only after the "refugee" had left the legation. In many instances only women and children are involved, while in other cases, there appears to have been no government which was clearly in control. Where such cases have been known to the government of the territorial state, in all probability they were not considered of sufficient importance to raise a controversy.

3. *Cases where it appears that the territorial state prefers to expel the "refugee" from the country rather than inflict other punishment and, therefore, willingly cooperates in granting safe conduct, sometimes referring to it as "expulsion" rather than a grant of safe conduct.* In such cases it will be noted that the "refugee" in the legation often experiences the same fate as his cohorts who were unable to reach a legation before they were apprehended and placed in prison pending exile. In 1899 a number of unsuccessful revolutionaries received asylum in the United States legation in Haiti. With but one exception, no controversy arose over a "right of asylum" inasmuch as it does not appear that the government of Haiti was anxious to apprehend these persons except for purposes of expelling them from the country. Exile was the sentence decreed against those persons whom the government had arrested and imprisoned and a similar decree provided for *expulsion* of those who had taken refuge in the United States and other legations. Throughout, the government of Haiti spoke of their action as "expulsion" rather than a grant of "safe conduct." [1]

4. *Cases where "asylum" is granted with the full approval of the territorial state, often being welcomed as a means of protecting the "refugee" from violence until he can be removed from the county.* In other cases it is apparent that the "new" or "revolutionary" government of the territorial state welcomes the grant of asylum as an alternative to inflicting the "just punishment" which it has promised to mete out to the members of a deposed regime in a bid for public support but which it has no real desire to do. A despatch from the American *Chargé* in Cuba tells of a case in this category.

I asked Dr. Ferrara [Cuban Minister of Foreign Relations] about Carlos Manuel de la Cruz, leader of the Orthodox Conservative faction in the House, who is also in hiding and who was insistently reported to have sought refuge in this

---

[1] See numerous exchanges between U. S. Minister to Haiti and the Haitian Secretary of State for Foreign Affairs and between the former and the U. S. Secretary of State in *For. Rel. of the U. S.*, 1899, pp. 376–396.

Embassy. The Secretary replied that he understood that de la Cruz was in the Uruguayan Legation and that if this were true, the Cuban Government would raise no objection. He regarded such asylum as entirely justifiable in the circumstances, *since it might protect the refugee from acts which the Cuban Government would be the first to condemn. Furthermore, de la Cruz was not a fugitive from justice.*[1]

That this is an indication of "toleration " rather than recognition of a "rule incumbent" is further emphasized by a case involving "hospitality" granted to President Alessandri of Chile in the American embassy. In this case enlightened action on the part of the United States minister avoided any claims of asylum. Nevertheless, the protection given was respected *as in the cases generally referred to as "asylum cases."* The United States minister reported to the Secretary of State that although Alessandri had stated that he felt that his life

---

[1] Reed, United States *Chargé* in Cuba, to the Secretary of State, Sept. 29, 1932, Dept. of State file 837.00/3359, *For. Rel. of the U. S.*, 1932, V, p. 558. (My italics.) The United States Minister to Haiti commented similarly: "Allow me also to state in this connection that shelter often given to these refugees is at times a great help to the Government itself. Heated passions are allowed to cool, and the Government is allowed to extricate itself from a serious dilemma ... This, in fact, was the case of the refugees who were with us. They started for Santiago, but the military authorities refused permission for them to land. They had to return here and left for St. Thomas. After their departure, the Government found the charges made against them to be false. Passports allowing them to return were sent ..." Powell to Hay, Secretary of State, Nov. 15, 1899, *For. Rel. of the U. S.*, 1899. pp. 395–396. In 1931, a former President of Panama, Rudolfo Chiari, was brought to the Ecuadorian Legation *by the Minister of Foreign Relations* who requested protection for him. The more zealous "revolutionist" of the government in power were directing their spite against him. Davis, U. S. Minister to Panama, to the Secretary of State, Jan. 6, 1931, Dept. of State file 819.00 Revolutions/29, *For. Rel. of the U. S.*, 1931, II, p. 900. See also Curtis, U. S. Minister to the Dominican Republic to the Acting Secretary of State, tel., Feb. 24, 1930, 839.00 Revolutions/2, *For. Rel. of the U. S.*, 1930, II, p. 699. For a case involving a request by the recognized government of Haiti that protection be given to the Minister of the Interior and his family during their departure from the country see the several telegrams from consul Livingston to the Secretary of State in *For. Rel. of the U. S.*, 1914, pp. 385-386. During one of the many periods of unrest in Bolivia, the Chilean legation received a telephone call from the family of General Montes stating that his arrest had been ordered and asking for asylum. The Chilean *Chargé* immediately went to the President stating that he wished to grant asylum to said general and that he would guarantee his departure from the country on the following day. Upon receiving the *President's consent* the *Chargé* went to the General's home, which had already been surrounded by the police, and personally escorted him to the legation. The refugee left the country on the following day escorted by the Chilean *Chargé*. Hubbard, U. S. *Chargé ad interim* in Bolivia, to the Secretary of State, Oct. 11, 1939, MS Dept. of State file 824.00/ 473. In 1878, *the government of Haiti suggested* as a means of ending a revolt, that General Tanis who was besieged in a fort, be given asylum in the British legation after which he would be free to surrender himself to the laws of the country or to leave Haiti along with his companions. See exchanges between Carrie, Haitian Secretary of State for Foreign Affairs, and the British and American Ministers to Haiti, printed in *For. Rel. of the U. S.*, 1878, pp. 439–443. For asylum granted to a President of the Dominican Republic who was "under impeachment" and where *prior approval* of the grant had been given by the cabinet and Vice President, on condition that he resign and leave the country, see exchanges included in Dawson, U. S. Minister to the Dominican Republic, to the Secretary of State, extracts, Jan. 16, 1906, *For. Rel. of the U. S.*, 1906, I, pp. 543–549.

and the lives of his family were imperilled, he gave the following statement to the press:

> Don Arturo Alessandri came to the American Embassy after midnight accompanied by members of his family stating that he had resigned as President of Chile. He asked the hospitality of the Embassy. It was granted to him. No Chilean ever asked the hospitality of the Embassy and was refused.[1]

The following telegram gives the response of the government of Chile.

> Minister of Foreign Affairs called to thank me personally and in name of government for hospitality extended to Señor Alessandri and for form of communication to press ... Hundreds of people including many of opposition have called with full permission of Government to pay respects to Alessandri and all seem deeply touched by fact that I refrained from stating that I was giving him asylum and said that I was extending him hospitality thus avoiding implications that his life was threatened ...[2]

5. *Cases in which it seems clear that the diplomatic representative has exercised the "right of asylum" far in excess of what his government normally would claim.* Once asylum has been granted, however, admitting the error and turning the refugee out becomes a very delicate matter and the diplomat's government often has little choice but to support him and press for guarantees for the refugee's safety. In such cases the claims made will be vague and evasive, avoiding any precise legal position. An excellent example of this is demonstrated in a note from the United States Secretary of State to the United States minister to El Salvador. The latter had reported that he had granted asylum to a Salvadoran subject who had voluntarily agreed to leave shortly thereafter.

> Nothing will at this time be said as to the propriety or expediency of your having granted that asylum; you are, however, referred for the general views of the Department upon the subject to instruction No. 24 ...
>
> Having, however, whether for sufficient reason or otherwise, granted a refuge to Mr. Duenas, you thereby incurred an obligation, which it might be said, more or less implicated the honor of this government in its exact fulfilment.[3]

---

[1] Collier, U. S. Minister to Chile, to the Secretary of State, tel., Sept. 9, 1924, MS Dept. of State file 825.00/297.

[2] Collier to the Secretary of State, tel., Sept. 9, 1924, MS Dept. of State file 825.00/282.

[3] Fish, U. S. Secretary of State, to Torbert, U. S. Minister to El Salvador, May 18, 1871, *For. Rel. of the U. S.*, 1871, p. 695. For a similar case in Haiti, see numerous exchanges between U. S. Secretary of State and Minister Furniss in *For. Rel. of the U. S.*, 1908, pp. 429–435. In 1929, the Vice President of Bolivia received information that he was to be arrested immediately upon leaving the Senate. He telephoned the Mexican ambassador requesting that he come to the Senate at once. Upon the latter's arrival at the Senate, the Vice President stated that he wished to seek asylum in the Mexican legation. When they left the Senate, the police attempted to arrest the Vice President in spite of efforts on the part of the Mexican ambassador to claim immunity for both of them. In the confusion which followed the

The rebuke despatched to the U. S. minister to Haiti by the government in Washington is even more to the point.

> It is regretted that you deemed yourself justified by an impulse of humanity to grant such asylum. You have repeatedly been instructed that such a practice has no basis in public law, and, so far as this Government is concerned, is believed to be contrary to all sound policy . . .
> Mr. Preston [Haitian minister to the United States] has been here by order of his Government to ask that you may be directed to set at large the refugees who have sought your protection. I answered him, however, that though it might have been preferable that you should not have received those persons, it was not deemed expedient to comply with his request.[1]

6. *Cases where the territorial state clearly objects to the grant of asylum, but since the granting state will not surrender the refugee and since the territorial state does not wish to resort to the extreme of violating the immunity of the embassy or legation (or of breaking diplomatic relations), safe conduct out of the country is finally granted out of what appears to be political expediency.*[2] Controversies such as this will provide one means of determining whether or not the parties involved considered their action in accordance with a rule of law and will be discussed in chapter V.

Thus it must be concluded that a variety of motives have prompted both the granting of asylum on the part of the state of refuge and the failure to raise objections on the part of the territorial state (or inability to secure a remedy even when objections are raised). In a large number of cases the action gives no indication of having sprung from any recognition of legal right or duty under international law – American or general. This, of course, does not prove that a feeling of legal obligation was *not* present in any of them. But it does show that the mere citation of a long list of cases where protection has been afforded and respected in one form or another cannot of itself serve as the basis for a rule of law which would be applicable where circum-

---

Mexican ambassador was roughly treated and the Vice President placed under arrest. The Mexican government protested and demanded the proper apologies. The Mexican ambassador was unable to gain support of the diplomatic corps in demanding that the Vice President be surrendered to his legation. Official apologies were published but they implied that there had been no attempt on the part of the Mexican ambassador to exercise a "right of asylum." Hubbard, *Chargé ad interim* in Bolivia, to the Secretary of State, Oct. 11, 1929, MS Dept. of State file 824.00/473.

[1] Fish, U. S. Secretary of State, to Bassett, U. S. Minister to Haiti, June 4, 1875, *For. Rel. of the U. S.*, 1875, II, p. 701.

[2] This category of cases is bound up with the problem of "political" and "criminal" offenses and the allied problem of who shall qualify the nature of the offense.

stances such as those described above (especially in categories one through four) do not prevail. It was considerations such as this which prompted the International Court of Justice to remark with regard to the cases cited in the Colombian *Memoria* in the *Colombian-Peruvian Asylum Case:*

> In the absence of precise data, it is difficult to assess the value of such cases as precedents tending to establish the existence of a legal obligation upon the territorial state to recognize the validity of asylum *which has been granted against the proceedings instituted by local juridical authorities.*[1]

It is imperative then to seek out clear declarations of state policy in connection with contentious cases and other circumstances in order to determine whether there has been a consistent recognition of an obligatory rule on the part of the states involved. But before this can be done, one further category of cases must be recognized.

In a number of cases an obligation growing out of conventional arrangements is clearly recognized and no question of international law, apart from treaty obligations, is raised. At other times claims are made that these conventions are themselves merely declaratory of "American International Law" or that they have established a general rule of law which is binding even upon those states in Latin America which are not parties to them.[2] Thus, the next step must be a study of the relevant treaties in order to ascertain to what extent they establish a legal obligation to respect the practice of asylum, either among the parties to such treaties or among Latin American states generally.

---

[1] *Op. cit.,* p. 286. (My italics)
[2] Espinoza, Cuban *Chargé d'Affaires* in Peru, to Díaz Dulanto, Peruvian Minister of Foreign Relations, March 31, 1949, in *Revista peruano de derecho internacional,* IX (1949), p. 164.

CHAPTER IV

ESTABLISHING A LEGAL BASIS THROUGH MULTILATERAL CONVENTIONS AND TREATIES[1]

Abuses in the practice of asylum have led the Latin American states on a number of occasions to attempt to formalize, regulate or even abolish the practice by means of multilateral agreements. It is worth noting some excerpts from the proceedings of one such conference held by the diplomatic corps at Lima in 1867. They offer an explanation as to why some of the agreements which have finally materialized have really done very little to clarify the legal status of the practice.

Señor Benavente [Bolivia] said that . . . he was not authorized to accept the complete abolition of the right of asylum, but that he would contribute most willingly to regulate its exercise . . .

Abstaining, said Mr. Martínez [Chile], from entering into the discussion of the principles of the case, and limiting myself to the consideration of the right of asylum as a usage . . . the thought of the Chilean government has been not to abolish completely this humane and established custom, but to confine it to certain cases . . .

Señor Pacheco [Peruvian Minister of Foreign Relations] answered that having carefully studied the subject of asylum, the Peruvian government thought that custom had no precedent foundation in law. . . .

Señor Varnhagen [Brazil] . . . said that . . . although it be not a principle but a mere practice, to abolish it when it is necessary and when those cases occur so frequently . . . would be to deprive the house of the foreign ministers of the respectability which they enjoy, and to endanger their privileges. . . .

General Hovey [United States] replied that the practice of asylum did not exist in the United States, and that if a case had occurred and the government had demanded the delivery of the transgressor, he would have been given up by the foreign minister who had him in his house. . . .[2]

---

[1] This writer has been unable to find any bilateral treaties on diplomatic asylum signed by Latin American states, nor has he observed any reference to such treaties in any of the cases on diplomatic asylum which have come to his attention. He has not checked every bilateral treaty on *extradition* among Latin American states but in those which have been observed there is no evidence to indicate that the parties intended to include diplomatic asylum within the scope of said treaties. It may also be observed that no bilateral treaties on asylum were cited in the recent *Colombian-Peruvian Asylum Case.*

[2] Translation (enclosure in Hovey, U. S. Minister to Peru, to Seward, Secretary of State, February 14, 1867), *Dip. Cor. of the U. S.,* 1867, II, pp. 740–742.

This was the tone of the entire proceedings. The closing comment by the French envoy is instructive inasmuch as it explains why "agreements" eventually emerge from the obvious disagreement.

M. de Lesseps continued, saying that he had not expected that the present meeting would produce the result of placing the members of the conference on different standpoints ... that public opinion was already being heard on the subject; that the public and the press were saying that a respectable conference, referring to the present one, in which there were persons of great ability, was discussing the question of asylum; that it would be regretted that it should come to an end without obtaining a practical result .... [1]

The results were hardly spectacular. The Peruvian Minister of Foreign Relations was prepared to submit a set of principles but "when the *Memorandum* was about to be read, some of the honorable members remarked that the hour was rather late, and it was agreed that the secretary should send it to the senior member of the body ..." [2] This, for all practical purposes, was as close as the members came to an agreement.

In some cases certain members of the diplomatic corps have reached agreements on procedures for accepting refugees but such agreements have not attempted to establish any legal basis for the practice. [3] The Argentine *Project of Convention on the Right of Asylum* [4] which grew out of the controversies over asylum during the Spanish Civil War was widely circulated but apparently not opened for signature and ratification. It did, however, contribute to the Treaty on Political Asylum and Refuge signed at Montevideo, in 1939. [5]

A number of American conferences and congresses have dealt with the question of asylum and have succeeded in drafting treaties and conventions which have been signed by all or nearly all of the participating members. In most cases, however, ratifications have been far less numerous than signatures.

The first multilateral agreement dealing with diplomatic asylum was the Treaty on International Penal Law, signed at Montevideo, 1889. The relevant part of this treaty is Article 17 of Title II.

---

[1] *Ibid.*, p. 742.

[2] *Ibid.*

[3] In 1898, in Bolivia. See Bridgman, U. S. Minister to Bolivia, to Hay, Secretary of State December 24, 1898, *For. Rel. of the U. S.*, 1898, p. 171, for a text of the agreement. An accord was signed by Germany, Argentina, Spain, Bolivia, Brazil, Cuba, the United States, France, Great Britain, Peru, and Uruguay regulating procedures in Paraguay on June 5, 1922; Perú, *Proceso*, p. 380.

[4] Argentine Republic, Ministry of Foreign Affairs and Worship, *Project of Convention on the Right of Asylum* (Buenos Aires, 1937).

[5] Morena Quintana, *op. cit.*, pp. 53, 57.

The common criminal who is given asylum in a legation, must be surrendered by its chief to the local authorities, after negotiations with the Minister of Foreign Relations, when it is not effected spontaneously.

Said asylum will be respected with regard to persons pursued for political reasons; but the chief of the legation is obligated to inform immediately the Government of the State to which he is accredited, who can demand that the refugee be placed outside the national territory, within the shortest time possible.

The same principle will be observed with respect to refugees on warships anchored in territorial waters.[1]

The treaty was signed by five of the states attending the congress and as of November 14, 1957, only those five states had ratified (or adhered to) it.[2]

At the Second American Congress on Private International Law held at Montevideo in 1939, Argentina, Bolivia, Chile, Paraguay, Peru and Uruguay signed a Treaty on Political Asylum and Refuge.[3] According to the preamble of the treaty, "the principles governing asylum which were established by the Treaty on International Penal Law signed at Montevideo on January 23, 1889, require amplification in order that they may cover the new situations which have arisen and may serve to confirm the doctrines already sanctioned in America ...[4]

The sections concerned with the amplification of the 1889 Treaty will be dealt with in another chapter. Those intended to "confirm doctrines already sanctioned in America" are the following:

Article I. Asylum may be granted without distinction of nationality, and without prejudice to the rights and obligations of protection appertaining to the State to which the refugees belong. ...

Article II. Asylum may be granted only in embassies, legations, men-of-war,

---

[1] Perú, Ministerio de Relaciones Exteriores, *Congresos y conferencias internacionales en que ha tomado parte el Perú* (Lima: Oficina de "La Opinión Nacional," 1910), p. 296; Martens, *op. cit.*, XVIII (2me série par Stoerb, 1893), p. 432. Apparently this treaty has not been registered with the Secretariat of the League or the U. N.

[2] Letter from Mary P. McWalters, Cultural Affairs Assistant, American Embassy, Montevideo, Uruguay, November 14, 1957. The Ministry of Foreign Affairs of Uruguay is the depository for the instruments of ratification of this treaty. See also Universidad de Buenos Aires, Facultad de Derecho y Ciencias Sociales, *Segundo congreso sudamericano de derecho internacional privado de Montevideo* (Buenos Aires, 1940), p. 5. The latter source shows seven signatories but the letter cited above shows but five. Colombia also cited five signatories in the *Colombian-Peruvian Asylum Case* and it appears that this was not contested by Peru; Perú, *Proceso*, p. 121. Apparently the treaty is still in force. Both parties treated it in this manner before the International Court of Justice. See *ibid.*, pp. 121, 162–163. See also Moreno Quintana, *op. cit.*, p. 81, where it is asserted that the treaty is in force among the five ratifying states.

[3] Manley O. Hudson, ed., *International Legislation* (Washington: Carnegie Endowment for International Peace, 1949) VII, pp. 405-6.

[4] *Ibid.*, p. 405.

military camps or military airplanes, and exclusively to persons pursued for political reasons or offenses, or under circumstances involving concurrent political offenses, which do not legally permit of extradition. The chiefs of missions may also receive refugees in their residences, in cases where the former do not live on the premises of the embassies or legations.

Asylum shall not be granted to persons accused of political offenses, who shall have been indicted or condemned previously for common offenses, by the ordinary tribunals. ...[1]

The significance of this treaty, insofar as the contractual status of diplomatic asylum is concerned, is indicated by the fact that only Uruguay and Paraguay have ratified to date.[2] But this does not necessarily indicate a rejection of the principles of the 1889 treaty, inasmuch as the 1939 treaty was equally concerned with the amplification of the former, one aspect of which dealt with the highly controversial question of the qualification of the offense.

By far the most important of the contractual arrangements are the Convention on Asylum signed at Havana, February 20, 1928,[3] the Convention on Political Asylum signed at Montevideo, December 26, 1933 [4] and the Convention on Diplomatic Asylum signed at Caracas, March 28, 1954.[5] These are the only conventions signed at international conferences embracing all the American republics.[6]

---

[1] *Ibid.*, pp. 406–407.

[2] Letter from Mary P. McWalters, Cultural Affairs Assistant, American Embassy, Montevideo, Uruguay, November 14, 1957. The Uruguayan Ministry of Foreign Relations is the depository of the instruments of ratification of this treaty. See also the Bolivarian Agreement on Extradition of 1911, signed by Bolivia, Colombia, Peru and Venezuela. The relevant part of this treaty is Article 18: "Aside from the stipulations of the present agreement, the signatory States recognize the institution of asylum in conformity with the principles of international law." Perú, Ministerio de Relaciones Exteriores, *Congresos y conferencias internacionales en que ha tomado parte el Perú* (Lima: Imp. Americana, 1920), p. 627. In the *Colombian-Peruvian Asylum Case* Peru pointed out, correctly in this writer's opinion, that this was an extradition treaty and as such, referred only to territorial asylum. Perú, *Proceso*, pp. 165–166. In any event, the Court gave it only passing attention, implying that the contracting parties had agreed to recognize the institution of asylum *insofar* as it is recognized in international law. *Op. cit.*, pp. 274–275.

[3] Manley O. Hudson, ed., *International Legislation* (Washington: Carnegie Endowment for International Peace, 1931), IV, p. 2412. *League of Nations Treaty Series*, CXXXII, p. 323; Martens, *op. cit.*, XL (3e série, 1943), p. 357. International Conference of American States, Sixth, *Final Act: Motions, Agreements, Resolutions and Conventions* (Havana, 1928), p. 166; International Conference of American States, Sixth, *Report of the Delegation of the United States of America* (Washington: G. P. O., 1928), p. 225.

[4] Martens, *op. cit.*, XL (3e série, 1943), p.446; Hudson, *op. cit.*, VI, p. 607; International Conference of American States, Seventh, *Report of the Delegates of the United States of America to the Seventh International Conference of American States* (Washington: G.P.O., 1933), p. 141; International Conference of American States, Seventh, *Final Act*, ([Montevideo]), p. 162. This convention has not been registered with the League of Nations or United Nations Secretariats.

[5] International Conference of American States, Tenth, *Report of the Pan American Union on the Conference*, Conferences and Organizations Series, No. 36 (Washington, 1955), p. 39; Pan American Union, [Division of Law and Treaties], *Convention on Diplomatic Asylum*

Only Articles 1 and 2, of the Havana Convention are relevant here.

Article I. It is not permissible for States to grant asylum in legations, warships, military camps or military aircraft, to persons accused or condemned for common crimes, or to deserters from the army or navy.

Persons accused or condemned for common crimes taking refuge in any of the places mentioned in the preceding paragraph, shall be surrendered upon request to the local government. ...[1]

In the *Colombian-Peruvian Asylum Case* the Court pointed out that this convention was primarily a *limiting* document, "concluded with the manifest intention of preventing the abuses which had arisen in the previous practice, by limiting the grant of asylum." [2] With the exception of Article 2, it is clear that the remainder of the convention attempts to lay down certain rules to regulate and formalize a general practice. It was in this tone that the Mexican delegate to the Sixth International Conference of American States reported on Project X of the International Commission of American Jurists. Project X served as the basis for the Convention.

Under such terms, the ultimate result of the aforementioned project is a limitation affecting persons, in regard to places, and concerning time. Besides, it takes precautions, prudently and discretely, which are necessarily [sic, necessary?] in order to prevent the undue exercise of the right of asylum.[3]

It cannot be deduced from this, however, that the convention *assumes* a "right of asylum" and then simply proceeds to establish certain limits. Article 2, deals with asylum in a more positive way.

Article II. Asylum granted to political offenders in legations, warships, military aircraft, shall be respected to the extent in which allowed, as a right or through humanitarian toleration, by the usages, the conventions or the laws of the country in which granted. ...[4]

Signed at the Tenth Inter-American Conference, Caracas, March 1–28, 1954, Law and Treaty Series (Washington, 1954). Conventions and treaties are not printed in the *Final Act* of this Conference.

[6] Excluding Canada.

[1] Hudson, *International Legislation,* IV, p. 2414.

[2] *Op. cit.,* 275.

[3] International Conference of American States, Sixth, *Minutes and Reports of Committees,* Part I, Binders Title (Havana, 1928), various pagings.

[4] Hudson, *op. cit.,* IV, p. 2414. The English version is open to an interpretation quite different from that of the Spanish and French versions, as regards the words "of the country in which granted." The Spanish "del país de refugio" and the French "du pays de refuge" would clearly translate into "the country of refuge" which was the interpretation given by the International Court of Justice. The English version could easily be interpreted to mean the laws of the territorial state rather than of the country of refuge. For the French and Spanish versions, see respectively, *ibid.,* and Carnegie Endowment for International Peace, Division of International Law, *Conferencias internacionales americanas,* 1889–1936 (Was-

In its arguments before the International Court of Justice, the Peruvian government insisted that the text of this article did not comprehend any general or unconditional recognition of asylum: "Its admission is subordinated to the existence of a *usage*, of conventions, or of the laws of the country of refuge. But in no way is it stated that it can be based upon custom." [1] In fact, according to the Peruvian argument, "this custom, admitting that it may have existed, is substituted and abolished by convention." [2]

The Colombian arguments gave an implicit recognition of this in asserting that "the customs, conventions and the laws of Colombia as concerns asylum, constitute in fact the code that ought to rule, obligatorily, all the measures which regulate the application of norms in the present case." [3]

The decision of the Court in this case offered very little in the way of clarification. Noting the above mentioned Colombian argument that the territorial state was bound to recognize the usages, conventions, and laws of the state of refuge, the Court observed that "this interpretation, which would mean that the extent of the obligations of one of the signatory states would depend upon any modifications which might occur in the law of another, cannot be accepted." [4] But then after asserting that the provision must be regarded as "a limitation of the extent to which asylum shall be respected," it seemed to reverse itself.

> What the provision says in effect is that the state of refuge shall not exercise asylum to a larger extent than is warranted by its own usages, conventions or laws, and that the asylum granted must be respected by the territorial state only where such asylum would be permitted according to the usages, conventions or laws of the State of refuge. Nothing therefore can be deduced from this provision in so far as qualification is concerned. [5]

About all that can be deduced from this is that the Court felt that "qualification of the offence" cannot be considered a part of "the extent to which asylum is recognized." The meaning of the words "extent to which asylum is recognized" was not provided. In any event, all parties were agreed that no general recognition of asylum had been established by the treaty.

hington: Carnegie Endowment for International Peace, 1938) p. 387. See also Martens, *op. cit.*, XL, (3e série), p. 357.

[1] Perú, *Proceso*, p. 163. (My translation.)
[2] *Ibid.*
[3] *Ibid.*, p. 116. (My translation.)
[4] *Op. cit.*, p. 276.
[5] *Ibid.*

The antecedents of the Sixth International Conference of American States, the conference at which this treaty was signed, lend support to this interpretation. Project X of the International Commission of Jurists which met in Rio de Janeiro in 1927, formed the working basis for the treaty.[1] Article 2 of this project provided that:

Asylum granted to persons accused of political crimes, in national territory, in legations, on war vessels, or in military camps or aircraft, must be respected.[2]

The significantly different wording in Article 2 of the Treaty of Havana is explained in the report of the Mexican delegate, González Roa, Chairman of the committee which prepared the latter document.

After the project was discussed, the chairman noted that some delegations, among them the United States, were opposed to the acceptance of the right of asylum and then proposed the substitution of another article for Article 2 of the project, declaring that asylum would be respected to the extent to which, as a right or through humanitarian tolerance, it might be admitted by practice or conventions in force in the countries in which it might be conceded.[3]

A final observation in this same report makes this even more clear:

In spite of the fact that in this form the contracting States remained at liberty to follow their own policy [política] in the matter of asylum, the U. S. Delegation added a reservation on this point. . . .[4]

The report of the Brazilian delegation indicates that that government was one of those desiring the change.

Article 2 of the project on convention approved by the International Commission of Jurists, had consecrated the right of asylum, which Brazil, for its part, has permitted in special cases, through considerations of humanity.
On the proposal of the reporter, who accomodated the text to situations such as that of Brazil, Article 2 became the following . . .[5]

---

[1] International Conference of American States, Sixth, *Minutes and Reports of Committees.*
[2] *American Journal of International Law*, XXII, Special Supplement (January, 1928), p. 265.
[3] Mexico, Secretario Relaciones Exteriores, *La participación de México en la sexta conferencia internacional americana*, informe general de la delegación de México (México; Imprenta de la Secretario de Relaciones Exteriores, 1928), p. 145. (My translation.) The punctuation has been changed slightly in this translation for purposes of clarity. The Spanish version makes the above interpretation even more clear. "Antes de que se discutiera el proyecto, el ponente tuvo conocimiento que algunas delegaciones, entre ellos la de los Estados Unidos, se opondrían a la aceptación del derecho de asilo, y entonces propuso que se substituyera el Artículo 2 del proyecto por otro, declarando que el asilo se respetaría en la medida en que por un derecho o por humanitaria tolerancia lo admitieran el uso o los convenciones en vigor en los países en que fuere concedido." But note that this uses language much closer to that of the English version of the Treaty.
[4] *Ibid.*
[5] Brazil, Ministerio de Estado, *Relatório apresentado ao Ministro de Estado das Relações Exteriores pelo Presidente da Delagação do Brasil a 6ª conferencia internacional americana*

The practice of Latin American states offers little in the way of interpretation. In a great many cases treaties are not invoked even though binding upon both parties. A recent case involving Cuba and Peru provides an excellent demonstration of this. On December 29, 1948, the dean of the diplomatic corps in Lima notified the Peruvian Minister of Foreign Relations that, inasmuch as Cuba did not maintain relations with the present government, it had requested the dean of the corps to solicit safe conduct for two refugees in the Cuban embassy. No treaty, practice or custom was invoked even though both Cuba and Peru had ratified the Havana convention.[1] On January 18, 1949, the Cuban *chargé d'affaires* addressed a note directly to the Peruvian Minister of Foreign Affairs and Worship again soliciting safe conduct but without invoking any treaty.[2] It was not until February 21, 1949 that the Convention of Havana was finally invoked.[3]

In 1938, *after having ratified the treaty*, the Brazilian foreign office sent a circular to the foreign diplomatic missions stating that asylum in legations or embassies " does not constitute a right, although practice has admitted it in certain circumstances as a reasonable measure, determined by purely humanitarian motives." [4] The circular then pointed out that, with these considerations in mind, Brazil had given its frank adhesion to the conventions of Havana and Montevideo "and will loyally respect them, while they are in force, in her relations with the rest of the ratifying governments." [5]

In contrast to this the government of Cuba pointed out as an interested party before the International Court of Justice that "the Convention of Havana of 1928, clearly establishes the legitimacy of asylum conceded to political delinquents." [6]

Where treaties are invoked the interpretation is given only in

realizada em Havana, em 1928 (Rio de Janeiro: Imprensa Nacional, 1929), p. 39. (My translation.)

[1] Irrazabal, Paraguayan Ambassador and Dean of the Diplomatic Corps, to Díaz Dulanto, Minister of Foreign Relations and Worship, December 29, 1948, full text of note in *Revista peruana de derecho internacional*, Toma IX (1949), pp. 148–149.

[2] Espinoza, Cuban *Chargé d'Affaires*, to Díaz Dulanto, January 18, 1949, *ibid.* p. 150.

[3] Espinoza to Díaz Dulanto, February 21, 1949, *ibid.*, pp. 150–152.

[4] Perú, *Proceso*, p. 155. (My translation.)

[5] *Ibid.*

[6] "Exposition Presented to the International Court of Justice by the Government of the Republic of Cuba," February 15, 1951, *ibid.*, p. 71. (My translation.) Cuba argued that as a signatory to the Treaty of Havana she had an interest in the interpretation which would be given to that treaty and submitted her views according to Article 63 of the Statute of the International Court of Justice. "Note from the Minister of State of the Republic of Cuba to the Secretary of the International Court of Justice," February 15, 1951, *Proceso*, II, pp. 69–70.

ambiguous terms. The matter is even further confused by the fact that a number of conventions are often referred to simultaneously in diplomatic notes with little regard to whether or not the author or recipient state has signed or ratified any or all of the conventions. Typical of this is the Chilean position given in its *Memoria* for 1936, with reference to the controversy over asylum in Spain. It was reported that Chile had "firmly maintained its thesis in favor of the right of asylum, consecrated in the conventions of Montevideo, 1889; Havana, 1928, and of Montevideo of 1933, in which it is indicated to whom it can be fully applied, through elimination of those to whom it cannot apply." [1] Spain had neither signed nor ratified any of these conventions and Chile had signed only (but had not ratified) the conventions of 1889 and 1928. [2]

Similarly, in connection with asylum granted in Bolivia in 1946, a memorandum of the Paraguayan embassy did not invoke the Montevideo treaty of 1889, the *one* treaty binding both parties, but invoked the Convention of Havana, the Convention of Montevideo, 1933, and the Treaty of Montevideo, 1939, none of which Bolivia had ratified. [3] In the latter case, *neither* party had ratified the treaty. [4]

In answer to an inquiry by Chile in 1937, Ecuador referred to the "Latin American principle of internal asylum defined by the conventions of Havana and Montevideo." [5] In 1949 the same government reported that it had "informed public opinion through the press that it considered that asylum is consecrated and defined, not only by American international conventions but also by international custom." [6] Similarly, the Bolivian delegate to the League of Nations said that "there exists a right, an American right perpetuated by age long traditions and confirmed by the conventions of Montevideo and Havana." [7] Bolivia had signed but had not ratified the Havana Convention and had neither signed nor adhered to the Montevideo Convention. [8]

Thus the only conlusion one can reach concerning the interpretation

---

[1] Chile, *Memoria*, 1936, p. 570. (My translation.)

[2] See appendices I–III.

[3] "Memorandum," September 24, 1946, Bolivia, Ministerio de Relaciones Exteriores, *Boletín del Ministerio de Relaciones Exteriores* (julio-diciembre, 1946), pp. 62–64.

[4] See Appendices I, II.

[5] "Memorandum ,"June 2, 1939, Perú, *Proceso*, p. 271. (My translation.)

[6] Ecuador, *Informe a la nación* (Quito: junio, 1949), p. 68. (My translation.)

[7] League of Nations, Council, *Official Journal*, 95th session, fourth meeting, December 12, 1936, p. 20.

[8] See Appendices I, II.

given to this article by Latin American states is that there has been considerable disagreement; it has been largely a matter of expediency and offers little help in determining the intended meaning. The general lack of agreement plus the interpretation rendered by the International Court of Justice and the antecedents of the Sixth International Conference of American States showing that the present article was substituted for an article clearly recognizing a right of asylum would certainly indicate, however, that the treaty was not intended to establish any general right of asylum even among the signatories – much less in "Latin American International Law."

The English version of the Montevideo Convention of 1933 states that its purpose is "to *define* the terms of the one signed at Havana." [1] The Spanish and Portuguese versions use the words *modifica* [2] and *modifique* [3] respectively. Thus the International Court of Justice ruled in the *Colombian-Peruvian Asylum Case* that inasmuch as it "modifies" the Havana Convention "it cannot therefore be considered as representing merely an interpretation of that convention." [4] This fact is parhaps of no great significance for the interpretation of the point under consideration here inasmuch as the relevant part of this treaty does not seem to bind the signatory states to any generally accepted rule any more than does the Havana Convention. Article 1 specifies certain conditions under which asylum shall *not* be granted and Article 2 deals with the qualification of the offence,[5] both of which will be dealt with below. Article 3 would correspond most closely to Article 2 of the Havana Convention.

Political asylum, as an institution of humanitarian character, is not subject to reciprocity. Any man may resort to its protection, whatever his nationality, without prejudice to the obligations accepted by the State to which he belongs; however, the States that do not recognize political asylum, except with limitations and peculiarities, can exercise it in foreign countries only in the manner and within the limits recognized by said countries.[6]

It will be noted that this is almost exactly the interpretation given

---

[1] Hudson, *International Legislation*, VI, p. 608.
[2] *Ibid.*
[3] Brazil, Ministro de Estado das Relações Exteriores, *Relatório apresentado ao Dr. Getulio Vargas Presidente da República dos Estados Unidos do Brasil pelo Dr. Alfranio de Mello, Ministro de Estado das Relações Exteriores: Ano de 1933*, (Rio de Janeiro: Imprensa Nacional, 1939), anexo especial, 3° Volume, p. 132.
[4] *Op. cit.*, p. 277.
[5] Hudson, *International Legislation*, VI, pp. 609–610.
[6] *Ibid.*

to Article 2 of the Havana Convention by the International Court of Justice.[1]

The meaning of this article seems even more obscure than that of Article 2 of the Havana Convention. To say that "any man may resort to its protection [asylum], without prejudice to the obligations accepted by the State to which he belongs," seems to imply that the territorial state is not necessarily obliged to respect it. Lauterpacht's analysis of the meaning of Article 14 of the Universal Declaration of Human Rights is instructive in this respect. The provision there that "everyone has a right to *seek* and to *enjoy* in other countries asylum from persecution," according to his interpretation, "does not confer a right to receive asylum." [2] Furthermore, the words "any man may resort to its protection ... without prejudice to the obligations accepted by the State to which he belongs" seem considerably weaker than the words "everyone has a right to *seek* and to *enjoy* in other countries asylum from persecution." The fact that one provision refers to territorial asylum and the other to diplomatic asylum would not invalidate the analogy in this case. Both of these provisions are concerned with claims of an individual and with the action of a state within its own territory, at least insofar as the Montevideo Convention creates an obligation for the territorial state.

What follows seems to imply two conflicting ideas: "the states that do not recognize political asylum, except with limitations and peculiarities, can exercise it in foreign countries only in the manner and within the limits recognized by said countries." On the one hand this implies that the extent to which asylum can be granted in any particular case will depend upon the manner and limits recognized by the state of refuge. On the other hand it admits that some states "do not recognize political asylum except with limitations and peculiarities." If a state in this latter group is in the role of the *territorial* state, is it then obliged to recognize asylum to the extent that it is recognized by the usage, laws and conventions of the state which *grants the refuge* even if that may be in its fullest and most extreme form? Such an interpretation would hardly seem acceptable in view of the antecedents of the convention itself. The chairman of the sub-committee that wrote the text of the convention reported that "some states do not recognize asylum, *or* they accept it with modifications and specific

[1] *Op. cit.*, p. 276.
[2] *Op. cit.*, pp. 677–678.

characteristics. The sub-committee has anticipated the case and proposes an express declaration in this regard." [1]

If this declaration was intended to meet the objections of states which did not recognize asylum it is extremely doubtful if such an interpretation of the declaration would have satisfied their objections. In this way each state would have agreed to be bound by the practice of the state recognizing asylum in its most extreme form should that state decide to grant asylum within its territory.

Thus it is safe to conclude that, while it is by no means clear what obligations are incurred in the conventions of Havana and Montevideo (1933), neither of them establishes a general right of asylum. The clearest statement of this was presented in the dissenting opinion of M. Caicedo Castillo, Judge *ad hoc* for Colombia in the *Colombian-Peruvian Asylum Case*. Speaking only of the Havana Convention he said:

> No effort is made to find a definite basis for asylum from the legal point of view, so that some contracting States may consider asylum as an institution based strictly on law, while others may consider it as a custom or merely a humanitarian toleration. [2]

The Convention of Diplomatic Asylum signed at the Tenth Inter-American Conference at Caracas, March 28, 1954, clearly establishes an obligation to respect a "right of asylum" with regard to political offenses. [3]

Article I
Asylum granted in legations, war vessels, and military camps or aircraft, to persons being sought for political reasons or for political offenses shall be respected by the territorial state in accordance with the provisions of this Convention ...

Article II
Every State has the right to grant asylum; but it is not obliged to do so or to state its reasons for refusing it.

Asylum is not to be granted to deserters from the armed forces or to persons indicted or convicted for common crimes at the time of the request for asylum. [4] But limitations similar to those provided in

---

[1] International Conference of American States, Seventh, *Minutes and Antecedents with General Index* (Montevideo, 1933), p. 172.
[2] *Op. cit.*, p. 361.
[3] Pan American Union, *Convention on Diplomatic Asylum*, Law and Treaty Series (Washington, 1954), p. 1.
[4] *Ibid.*

Article 2 of the Havana Convention and in Article [1] of the Montevideo Convention of 1933 are not included here.

Signatories included all the Latin American states with the exception of Peru. As of September, 1963 eleven of these states had ratified. Since the signing of this treaty, the Dominican Republic has denounced the treaties of Havana and Montevideo, 1933. The 1954 convention was not mentioned in the denunciation but it can be assumed that this was considered unnecessary inasmuch as it had not been ratified by the Dominican government at that time.

RATIFICATION OF MULTILATERAL AGREEMENTS,
CONVENTIONS, AND TREATIES ON ASYLUM

	Montevideo 1889 [2]	Havana 1928 [3]	Montevideo 1933 [4]	Montevideo 1939 [5]	Caracas 1954 [6]
Argentina	X				
Bolivia	X				
Brazil		X	X		X
Colombia		X	X		
Costa Rica		X	X		X
Cuba		X	X		
Chile			X		
Ecuador		X	X		X
El Salvador		X	X		X
Guatemala		X	X		
Haiti		X	X		X
Honduras		X	X		
Mexico		X	X		X
Nicaragua		X	X		
Panama		X	X		X
Paraguay	X	X	X	X	X
Peru	X	X	X		X
Dominican Republic					X
Uruguay	X	X		X	
Venezuela					X

[1] See Appendix III.

[2] Letter from Mary P. McWalters, Cultural Affairs Assistant, American Embassy, Montevideo, Uruguay, November 14, 1957. The only date of ratification available is that for Uruguay: Oct. 17, 1892.

[3] Pan American Union, *Status of Inter-American Treaties*, Treaty Series No. 5, Revised to September 1, 1963 (Washington, 1963), p. 5.

[4] *Ibid.*, p. 7.

[5] Letter from Mary P. McWalters, Cultural Affairs Assistant, American Embassy, Montevideo, Uruguay, November 14, 1957. See also Hudson, *International Legislation*, VII, p. 104. Uruguay ratified Nov. 12, 1942; other dates of ratification are not available.

[6] Pan American Union, *Status of Inter-American Treaties*, Treaty Series No. 5, Revised to September 1, 1963 (Washington, 1963), p.9.

Only the Montevideo treaties of 1889 and 1939 and the Caracas Convention of 1954 clearly establish among the signatories the recognition of a general right of asylum. The Montevideo conventions of 1889 and 1939, were signed by only five and six states respectively and ratified by five and two states respectively. The Caracas Convention, although signed by nineteen states, has been ratified by only eleven. Thus Argentina, Bolivia, Brazil, Costa Rica, Ecuador, El Salvador, Haiti, Mexico, Panama, Paraguay, Peru, Dominican Republic, Uruguay and Venezuela have agreed to respect a general right of asylum. But not all of these states are bound by the same treaty. It must be concluded that, so far as any contractual obligation to recognize a general right of diplomatic asylum is concerned, it is in force only among two different groups of five and eleven states respectively.

CHAPTER V

DIPLOMATIC ASYLUM
IN LATIN AMERICAN PRACTICE

A singular feature of most asylum cases in Latin America is the fact that the controversy seldom centers around the question whether or not the state of refuge, in granting protection to persons pursued for political offences, is exercising a right which the territorial state is legally bound to respect. This study has already indicated that, in a great many cases, political expediency and lack of concern on the part of the territorial state seem to be the primary considerations and there is no evidence that legal issues were ever discussed.

Where the case is sufficiently important to evoke strong objections on the part of the territorial state the controversy will usually center around the question as to whether or not a particular refugee falls within the category of those to whom asylum may be afforded. This suggests that the right of asylum for political offenders is simply taken for granted and regarded as a rule incumbent upon the territorial state. There are reasons, however, why such an assumption cannot be made without further investigation. The rights and obligations in a particular instance may rest upon a treaty in which case there is no question of law apart from the provisions of the agreement. It could also mean that the territorial state regards asylum for political offenders as a mere toleration on its part and that it is unwilling to extend this toleration to "common criminals."

This chapter will attempt to determine, on the basis of cases and other instances where state policy has been expressed, upon what grounds (i.e. mere toleration of a practice or recognition of an obligatory rule based upon a custom recognized as law) is the granting of asylum in embassies and legations practiced and respected in Latin America.

Until 1946 the statements of the Venezuelan Foreign Ministry were remarkably consistent in denying any legal status to the practice of asylum. This position was first outlined in connection with a controversy over asylum granted to General Monagas in the French legation in Caracas in 1858. In this case the Venezuelan government pointed out that a right of asylum was not recognized among European states and that a different rule would be inadmissible in Venezuela.[1] Continuing this policy, the Venezuelan *Memoria* for 1880, stated that "as concerns the houses of public ministers and ships of war, no one doubts the right of the State concerned, to claim, with all consideration of the case, the surrender of the one who takes refuge there in order to remove himself from the action of the authorities." [2]

In 1928, the Colombian minister informed the Venezuelan Minister of Foreign Relations that asylum had been granted in the Colombian legation to a Venezuelan student and stated his desire to reach an agreement on the matter.[3] The Venezuelan Minister of Foreign Relations replied that there were no charges against said student and consequently there was no reason for his seeking asylum. Nevertheless, the minister said that he considered it opportune to reiterate Venezuela's position on this matter.

> ...The Republic does not recognize asylum as a right whose juridical result would be to withdraw from action of the civil and judicial authorities, nationals in its very own country, diminishing and compromising the sovereignty of the latter.
>
> If for reasons of simple humanity, asylum is conceded to persons in grave and imminent risk of loss of life, such asylum could not be respected as a juridical situation, according to international principles, except where there arises a positive conventional right, clearly defined between the country whose legation concedes asylum and the country in which it functions ...
>
> Venezuela, for its part, following a tradition founded on experience, considers asylum as an institution of purely humanitarian tendency without the character of law, dangerous to sovereignty and to the good and friendly relations among States ...[4]

This same position has been maintained on a number of occasions.

---

[1] Toro, Venezuelan Minister of Foreign Relations, to the Diplomatic Representatives of France and Great Britain, April 30, 1858, in Venezuela, Ministerio de Relaciones Exteriores, *Cuestión promovida a Venezuela por los agentes de Francia y de la Gran Bretaña* (Caracas, Imprenta de Jesús María Soriana, 1858), pp. 28–53.

[2] P. 15. (My translation.)

[3] Zuelta, to Itraigo Chachin, April 12, 1928, in Venezuela, Ministerio de Relaciones Exteriores, *Boletín del Ministerio de Relaciones Exteriores de los Estados Unidos de Venezuela*, año IV, nos. 4, 5, 6, y 7 (abril, mayo, junio y julio, 1928), pp. 277–278. (My translation.) Hereafter cited as Venezuela, *Boletín*.

[4] *Ibid.*, pp. 278–279. See also Venezuela, Ministerio de Relaciones Exteriores, *Libro Amarillo de los Estados Unidos de Venezuela presentado al Congreso Nacional en sus sesiones de 1929 por el Ministerio de Relaciones Exteriores* (Caracas: Tipográfica Americana, 1929), pp. 203–204. (My translation.) Hereafter cited as Venezuela, *Libro Amarillo*.

In connection with the controversy over asylum during the Spanish Civil War, the Venezuelan Minister of Foreign Relations advised its legation in Santiago, Chile, that "the government of Venezuela has always maintained that asylum is not a right but a humanitarian practice." [1] But it advised, with regard to the Chilean solicitation for support of the policy the latter government was maintaining in Madrid, that it could support "whatever humanitarian action the embassy of Chile may take." [2]

Two months later the Foreign Office gave a more explicit account of the Venezuelan position. Referring first to the previous telegrams, quoted above, it again informed the minister in Santiago that:

> Consistent with this doctrine, the government of Venezuela considers that asylum can only be considered as a right in the countries that have expressly admitted it and are parties to the international instruments formulated in order to recognize and regulate such right. Venezuela is not a party to such agreements and does not admit that the foreign missions accredited here can accord asylum nor invoke it or demand it as an admitted and recognized juridical principle. For that reason our government would not be able to collaborate in any collective action which has as an object a claim of such principles before a third power.[3]

After 1946, the policy of the Venezuelan government became far more ambiguous. As a result of the 1946 revolution in Bolivia a large number of refugees received asylum in legations in La Paz. The Venezuelan ambassador, as dean of the diplomatic corps, took charge of the negotiations with the *de facto* government of Bolivia in demanding safe conduct out of the country for all of said refugees. As is so often the case, the controversy revolved around the question as to whether or not these were political refugees or common criminals and the question of a "right of asylum" was not really an issue. A memorandum of the diplomatic corps noted that said corps had met in the residence of the Venezuelan ambassador and by unanimous agreement empowered him to present a list of the refugees in the legations and "to solicit for all of them, without exception, the respective safe

---

[1] Borges, Venezuelan Minister of Foreign Relations, to the Venezuelan Legation in Santiago, Chile, June 17, 1939, Venezuela, *Libro Amarillo* 1940, I, p. 129. The text of this was also sent to the Venezuelan minister in Spain, see *ibid.*, p. 130. (My translation.)

[2] *Ibid.*, p. 129. (My translation.)

[3] Borges, Venezuelan Minister of Foreign Relations to Carnivali, Venezuelan Minister to Chile, August 23, 1939, *ibid.*, p. 131. (My translation.) For a similar statement in the "Position of Venezuela on the Problems of the Conference," prepared for the Eighth Inter-American Conference at Lima, 1938, see *Libro Amarillo*, 1939, I, pp. 81–83. (My translation.) For a similar statement by the Minister of Foreign Relations printed in the *Memoria* (now superseded by *Libro Amarillo*), see Simón Planas-Suárez, *op. cit.*, p. 505.

conduct in order that, in conformity with international conventions signed by Bolivia, the principles of international law and of customary Latin American law, they can leave the country with due security and protection." [1] Bolivia was bound only by the Treaty of Montevideo, 1889, and only three other members of the diplomatic corps who had granted asylum (Argentina, Paraguay and Peru), were parties to this treaty.[2]

The Venezuelan *Libro Amarillo* gave very little attention to the case in its 1947 edition and, indeed, emphasized that the Venezuelan ambassador had acted as the representative of the diplomatic corps as much as representative of Venezuela.

> The exit of all the refugees from Bolivian territory was authorized after active measures by the resident diplomatic corps in La Paz, *in which there was detached action on the part of Lieutenant Colonel Estaban Chalbaud Cardona*, in his role of ambassador from Venezuela and dean of that corps.[3]

In January of 1949, the ambassadors of Chile and Guatemala asked the Council of the Organization of American States to take action concerning the refusal of the Venezuelan government to grant safe conduct passes to Rómulo Betancourt, who had received asylum in the Colombian embassy in Caracas.[4] While this controversy again revolved primarily around the question of safe conduct rather than the legal basis of the institution of asylum, the Venezuelan position regarding the latter question was stated in a note to the government of Chile.

> The problem of asylum in its entirety presents two aspects: one is the acceptance of the rule of asylum, that which is manifested as a right, by the signing of the pertinent conventions and *de facto*, when the existence of refugees in the diplomatic missions is tolerated.
> The country which refuses to become a party to treaties on this matter would reject the principle of asylum; the country which, having contracted such agreements, refuses to permit the access by refugees to such missions would violate its international agreements on asylum.[5]

The note then pointed out that neither of these was the case with Venezuela because it had "concluded last year, precisely with Colom-

---

[1] July 30, 1946, Chile, *Memoria*, 1946, p. 51. (My translation.)

[2] *Supra*, p. 64. It is not known which members of the diplomatic corps were present at this meeting. Venezuela, Paraguay, Peru, Argentina, Ecuador, Holy See, and Mexico had granted asylum in their legations; see Memorandum of the Diplomatic Corps, August 19, 1946, Bolivia, *Boletín Oficial* (julio-diciembre, 1946), pp 51–52.

[3] Venezuela, *Libro Amarillo*, 1947, pp. v–vi. (My translation and italics.)

[4] See full text of notes in *Annals of the Organization of American States*, I (1949), pp. 216–217.

[5] January 28, 1949, quoted in Planas-Suárez, *op. cit.*, p. 610. (My translation.)

bia, a convention through exchange of notes which are in force through the Military Junta's having declared its will to carry out the international agreements." [1] Thus, according to the Venezuelan explanation, safe conduct had already been granted and, in doing so, that government had acted "in strict conformity with the Treaty of Montevideo, applicable by virtue of the agreement concluded by an exchange of notes in June 1948 between the republics of Venezuela and Colombia." [2]

Planas-Suárez points out that these notes had not been made public and, indeed, questions their validity under Venezuelan law.[3] While it may well have been an expedient means of resolving a difficult situation by offering some legal obligation in order to save face, what is important is that the government chose to base its obligation on convention and clearly denied any legal obligation arising from a customary rule.

The Military Junta explained its policy regarding asylum in an official report.

On various occasions the Ministry of Foreign Relations has ratified the adherence of the Republic to the fundamental principles of the humanitarian institution of diplomatic asylum, and has demonstrated in practice its will to cooperate in the resolution of problems of this kind, fulfilling the customary American norms [las pautas consuetudinarias americanas], all within the spirit of respect to the sovereignty of others, and without the State of refuge interfering with the internal jurisdiction of the territorial State.[4]

The unhappy state of political affairs in Haiti has resulted in perhaps more grants of asylum in the foreign embassies and legations there than anywhere else in Latin America. The government in power at a given time, forced to reckon with its own shaky existence and often with cases involving one or more of the great powers (who at times backed their "requests" for safe conduct with threats of naval power while still insisting that they were not claiming this as a right but only as a "practice" tolerated in Haiti), could do little else but capitulate. In spite of this, however, Haitian governments have on a number of occasions refused to recognize the practice as forming an obligation on Haiti's part.

---

[1] *Ibid.*

[2] "Communication of the Ministry of Foreign Affairs of the United States of Venezuela," January 22, 1949. *Annals of the Organization of American States*, I (1949), p. 217.

[3] *Op. cit.*, pp. 576–577.

[4] *Síntesis de las labores realizadas pro la Junta Militar de Gobierno de los Estados Unidos de Venezuela durante un año de gestión administrativa: 1949–1950*, quoted in Planas-Suárez, *op. cit.*, p. 652. (My translation.)

In 1868, the United States minister in Port-au-Prince reported that "danger from disease" made it necessary for him to secure a promise of amnesty and safe departure for some 150 men, women and children sheltered in the legation. The President reluctantly agreed, according to the minister, "out of personal regard for me, for Mr. and Mrs. Conard, and for our government ..." [1] The United States minister had recommended to the State Department earlier that "it is no longer expedient to practice the right of asylum in the Haytien republic." [2]

In a long controversy which developed in 1875 over the grant of asylum in the United States legation to ex-President Boisrand Canal, the Haitian Secretary of State for Foreign Affairs said that the inviolability of the persons and residences of the foreign powers "does not acknowledge their power to give asylum to and to protect any category of criminals belonging to the country where they are accredited." [3] The United States refused to surrender the refugee without first securing adequate guarantees for his safety and the Haitian government finally decided to transfer negotiations to its minister in Washington.

The United States Acting Secretary of State admitted to the Haitian minister that, so far as the grant of asylum was concerned, "this act on his part has not been approved by the Department, as it is not sanctioned by public law, though it is in conformity with precedents in that quarter." [4] The Haitian minister replied "that the opinions of the Government of the United States in regard to the pretended right of asylum agree entirely with those of the Government of Hayti." [5]

After nearly four months of fruitless negotiations the case remained unresolved. A memorandum of a conversation between the Haitian minister and the United States Acting Secretary of State indicate very clearly the former's desire to settle the controversy without giving way on the legal issue.

Mr. Preston then suggested that, as a means of the disposition of the question, without on the one side committing the United States to a *practical* abolition of the right of asylum, and the Haytian government to a recognition of the right, that the government of Hayti might be prepared to grant, from good will, what they would not be willing to acknowledge as a right. [6]

---

[1] Hollister, U. S. Minister to Haiti, to Seward, Secretary of State, June 29, 1869, *Dip. Cors. of the U. S.*, 1868, II, p. 360.

[2] *Ibid.*, p. 358.

[3] Mr. Excellent, Secretary of State for Foreign Affairs of Haiti, to Mr. Bassett, U. S. Minister to Haiti, trans., May 8, 1875, *For. Rel. of the U. S.*, 1875, II, p. 699.

[4] *Ibid.*, p. 739.

[5] Mr. Preston, Haitian Minister to the U. S., to Mr. Cadwalader, Acting Secretary of State, August 14, 1875, *ibid.*, p. 740.

[6] "Memorandum," August 18, 1875, *ibid.*, p. 742. (My italics.)

The case was eventually settled with a grant of pardon to the ex-President and his permanent exile from the county.[1] The significance of the Haitian refusal to admit any *right* of asylum in this case can better be understood knowing that the case lasted nearly five months and that the United States at one point informed Haiti that a United States war vessel was being dispatched to Port-au-Prince.[2]

Since the foreign powers insisted they could not unilaterally renounce the "right of asylum" so long as it was a practice tolerated in Haiti, the latter attempted to gain such agreement. The memorandum forewarded to the United States said:

> The President of Hayti thinks it his duty to propose to the Government of the United States to give its consent to the abolition of the right of asylum which has hitherto been exercised by the heads of legations accredited to the cabinet at Port-au-Prince.[3]

While the proposal did provide for asylum in special circumstances it left it *to the government of Haiti* to evaluate such circumstances, the net result of which would be to leave it at the toleration of the territorial state.[4]

In 1908, after a similar case with similar results, the Haitian government again attempted to abolish the practice.

> I have the honor to inform your excellency that the Haitian Government has decided to put an end to the custom of asylum in legations and consulates established in this country.
>
> Your legation will kindly take note therefore, and issue to your consular agencies precise intructions, that they may comply with that decision.[5]

It has already been noted that at the 1927 meeting of the International Commission of American Jurists, the Haitian delegate opposed the strong statement of the project on asylum and proposed an amendment that "each state is free to recognize a right of asylum, but if it does so it, [*sic*] will observe the following rules."[6] It should be pointed out here that the purpose of this meeting was "the codifi-

---

[1] "Memorandum of Agreement," September 27, 1875, *ibid.*, p. 748.

[2] Preston, to Fish, U. S. Secretary of State, trans., September 27, 1875, and Fish to Preston, September 27, 1875, *ibid.*, pp. 747–748.

[3] "Memorandum," trans. October 25, 1875, *For. Rel. of the U. S.*, 1876, pp. 341–342.

[4] *Ibid.*, p. 342.

[5] Borno, Haitian Minister for Foreign Affairs, to Furniss, U. S. Minister to Haiti, trans., May 20, 1908, *For. Rel. of the U. S.* ,1908, p. 438.

[6] Brazil, Minister of State for Foreign Affairs. *International Commission of Jurists: 1927 Meeting*, Vol 2 (Rio de Janeiro, Imprensa Nacional), minutes of the 10th session, May 19, 1927, p. 113.

cation of public and private international law . . ." [1] Thus the Haitian delegate pointed out that "in his opinion, the right of asylum should be made the object of treaties." [2] This, of course, cannot be regarded as an official pronouncement by the government of Haiti. The nature of the International Commission of Jurists makes it clear, however, that each delegate would of necessity take into account the views of his government.[3]

But Haitian governments have also followed the opposite policy. Morgenstern quotes the following statement by the Haitian Secretary of State for Foreign Affairs in 1859.

> Le Gouvernement . . . n'a nullement l' intention de méconnaître, de changer, ou d'altérer ce droit d'asile sacré dès l'antiquité . . . et qui, dans nos temps modernes si agités, a reçu tant et de si fréquentes applications.[4]

A note from the United States minister to Haiti in connection with the above mentioned controversy over asylum granted to Boisrand Canal points to a similar attitude.

> . . . Each successive administration has clung to the right, and practically, once or twice formally, refused to assent to its discontinuance. Only lately, as I had the honor of stating to you personally, when I was at the Department in November last, the work of completing our consular treaty with this government was arrested because the Haytian plenipotentiary would not agree to having the exercise of this right taken away from even our consulates in the inferior ports.[5]

The government of Peru was unwilling either to admit or deny a right of asylum in connection with a case in 1848. A note to the United States minister said:

> One so well informed as yourself must be aware of the extent to which a right of asylum is recognized by international law.[6]

---

[1] *A.J.I.L.*, Special Supplement, XXII (January, 1928), p. 234.

[2] Brazil, Minister of State for Foreign Affairs, *International Commission of Jurists* . . ., p. 114.

[3] Article 1 of the Convention Establishing an International Law Commission, adopted at the Third International Conference of American States, Rio de Janeiro, August 23, 1906, provides: "there shall be established an International Commission of Jurists, composed of one representative from each of the signatory states, appointed by their respective governments, which commission shall meet for purposes of preparing a draft of a code of private international law and one of public international law regulating the relations between the nations of America . . . ." *A.J.I.L.*, Special Supplement, XX (July and October, 1926), p. 296.

[4] F. O. 55/309, *op. cit.*, p. 244.

[5] Bassett, U. S. Minister to Haiti, to Fish, U. S. Secretary of State, May 19, 1875, *For. Rel. of the U. S.*, 1875, II, p. 697.

[6] Pardo, Secretary of Foreign Relations of Peru, to Clay, U. S. Minister to Peru, February 12, 1849 (inclosure in Clay to the U. S. Secretary of State no. 23, March 10, 1849), Despatches, Peru, Vol. 8. (My translation.)

The Secretary of Foreign Relations then indicated that he would not enter into this question for the present and merely asked if any persons had been granted protection in the legation.[1] He was equally unwilling to admit that any rule other than that of the law of nations could be applied in Peru. In reply to a subsequent note from the United States minister, pointing out that asylum had been respected without question in Peru, the latter government replied:

> I do not need to examine what is the right of asylum which the government of Peru has recognized with regard to foreign diplomatic agents ... I have put this question aside, since you and I are in agreement that this asylum cannot be indefinite ...[2]

Revolutions continued and so did the granting of asylum. Eighteen years later, throughout a long and bitter controversy with the French legation in Lima, Peru insisted that diplomatic asylum was a mere toleration or practice rather than a right.[3] After an unsuccessful attempt to reach an agreement with the foreign diplomatic corps abolishing the practice of asylum, the Peruvian Secretary of Foreign Relations issued a memorandum on the subject. Following a masterful discussion of the origin and principles of the practice of asylum was a declaration that it would no longer be recognized in Peru.

> Considered from a humane point of view, diplomatic asylum would be a favor extended to citizens or subjects of the state where the legation may be resident; ... but the logical consequence is, that if a state has allowed such protection to be exercised by a foreign legation within its limits, the state can at pleasure, for itself and its citizens or subjects, deny the further exercise of any such protection. The admission of a favor is no obligation, and the person receiving the favor may renounce it at any time ...
>
> Therefore the Peruvian government deems it its duty and right to declare, as it does declare, first, that it will not recognize, in the future, diplomatic asylum, as practiced until now, in Peru, but only within the limits assigned to it by the law of nations, which are sufficient to resolve the question that, in exceptional cases, may occur; second, that, as diplomatic asylum exists in the South American states, the legations of Peru in such states exercising the right, Peru now renounces, on her part, this privilege, and denies it to the legations of such states in Peru.[4]

---

[1] *Ibid.*

[2] March 10, 1949, (inclosure in Clay to the Secretary of State, No. 25, April 10, 1849), *ibid.* (My translation.)

[3] See the numerous and lengthy diplomatic exchanges published in Perú, Secretario de Relaciones Exteriores, *Correspondencia diplomática relativa a la cuestión sobre asilo*, publicado por orden de S. E. El Jefe Supremo Provisorio para ser presentada al Congreso Constituyente. (Lima: Imprenta del Estado por Enrique del Campo, 1867).

[4] "Memorandum Relative to Diplomatic Asylum," Translation, January 29, 1867, *Dip. Cor. of the U. S.*, 1867, II, p. 745. Also in Perú *Correspondencia diplomática relativa a la cuestión sobre asilo*, pp. 34–37. The reference to asylum as practiced within the limits assigned to

In 1913, upon being informed that the Italian legation in Lima had granted asylum to Roberto Leguía, the Peruvian government stated that asylum for political delinquents was recognized only as "a practice founded on reasons of humanity." It was "not founded on any right [*derecho*]" but "only accepted as a practice." [1]

In the role of the state *granting* asylum, the position taken by Peru became ambiguous and evasive to say the least. During the Spanish Civil War asylum was granted in both the Peruvian legation and the consulate in Madrid. [2] The first notes exchanged avoided any implication of legal status for its action. It was referred to as the "institution of asylum" and as being "inconformity with the traditon of chivalrous generosity." At another point it was referred to as corresponding "to humanitarian principles which are applied in accordance with the juridical status of the legations." [3] A short time later the Peruvian Minister of Foreign Relations informed the Spanish government that Peru maintained "the juridical and moral fundamentals of that institution." [4]

Not only are all of these statements masterpieces of evasion but Peruvian *action* also added to the ambiguity of the situation. In 1939, the *Memoria* of the Minister of Foreign Relations stated that the ambassador to Spain had been instructed to express to the government of Spain "the sympathy with which Peru – which had always defended and respected the right [*derecho*] of asylum, to the point of breaking diplomatic relations with the deposed Republican government, among other causes for having disregarded that right and having violated the consulate of Peru in Madrid – would receive a favorable solution to the incident with Chile." [5] To say that recognition of the asylum grant-

---

it by the law of nations" apparently refers to a very limited and distinctly temporary resort to the practice where the refugee would be surrendered at the request of the local authorities. See especially "Pacheco, Peruvian Secretary of Foreign Relations, to Vion, French Representative in Peru," January 2, 1866, *op. cit.*, pp. 8–13.

[1] Perú, Ministerio de Relaciones Exteriores, *Memoria del Ministerio de Relaciones Exteriores, 1914* (Lima, Imprenta Americana, 1914), pp. 64–68. Hereafter cited as Perú, *Memoria*.

[2] Peruvian diplomatic exchanges did not treat asylum in legations and consulates as being founded upon any different bases or as having any different legal foundation.

[3] Ulloa, Peruvian Minister of Foreign Relations, to the Spanish Minister of Foreign Relations, September 2, 1936, Perú, *Memoria*, 13 abril–22 octubre, 1936, pp. 94–95. (My translation.) The correct title should be Spanish Minister of State instead of Minister of Foreign Relations. Exact titles vary and are sometimes misquoted in Latin American diplomatic literature. The practice here will be to *reproduce them as quoted in the source used.*

[4] Ulloa to the Spanish Minister of State, October 22, 1936, Perú, Ministerio de Relaciones Exteriores, *Boletín del Ministerio de Relaciones Exteriores* (4 trimestre de 1936), p. 105.(My translation.) Hereafter cited as Perú, *Boletín*.

[5] Perú, *Memoria*, 20 de abril–8 de diciembre de 1939, pp.X–XII. (My translation.)

ed was claimed not as a legal right but as a humanitarian practice and then demand that the territorial state recognize this claim as though it were a legal right is to obscure all distinction between a tolerated practice and a binding rule. This would seem to be particularly true when the state granting asylum goes to the extreme of breaking diplomatic relations when its claims are not recognized.

A statement published in *El Peruano*, official organ of the Peruvian government, explained the government's policy regarding a number of cases settled in 1948:

> Diplomatic asylum, which until some years ago was only an international practice, fully accepted by some and conditionally by others, in actuality assumes the characteristics of a true institution of American international law, *limited* and *regulated* by norms that are recorded in conventions in force which are fully obligatory for the participating countries.[1]

This clearly implies that the law is not *established* by the conventions but only *limited* and *regulated* by them. The only interpretation would seem to be that international practice had ripened into a customary rule of law. After a review of the relevant conventions and treaties, however, the concluding statement seems to rely primarily upon them.

> Concerning the leaders of the Popular Revolutionary Alliance to whom asylum has been conceded in the embassies of friendly countries, the government, without losing sight of the necessity that the instigators of the military rebellion ... do not remain unpunished has proceeded in accord with the already mentioned conventions in force, respecting the word pledged in them and declaring an express reservation of its right to solicit extradition in virtue of the prerogatives of national jurisdiction.[2]

The positon taken in the *Colombian-Peruvian Asylum Case* was the complete reverse of this:

> The Colombian *Memoria* in no way demonstrates that "the institution of asylum" ... is based upon a customary right [or law – *derecho*] ...
> ... We think that asylum, precisely through its humanitarian character, is a practical ideal but it lacks, even in America, the circumstances necessary in order to be realized juridically.[3]

The unsuccessful attempt of members of the diplomatic corps, in 1867, to reach an agreement on the granting of asylum in Peru has already been discussed. In the course of the meeting, the United States representative, noting the divergence of opinion, suggested that

---

[1] *El Peruano:* Diario oficial (Lima), 26 de octubre de 1948. (My translation and italics.) Also reprinted in Perú, *Proceso*, pp. 124–126.
[2] *Ibid.*
[3] Perú, *Proceso*, p. 167. (My translation.)

each member communicate his position, in writing, to the Peruvian government in order that there could be no misunderstanding. The Brazilian minister replied that "he would really not send to the government a letter sustaining the right of asylum, which, though it could not be regarded as a right, was nevertheless a practice which ought to be maintained in order to avoid greater difficulties." [1]

More recent Brazilian practice has emphasized local toleration as the basis for the practice. The report of the Brazilian delegation to the Sixth International Conference of American States has already been alluded to in connection with the convention signed at that conference. It is of relevance to this discussion that the report pointed out certain changes made over the Project of Convention approved by the Commission of International Jurists.[2] These changes were made, according to the report, in deference to countries such as Brazil inasmuch as the Project had consecrated the right of asylum, which Brazil, on its part, has permitted in special cases, for considerations of humanity." [3]

In the Consolidation of Laws, Decrees and Decisions of the Brazilian Diplomatic Corps (1930), Article 47 provides that "in countries in which the conventions, laws or usages permit asylum for political criminals in the buildings of diplomatic missions, it may be conceded in accord with the following arrangements: ..." [4] This was repeated in virtually the same wording in a 1934 Decree on Regulation of the Diplomatic Service.[5]

Similarly, notes sustaining the thesis that asylum is not a right, and being a simple tolerance, ought not to be encouraged, are cited by Accioly for the years 1893, 1899, 1925 and 1935.[6] In a 1938 circular, already referred to, the Brazilian government notified the foreign diplomatic corps in Rio de Janeiro that "the Government of Brazil

---

[1] Dip. Cor. of the U. S., 1876, II, p. 741.

[2] Brazil, Relatório Apresentado ao Ministro de Estado das Relações Exteriores pelo Presidente da delegação do Brasil a 6ª Conferencia Internacional Americana, realizada em Havana, em 1928 (Rio de Janeiro: Imprensa Nacional, 1929), p. 39. (My translation.)

[3] Ibid.

[4] Brazil, Relatório, 1930, Anexo A, p. 173. (My translation.)

[5] Brazil, Relatório, 1934, 2 Vol., 1ª Parte, Annexo C, p. 239. (My translation.)

[6] Op. cit., p. 347. Apparently these are unpublished notes in the archives of the Brazilian Foreign Office. The author merely says: "Pueden citarse, en este sentido, la comunicación confidencial n. 3 de 24 de agosto de 1893, dirigida a la legación del Brazil en Lima y suscrita por el entonces ministro de Relaciones exteriores, J. Felipe Pereira; y la comunicación reservada no. 2, de 31 de enero de 1899, dirigida a la legación en La Paz, y suscrita por el entonces ministro de Relaciones exteriores, Olyntho de Magalhes. El mismo punto de vista fué sustentado también el 6 de abril de 1925, en el telegrama del Ministro de Relaciones exteriores a la legación del Brasil en Lima, y en diciembre de 1935, en telegrama a la legación del Brasil en Caracas."

understands that, in principle ... [asylum] does not constitute a right, although practice may have admitted it in certain circumstances as a reasonable measure, determined by purely humanitarian motives." [1]

This policy is also reflected in Brazilian action regarding the treaties on asylum discussed in the preceding chapter. The table on page 64 will show that Brazil has not ratified any of the treaties recognizing a general right of asylum and has not even signed the Montevideo treaty of 1939. [2]

In a case in 1851, the government of Chile implied that the granting of diplomatic asylum to persons pursued for political reasons was sanctioned by international law under certain strictly limited circumstances.

The law of nations establishes a great difference between asylum which a nation concedes in its own territory and that which, in some cases, a diplomatic minister accords in virtue of the immunities his house enjoys ... Asylum which a nation grants on its own soil is more ample, may be conceded in a greater number of cases and is, for that reasion, more effective. [3]

Thus it was pointed out that in societies where there is simply a *de facto* authority which constantly changes in the midst of political turmoil and where partisan vengeance obliterates the protection generally afforded by law, the granting of asylum "cannot be said to offend either an authority which lacks the character of legality or laws which have ceased to be respected." [4] But the situation in Chile was quite different, as were the offences of the delinquent: "what is discussed here is whether the privilege of fictitious extraterritoriality conceded to the house of a diplomatic agent, in protection of his person and his family, ought to be extended to delinquents guilty of grave crimes against the state or against society." [5]

A note from the Chilean Ministry of Foreign Relations to its minister in Lima, in 1856, implied that it was more a matter of local toleration.

---

[1] Perú, *Proceso*, pp. 155–156. Excerpts also quoted in Accioly, *op. cit.*, pp. 347–348. (My translation.)

[2] In discussions concerning the Draft Declaration of Human Rights before the Third Committee of the United Nations General Assembly in 1948, the Brazilian delegation "entirely agreed with the proposal of the delegations of Bolivia and Uruguay to extend the right of asylum to embassies and legations. The proposal was in accordance with current *practice* in Latin America. It would, however, be more appropriate for it to be inserted in the draft covenant." *Op. cit.*, p. 340. (My italics.)

[3] Varas, Chilean Minister of Foreign Relations, to the U. S. Minister to Chile, May 15, 1851. Chile, Ministerio de Relaciones Exteriores, *Jurisprudencia de la cancillería chilena*, p. 260. (My translation.)

[4] *Ibid.*, p. 262.

[5] *Ibid.*, p. 262.

... I am informed of the revolutionary movement which was attempted in Lima the 15th of last month and of the asylum conceded to those who had led it. Having acted according to the practice admitted in that Republic in such cases and having given due notice to that government, the conduct which you have observed in this case has merited the approval of the government.[1]

In 1867, in answer to the Peruvian memorandum on asylum, the Chilean minister to Peru frankly stated that it would be difficult to ascertain the practice in Chile. "As to the practice of asylum, the cases are so rare (perhaps not even two), and so lacking in alarming characteristics, which in other countries give rise to vexing questions, that it would be impossible to define what may be the practice in Chile." [2] The idea of comity was also stressed.

...In Chile there is not, with respect to diplomatic asylum, anything extraordinary or exceptional, nothing which goes beyond the law of nations. Aside from this, my government would not be disposed, in this or in any other case, to concede to friendly nations what they might deny to her.[3]

According to the American minister at Santiago, the Chilean Minister of Foreign Relations "stated that he recognized in the fullest manner that this legation had legitimately given asylum to the refugees now in the legation" as a result of the 1891 revolution in that country.[4] In this case, however, the legitimacy of the grant of asylum was based squarely upon exterritoriality.

"The asylum that emanates from the principles of extraterritoriality inherent in the person, the residence, and the vehicles of His Excellency the Minister does not extend ... to the streets ...[5]

In contrast to previous statements, a 1930 note to the minister from Uruguay, concerning asylum granted in that legation, pointed out that "in the conventions in force between some American countries as much as in international usages applied by those who, like Chile, *admit it only for reasons of humanitarian tolerance,* asylum is respected in cases of urgency and for the time strictly necessary for the refugee

---

[1] Varas to the Chilean Minister in Peru, Sept. 15, 1856, *ibid.*, p. 427.

[2] "Martínez, to the Peruvian Secretary of Foreign Relations," Feb. 6, 1867, Perú, *Correspondencia diplomática relativa a la cuestión sobre asilo*, p. 54. (My translation.)

[3] *Ibid.*, pp. 53–54.

[4] "Memorandum of Interview between Mr. Egan and Señor Matta," Oct. 3, 1891 (inclosure in Egan, U. S. Minister to Chile, to Blaine, U. S. Secretary of State, Oct. 6, 1891), *For. Rel. of the U. S.*, 1891, p. 183.

[5] Matta, Chilean Minister of Foreign Relations, to Egan, U. S. Minister to Chile, Sept. 29, 1891, trans. (inclosure in Egan to Blaine, Nov. 13, 1891), *For. Rel. of the U. S.*, 1891, p. 181.

to ensure in some other way his safety." [1] A few days later, a circular addressed to the Chilean diplomatic missions in America and circulated among the resident diplomatic corps in Santiago said that the Chilean position had always been that asylum could be invoked "for political causes, *not as a right* but as a recourse which may be useful for the country in which it is exercised, and advisable, at times indispensable, for reasons of humanity." [2]

The ambassador of Chile was the chief spokesman for the demands made upon Spain regarding asylum granted in the several legations there during the Spanish Civil War. In reply to the Spanish contention that it was not bound by the conventions invoked by Chile, he maintained "that the right of asylum has existed before the convention of Havana, and ... will always exist while humanitarian sentiments exist among nations." [3] Nearly a year later he again said: "The diplomatic asylum sustained by my government, is founded on principles of right and on reasons of humanity ..." [4] This plus the fact that the refugees who were not granted safe conduct were maintained in the Chilean embassy until the Republican Government of Spain fell [5] certainly indicates a claim of legal obligation.

In connection with the above mentioned controversy between Venezuela and Colombia the Chilean ambassador to the Organization of American States submitted the following note.

I have instructions from my Government to present before the Council of the Organization of American States and submit to it for examination the judicial case of the negligence with which the *de facto* Government of the Republic of Venezuela has viewed its duty to grant safe conduct to the ex-President of that country, Mr. Rómulo Betancourt, who has sought asylum for the past several weeks in the Embassy of a sister nation and is disposed to accept the refuge which is offered him in a foreign country. [6]

A note dated five days later more explicitly states the obligation on the part of Venezuela to recognize a "right of asylum."

---

[1] Barros C., Chilean Minister of Foreign Relations, to Martínez Thedy, Uruguayan Minister to Chile, October 28, 1930, Chile, *Memoria*, 1930, p. 415. (My translation and italics.)

[2] "Circular to the Chilean Diplomatic Missions in America (on asylum)," November 5, 1930, Chile, *Memoria*, 1930, pp. 416–417. (My translation and italics.)

[3] Nuñez Morgado, Chilean Ambassador to Spain, to del Vayo, Spanish Minister of State, October 19, 1936, Chile, *Memoria*, 1936, p. 571. (My translation.)

[4] Carlos Moria Lynch, Chilean *Chargé d'Affaires* to Giral, Spanish Minister of State, July 3, 1937, Chile, *Memoria*, 1937, p. 263. (My translation.)

[5] *Supra.*

[6] "Del Rio, Ambassador of Chile, to Corominas, Chairman of the Council of the OAS," January 20, 1949, *Annals of the Organization of American States*, I, (1949), p. 216.

... The Military Junta had delayed for two months the safe conduct of Señor Betancourt, violating thus the right of asylum.[1]

Following the Seventh International Conference of American States, the published report of the delegation of El Salvador observed that inasmuch as the Havana Convention had not yet been ratified "official action will have to study both conventions, considering them as a single whole, for purposes of giving or refusing definitive ratification." [2] As for practice:

Political asylum has come to be considered as a humanitarian institution in Latin America ... It does not have essentially a juridical foundation; and it is accepted as a custom which tends to be generalized, rather than a recognized right.[3]

In contrast to this, a note to the International Court of Justice in connection with the *Colombian-Peruvian Asylum Case* spoke of asylum as being *based* on justice and humanitarianism but *shaped* in customary law.

I wish in the first place, Mr. Secretary, to point out to you the profound interest which the Salvadorean government and people have in this problem which is without doubt one of primary importance for the definitive conservation or loss of one of the most precious achievements of the Inter-American System, an achievement which, being based on principles of inherent justice and pure humanitarianism, has been shaped in various inter-American conventions, and what is even more significant, in the customary law which has happily regulated the relations of American countries.[4]

Exactly what would be the status of a "conquest ... *based* on principles of ... justice and pure humanitarianism ... [and], *shaped* ... in the customary law" is not entirely clear.

Only a few days later, in connection with a controversy with Peru, El Salvador decided to submit the case to the Organization of American States. A note explaining its motives to the Peruvian government, seems to imply that the practice is *not yet* clearly regarded as having a juridical basis but that the government of El Salvador desired to see a ruling which would clearly provide such a basis.

---

[1] Partially quoted text in Planas-Suárez, *op. cit.*, p. 588. (My translation.)

[2] El Salvador, Ministerio de Relaciones Exteriores. *Informe de la delegación de El Salvador a la VII Conferencia Panamericana celebrada en Montevideo, Uruguay, del 3 al 26 de diciembre 1933* (San Salvador: Imprenta Nacional, [1934?]) pp. 44. (My translation.)

[3] *Ibid.*, pp. 45–46.

[4] Canessa, Minister of Foreign Relations of El Salvador, to the International Court of Justice, November 17, 1950, Colombia, *La opinión americana y el derecho de asilo*, (1951), p. 9. (My translation).

In taking this initiative, my government has only put into practice the unanimous and fervent desire of the Salvadorean people, that the institution of
asylum, based on the political reality of our people and inspired in high humanitarian sentiments, that which has already been consecrated in the Latin American
conscience, *may be converted* into one of the major contributions of the Continent
of the Liberty of International Law.[1]

This seems to express only a hope that "the *institution of asylum*,
based on the political reality of our people and inspired in high humanitarian sentiments ... *may be converted*" into law, if indeed a
"contribution of the Continent of the Liberty of International Law"
is necessarily a rule of law.

At one point in the long controversy with Spain over asylum granted
during the Spanish Civil War, the Dominican representative sent the
following note on order of his government.

I have the honor of communicating to you that my government is uniting
itself with the joint action of the diplomatic corps in Madrid, by expressing in
the collective note of the 19th, its adherence to the criterion of absolute respect
of the right of diplomatic asylum.

The Dominican Government believes that the right of asylum cannot be
subject to restrictions, contrary, [sic] to the principles of international law,
universally recognized and admitted in treaties, and that the Spanish Government maintained security and respect for this right, since the beginning of the
Spanish conflict.

Should the Spanish Government proclaim now that it has ceased to respect
this right, the Dominican Government will conclude that it has lost its authority
to enforce respect for the diplomatic missions and the legations of this country
in Madrid, will be in a very delicate situation.[2]

The statement that "the right of asylum cannot be subject to restrictions contrary to the principles of international law" certainly
implies the status of a rule of law. Legal obligation is made even more
clear in the last paragraph where it is asserted that failure to recognize
this "right" would mean that the government has lost its authority.
On the other hand, the Dominican envoy in addressing the diplomatic
corps implied that he was demanding recognition of something *not*
hitherto recognized as law.

The policy advocated by the Dominican Government is not the political
asylum as heretofore understood and regulated by international treaties; it is

---

[1] Canessa, Minister of Foreign Relations of El Salvador, to Gallagher Peruvian Minister
of Foreign Relations, December 5, 1950, *El Peruano: Diario oficial*, 7 de diciembre de 1950,
p. 1. (My translation.) The "Continent of the Liberty of International Laws" is used here
as a descriptive title for the Western Hemisphere.

[2] Tolentino, Dominican Minister to Spain, to del Vayo, Spanish Minister of State, Oct.
23, 1936 in Henry Helfant, *op. cit.*, p. 195.

a new form which Presidente [sic] Trujillo wishes to see established. For my part I shall remain here until the refugees of all the legations have been safely evacuated.[1]

Less enthusiasm was shown in a resolution of the National Congress of the Dominican Republic *promulgated* by the President and published in the *Gaceta oficial*, in 1954.[2] The resolution, as promulgated, proclaimed the denunciation of the treaties of Havana and Montevideo:

CONSIDERING: That in the present state of the struggle against communism it is necessary to affirm the self preservation of States against the elements which threaten the social harmony and institutions;

CONSIDERING: That diplomatic asylum permitted by the conventions of Havana (1928) and Montevideo (1933) is an obstacle to the domestic defense of states, inasmuch as it permits the most dangerous individuals to frustrate the course of justice and to pursue their dissolvent and subversive activity;

CONSIDERING: That said conventions give rise to real interventions among States, through the obscurity and uncertainty of the concepts which they lay down and the frequent contradictions in interpretation;

CONSIDERING: That such interventions constitute a cause of frequent friction among the States, legitimately jealous of their sovereignty and jurisdiction.

CONSIDERING: That the Convention of Montevideo in its Article 8, establishes, for each contracting State, the faculty of denunciation to the Pan American Union, with prior notice of one year.

CONSIDERING: That inasmuch as the Convention of Montevideo modified the Convention of Havana, the latter is susceptible to denunciation in the same terms as the former ...[3]

The precise significance of this is difficult to determine. It does not say that the Dominican Republic no longer regards respect of asylum granted in embassies and legations within its territory as obligatory (if, indeed, it ever did). It refers instead to "asylum permitted by the conventions of Havana (1928) and Montevideo (1933)." The resolution also emphasizes the "uncertainty of the concepts which they lay down and the frequent contradictions in interpretation." One thing is certain, however; the Dominican government does not regard these conventions as merely declaratory of a rule of international law as claimed by the Colombian government.

The opinion of an ex-Minister of Foreign Relations of the Dominican Republic is of interest here even though it may be of little legal significance inasmuch as he was no longer in office at the time of writing. In his article, however, it is clear that he is referring to

---

[1] Proceedings of the Diplomatic Corps, in Assembly, Session of March 31, 1937, Helfant, *op. cit.*, pp. 227–228.

[2] *Gaceta oficial*, (Ciudad Trujillo, 27 de septiembre de 1954), pp. 9–11. (My translation.)

[3] *Ibid.*

Dominican policy, particularly while he was Minister of Foreign Relations.

Few subjects of the law of nations are so delicate and uneven [escabrosas] as that of asylum. Although the notion of asylum has become better established, especially in America, it still continues to be an undefined matter, generally subject to the good will and good faith of the parties involved ... An institution of humanity, asylum depends, for that same reason, basically, on *Comitas Gentium*, that is, on a series of rules and principles of international courtesy, of mutual consideration and of respect, which is not written into any convention nor any positive instrument.[1]

The published papers relating to the foreign relations of some Latin American states are so sporadic and vary so much in the scope of materials published from year to year as to make an assessment of their policy over a long period of time impossible. But available materials do show that, at least in recent years, a number of these states have clearly claimed a juridical basis for the practice of diplomatic asylum. Whether this has been a consistent policy on the part of each of them cannot be ascertained.

Recent Guatemalan statements, some of them more evasive than others, must be placed in this category. In a meeting of the diplomatic corps in Madrid during the Spanish Civil War the Guatemalan representative asserted that "whenever a social revolution occurred, as at present in Spain, it was the duty of foreign representatives to strive for the right of asylum, from the country to which they were accredited, and from the belligerent forces, as well." [2]

A determined effort was made by Guatemala to secure such recognition in connection with the *Colombian-Peruvian Asylum Case*. A communication to the Secretary of the Court said:

... My government feels that the proceedings of this case and the final judgment of the International Court of Justice are of transcendental importance for the development of the juridical norms established and consecrated in American International Law, in relation to political asylum ...[3]

Following the Court's 1950 decision the government requested that the Council of the Organization of American States be convoked in order

---

[1] Manuel Arturo Peña Batlle, "Una sentencia de la Corte Internacional de Justicia," *El Caribe* (Ciudad Trujillo), 8 de abril de 1951. Reprinted also in Perú, *Proceso*, II, pp. 211-214. (My translation.)

[2] Proceedings of the Diplomatic Corps, in Assembly, Session of October 28, 1936, Chilean Embassy, in Henry Helfant, *op. cit.*, p. 168.

[3] González Arévalo, Guatemalan Minister of Foreign Relations, to Hambro, Secretary of the International Court of Justice, November 16, 1950, Colombia, *La opinión americana y el derecho de asilo*, p. 12. (My translation.)

to consider the problem. In the request, the Guatemalan position was outlined:

We believe that if the verdict were executed by handing over the asylee, in accordance with the interpretation given it by one of the Parties, the juridical and humanitarian tradition of the Right of Asylum would be violated and political asylum might become the object of future interpretations capable of impairing its noble intent and leaving it inoperative.[1]

Nearly four years later, it insisted that asylum was not only a right for the state of refuge but a duty as well. This was clearly indicated in the reservations attached by that government to the Caracas Convention on Diplomatic Asylum.

We make an express reservation to Article II wherein it declares that the States are not obliged to grant asylum; because we uphold a broad, firm concept of the right of asylum.[2]

As of September 1963, however, this convention had not been ratified by Guatemala.[3]

In May of 1954, the Guatemalan embassy in Nicaragua granted asylum to an officer of the Nicaraguan army. The Statement printed in the *Diario oficial* proclaimed the "New Guatemala" as "one of the nations which defends the right of asylum with the greatest firmness and energy ." [4] No doubt was left as to the juridical status. "Guatemala practices in her own house the thesis she defends in the field of public international law." [5]

In connection with the Chilean action during the Spanish Civil War, the Ecuadorean Ministry of Foreign Relations rendered a rather ambiguous opinion. On the one hand, it spoke of "its irrevocable adhesion to the Latin American principle of internal asylum, defined by the conventions of Havana and Montevideo." [6] On the other hand it took the position that "since it is a principle of jurisprudence still discussed by the nations of Europe, it is not in order to pronounce

---

[1] Goudbaud, Guatemalan Ambassador to the O.A.S., to Accioly, Chairman of the Council of the O.A.S., December 18, 1950, *Annals of the Organization of American states*, III (1951), p. 118. Recent translations have begun to use "asylee" for the Spanish word "asilado."

[2] Pan American Union, *Convention on Diplomatic Asylum Signed at the Tenth Inter-American Conference, Caracas, March 1-28, 1954*, Law and Treaty Series (Washington: Pan American Union, 1954), p. 5.

[3] See p. 64.

[4] "Derecho de asilo en el caso de Managua," *Diario de Centro-América*, 25 mayo, 1954, p. 1. (My translation.)

[5] *Ibid.*

[6] "Memorandum," June 20, 1939, Perú, *Proceso*, p. 297. (My translation.)

with respect to the specific case of asylum defended by Chile ..." [1]
In the first case it spoke of asylum as merely a "principle " rather than
a "principle of jurisprudence," but it contrasted this with a "still
discussed principle of jurisprudence" in Europe.

In 1949, the same Ministry provided a very clear statement of its
position. It pointed out first that, because of recent political transfor-
mations, cases of diplomatic asylum had been produced in the diplomatic missions accredited in the capitals affected by such movements.

> The Ministry of Foreign Relations of Ecuador informed public opinion through
> the press that it considered that asylum is consecrated [consagrado] and defined,
> not only by the pertinent American international conventions, but also by inter-
> national custom, valuable source of American law.
> The Ecuadorean diplomatic missions have been required, in various American
> countries, to offer asylum to persons affected by political events. In fulfilment
> of their duties, the Ecuadorean representatives afforded the asylum that was
> solicited from the respective authorities and governments, the guarantees and
> facilities necessary for departure from the country of the refugees.[2]

The following year, in a note to the government of El Salvador, it
declared itself "convinced of the necessity of reaffirming the right of
asylum [Derecho de Asilo], which signifies an irrenounceable a-
chievement in America," and declared its support of "every measure
or means which defends and facilitates this American principle." [3]

The Argentine *Memoria* for 1936–37 declares that "asylum in embassies is a right consecrated and sustained in America, especially by
Argentina." [4] While admitting that the doctrine was not accepted
by European powers as fully as in America it was deemed advisable
"to avoid all compromise ... in order to preserve intact the right of
asylum." [5] All of the difficulties encountered "in order to obtain
recognition of the right of asylum in the form sustained by the Argentine Government" had given rise to its *Project of Convention on the
Right of Asylum*.[6]

This project pointed to a number of cases where asylum had in fact
been granted and respected but did not provide any evidence as to

---

[1] *Ibid.*

[2] Ecuador, Ministerio de Relaciones Exteriores, *Informe a la Nación*, June, 1949, pp.
68–69. (My translation.)

[3] Neftali Ponce, Minister of Foreign Relations of Ecuador, to Canessa, Minister of Foreign
Relations of El Salvador, December 8, 1950, Colombia, *La opinión americana y el derecho
de asilo*, p. 9. (My translation.) The circumstances behind this note are not indicated in the
publication.

[4] Vol. I, p. 29.

[5] *Ibid.*, p. 32.

[6] *Ibid.*, p. 99.

whether these acts were accompanied by a conviction of legal right or obligation.[1] What is more, so far as Argentine practice was concerned, the Minister of Foreign Relations only pointed out that his government had insisted upon this right during the present controversy with Spain.[2] The following extracts from the *Project* show that, although Argentina recognized the fact that asylum was by no means a generally accepted principle of international law, it insisted upon claiming as a right precisely what it admitted was not generally accepted as such.

The opinions on the practice of asylum may vary according to the different views of writers on international law. But the feelings which since remotest times gave rise to the establishment of places of asylum for the persecuted remain unchangeable. Whether asylum, so necessary in the confusion of political struggles, is based or not on the extension of the nations' sovereignty, or on the idea of the extraterritoriality of warships, or on diplomatic immunities, the truth is that the realization of the noble ideal which inspires it becomes essential . . .

These deeds show, in the opinion of the Chancellery, that it is time to establish on a sound foundation this practice so worthily exercised in recent times. It is necessary to give it the definite forms of a convention thereby incorporating it to juridical rules . . .

This would show the maturity of that juridical evolution we have referred to, and would emphasize a universal desire which has the sufficient weight for it to be shaped into permanent international law . . .

With respect to the practical cases in which asylum has been conceded or recognized, in spite of it characteristics being more American than European, they have assumed a universal aspect with relation to the recent events in Spain. Indeed, whatever the opinions held by their Governments with respect to the right of asylum, the European and American embassies and legations could not help but respond to the humanitarian pleas of many persons . . .

As far as the Argentine Foreign Ministry was concerned, it expressly instructed its representatives in Spain to sustain with all firmness the right of asylum for persons who had invoked the protection of our flag . . .[3]

In reporting these activities to the Argentine Congress the *Memoria* for 1937–38 stated that such responsibilities were accepted, not only because of ties with neighboring states but for humanitarian reasons "and through the desire to maintain intact the right of asylum, in accord with the ample standard traditionally sustained by the Argentine Republic." [4]

Following the overthrow of the Argentine government in 1955, ex-President Perón was granted asylum on a Paraguayan gunboat. A

[1] Argentina, Ministry of Foreign Affairs and Worship, *Project of Convention on the Right of Asylum* (Buenos Aires, 1937), pp. 37–51.

[2] *Ibid.*, pp. 43–44.

[3] *Ibid.*, pp. 8, 10, 11, 37, 43.

[4] P. 45.

communique broadcast by the state radio said that the provisional government of Eduardo Lonardi "respectful of the right of asylum" pledges itself to grant Perón "every form of guarantees." [1] Three days later, in a written reply to questions submitted by a group of foreign correspondents General Lonardi said: "We have already declared publicly that we respect the right of asylum. The time of departure of General Perón is a problem that concerns the Paraguayan Government." [2]

In reply to the Argentine solicitation of opinions on its *Project of Convention on the Right of Asylum* in 1937, the Cuban government registered its "frank attitude of sympathy." [3] And in doing so it felt that it did "no more than contribute to the codification, and to the international force of diplomatic precedents of its own chancellery with respect to the right of asylum." [4]

When, in 1949, Cuba granted asylum to two revolutionaries in its embassy in Lima, the controversy was not primarily concerned with the legal basis of asylum inasmuch as both Peru and Cuba had ratified the Convention of Havana. This matter was alluded to, however, in some of the more general observations of the later government. The Cuban ambassador pointed out that, in conformity with instructions received from his government, his prolonged negotiations had been founded "on the nature of the right of asylum, which is humanitarian as well as juridical, of an emergent character, and, therefore, cannot be subjected to delays and procedures which unnecessarily retard its resolution.[5]

The Cuban interpretation of the Treaty of Montevideo, 1933, is of particular interest. It was asserted that the Cuban position, in invoking that treaty, had not claimed that both parties had ratified it, "but that the treaty established a general rule of law, which Peru as well as Cuba had given indications of considering morally binding." [6] Whether Cuba would attach any significance to the fact that it referred to this as a *"general rule of law"* which was considered *"morally"* binding

---

[1] *New York Times*, Sept. 25, 1955, p.1.
[2] *Ibid.*, Sept. 28, 1955, p. 15.
[3] Remos Secretary of State of Cuba, to Saavedra Lamas, Minister of Foreign Reiations of Argentina, August 18, 1937, Cuba, Secretario de Estado, *Documentos diplomáticos relativos a la guerra civil de España* (La Havana, 1939), p. 124.
[4] *Ibid.*
[5] Espinoza, Cuban Ambassador to Peru, to Díaz Dulanto, Minister of Foreign Relations and Worship of Peru, August 1, 1949, full text on *Revista peruana de derecho internacional*, Tomo IX (mayo-agosto, 1949), p. 175.
[6] Espinoza to Díaz Dulanto, March 31, 1949, *op. cit.*, p. 164.

rather than referring to it as a *general rule of law* which was considered *legally* binding would be difficult to say.

The statements of Cuba, as an interested party before the International Court of Justice in connection with the Haya de la Torre case, attribute to the practice the nature of a binding rule. Here it was asserted that the tradition of asylum "was incorporated into the juridical life of America through practice and custom, being recognized initially by customary law and submitted, afterwards, to the American international organizations, which determined its juridical structure." [1] Thus, for many years there had been in America "a juridical and humanitarian tradition of asylum, based upon certain principles which ought to be considered fundamental and immutable, which always have been practiced and sustained by Cuba and by the majority of the countries of America." [2] That it has now become an obligation to respect asylum was made very clear.

> ... Cuba has considered that, in accord with American International Law, no American State has the right to solicit the surrender of a political refugee who is in the *situación procesal* enunciated in the previous paragraph [against whom there were no proceedings for common crime at the time he sought asylum]...[3]

In 1892 the Colombian Ministry of Foreign Relations rendered an Opinion Relative to Diplomatic Asylum in response to a query by the French government. It asserted that "said concept does not have the character of an obligatory rule but that of a more or less probable theory." [4] It must be remembered, however, that the French query was prompted by a controversy between Chile and the United States. Thus the Colombian Minister observed that, while he had no objection to rendering such an opinion, it naturally constituted "an opinion and not the adoption of an obligatory rule." [5]

The Advisory Committee of the Colombian Ministry of Foreign Relations rendered the following opinion in 1931 in connection with a Chilean circular concerning the need to codify the practice of asylum.

> The so called right of asylum, which, as the Chilean chancellery very wisely says, cannot be considered as a right, but as a recourse, inspired by Christian and

---

[1] "Exposición presentada ante la Corte Internacional de Justicia por el Gobierno de la República de Cuba," Feb, 15. 1951, Perú, *Proceso*, II, p. 70.

[2] *Ibid.*, p. 71.

[3] *Ibid.*

[4] Colombia, *Anales diplomáticos y consulares de Colombia*, fundados y publicados por el Dr. Antonio José Uribe (Edición oficial; Bogotá, Imprenta Nacional, 1914) Tomo III, p. 602.

[5] Perú, *Proceso*, pp. 289–290.

humanitarian sentiments, has evolved with the passage of time like nearly all international practices and principles.[1]

Similarly, in connection with a controversy involving Cuba as the other party, it recommended "a conduct very discreet and reserved, which is based on the faithful interpretation of the tradition of the Republic and the law in force as regards diplomatic asylum." [2]

Judge M. Caicedo Castilla, in his dissenting opinion in the *Colombian-Peruvian Asylum Case*, pointed out that the Committee of Legal Advisors is merely a consultative body whose opinions are in no way binding upon the government.[3] But the decision of the Court took specific note of such an advisory opinion in pointing out that it expressed views contrary to those maintained by Colombia before the Court.[4]

The Colombian *Memoria* for 1939–1940, takes quite a different position in reporting its policy during the Spanish Civil War.

Colombia reaffirms the already expressed adherence to the thesis on the right of asylum which Chile has sustained, and which relies upon the unanimous support of America.[5]

Certainly nothing conclusive can be drawn from these antecedents, and Colombia offered the Court nothing more conclusive, so far as its own practice was concerned, than to cite a number of cases where Colombia had granted and/or respected asylum.[6] Nevertheless, the latter made it very clear that it regarded the right of asylum as being founded on a customary rule of law binding in America.[7] The clearest statement of this was offered during the oral proceedings. Colombia asserted that the foundation of this right was based "on the particular juridical nature of the American institution of asylum, recognized by positive American international law and by the practice of American states since the past century." It is very obvious that this did not refer to "practice" [8] in the sense of being distinct from "custom." Thus, it was founded "in general, upon the norms of positive and customary

---

[1] "Extractos del informe sobre asilo adoptado por la Comisión Asesora del Ministerio de Relaciones Exteriores de Colombia," Sept. 2, 1937, *Proceso*, p. 290.

[2] *Ibid.*, p. 159.

[3] *Op. cit.*, p. 363.

[4] *Ibid.*, p. 278.

[5] P. 102.

[6] See "Memoria del Gobierno de la República de Colombia," and "Réplica del Gobierno de la República de Colombia," Perú, *Proceso*, pp. 95–130, 327–414.

[7] *Ibid.*, 106–111.

[8] Perú, *Proceso*, p. 546.

American international law. Each one of these sources of obligation, which together constitute the *status juris* between Colombia and Peru." [1]

This position was again maintained in connection with a case of asylum granted in the Chilean legation in Colombia in 1952. [2]

In the 1946 case in Bolivia, that government emphasized both international agreements and practice as the basis for its action although only three of the states granting asylum were parties to the Montevideo Convention of 1889 – the only convention which Bolivia had signed and ratified. [3] In its memorandum to the diplomatic corps, the government declared that "at no time has the Government of Bolivia questioned the right of asylum. Faithful to its *international agreements* and respectful of its *diplomatic tradition*, it is disposed to grant immediately safe conduct for the political refugees." [4]

In the next paragraph, however, it puts forth certain reservations "in the exercise of the right that treaties in force and international practice confer on it." [5] In its declaration to the press, at the conclusion of the controversy, the Ministry of Foreign Relations again spoke only of treaty obligations: "At the very moment of its constitution, the *Junta Institucional de Gobierno* affirmed that it would respect treaties and international agreements, emphasizing on repeated occasions that this respect included the right of asylum." [6]

The Ninth International Conference of American States at Bogotá (1948), endorsed an American Declaration of Rights and Duties of Man. In connection with this, the Bolivian delegate spoke before the First Committee of guaranteeing the life and liberty of persons "by at least consecrating now, in a definitive way, the right of asylum." [7] But he clearly implied that, under present circumstances, it was not regarded as a juridical rule.

Previously, the fiction of exterritoriality has been spoken of; the respect which was necessary for protection of the diplomatic representative was also spoken of; it was said that opening the doors to the persons pursued was an indispensable act of humanity. But all this is a favor, it is an act of grace. On

---

[1] *Ibid.*, pp. 546–547.
[2] Colombia, Ministerio de Relaciones Exteriores, *Noticias de Colombia*, 18 abril, 1952. pp. 1–4.
[3] *Supra*, p. 64.
[4] August 19, 1946, Chile, *Memoria*, 1946, p. 60. (My translation and italics)
[5] *Ibid.*
[6] "Declaración que el Subsecretario de Relaciones Exteriores Doctor Julio Alvarado ha entregado a la prensa," November 2, 1946, Bolivia, *Boletín*, 1946, p. 98. (My translation.)
[7] Colombia, Ministerio de Relaciones Exteriores, *Novena Conferencia Internacional Americana, Bogotá, Colombia, marzo 30–mayo 2 de 1948: actas y documentos*, III (Bogotá, 1953), p. 140. (My translation.)

the other hand, if we recognize that man, as a subject of international law [persona de derecho internacional] has the right to demand protection ... in a legation or embassy. *I believe we will have given to the right of asylum a new expression, a new juridical foundation.*[1]

In any event, the amendment proposed by the Bolivian delegate fell considerably short of this ideal.

Everyone has the right of asylum, within the conditions stipulated by international conventions.[2]

It will be instructive to investigate this document and its antecedents further inasmuch as a reference to it in a resolution by the Council of the Organization of American States emphasizes the confusion and uncertainty in Latin American practice.[3] The Draft Declaration of the Rights and Duties of Man, presented as the working document by the Inter-American Juridical Committee, contained no provision relative to asylum in any form.[4] The amendment proposed by Bolivia has already been noted. The form finally submitted to the Sixth Committee in its seventh session provided that:

Everyone has the right to seek and receive asylum on foreign territory, in case of pursuit which is not motivated by common crimes and in accord with international conventions.[5]

At this point the United States delegate inquired as to whether or not this was intended to include diplomatic asylum and was assured by the Bolivian and Mexican delegates that the words "in accord with international conventions" had been added to meet objections in this regard.[6] The Dominican, Nicaraguan, Peruvian and Bolivian delegates further proposed that the article be amended to read:

...in accord with the legislation of each country and international conventions.[7]

The Guatemalan delegate objected to this because in his opinion "the article referred not only to refuge in foreign territory but also to asylum in legations, in which case national legislation could not be applied." [8]

---

[1] *Ibid.* (My translation.)

[2] O.A.S. Doc. CB–189/C. VI–Sub B–3. (My translation.)

[3] *Infra*, p. 145.

[4] International Conference of American States, Ninth, *Report of the Delegation of the United States with Related Documents* ([Washington, 1948]), pp. 115–120.

[5] Colombia, Ministerio de Relaciones Exteriores, *Novena Conferencia Americana* ..., V, p. 595.

[6] *Ibid.*

[7] *Ibid.*

[8] *Ibid.*

The Dominican delegate replied that "the article exclusively contemplated the case of refuge in foreign territory, and that the case of asylum in legations would be ruled by the stipulations of international treaties." [1]

It is obvious then, that there was disagreement as to the precise scope and meaning of the article. One thing seems certain, however: it was agreed that if diplomatic asylum was included it would be dependent upon previously existing treaty arrangements.

Following the Guatemalan request that the decision in the *Colombian-Peruvian Asylum Case* be considered in a special meeting of the Council of the Organization of American States, the latter resolved:

> To declare that the Right of Asylum is a juridical principle of the Americas set forth in international conventions and included as one of the fundamental rights in the American Declaration of Rights and Duties of Man, approved by the Ninth International Conference of American States in Bogotá. [2]

In view of the foregoing discussion of the American Declaration of the Rights and Duties of Man, it is difficult to determine what is the meaning of such a resolution. To say that "the Right of Asylum is a juridical principle of the Americas ... included as one of the fundamental rights in the American Declaration of Rights and Duties of Man" when *diplomatic* asylum is clearly intended seems contrary to any reasonable interpretation. The most that could possibly be said of the American Declaration is that the right of diplomatic asylum is included to the extent that it is provided for in existing treaties.

It must be emphasized, however, that neither the American Declaration of the Rights and Duties of Man nor the resolution of the Council are binding on the signatory powers. Furthermore, *all* decisions of the Council are by majority vote "except when otherwise provided for." [3] The most significant feature of these two documents,

---

[1] *Ibid.* It is difficult to see how any other interpretation could be given to the article. A literal translation of the article as approved, without changes in punctuation or in sentence construction would read: "Everyone has the right to seek and receive asylum on foreign territory, in case of pursuit which is not motivated by common crimes and in accord with the legislation of each country and with international conventions." The official translation is equally clear: "Every person has the right in case of pursuit not resulting from ordinary crimes, to seek and receive asylum in foreign territory, in accordance with the laws of each country and with international agreements." International Conference of American States, Ninth, *Report of the Delegation of the United States with Related Documents* ([Washington, 1948]), p. 246.

[2] Organization of American States, Council, *Decisions Taken at Meetings of the Council of the Organization of American States*, IV (Washington: Pan American Union, 1952), p. 26.

[3] Organization of American States, Council, *Regulations of the Council of the Organization of American States* (Washington: Pan American Union, 1953), p. 7. But on the legal force of resolutions, C. G. Fenwick, "The Tenth Inter-American Conference: Some Issues of

in the opinion of the writer, is the fact that they are very typical of the Latin American practice which has been discussed in this chapter. That practice may be summarized as follows:

1. In spite of eloquent statements proclaiming the virtues of the institution, there has been a reluctance on the part of a majority of the Latin American states to declare unequivocally that they regard the granting of diplomatic asylum to persons pursued for political acts as a right appertaining to the state of refuge and the respect of such asylum as a duty incumbent upon the territorial state in deference to a custom recognized as law.

2. Definitely conflicting statements of policy over a period of time have been offered by each of six Latin American states. El Salvador, Colombia, Chile, Haiti, Peru, and Venezuela are the states in this category.

3. Of these six states, three (Haiti, Peru and Venezuela) have clearly asserted on a number of occasions that they *do not* regard the practice of asylum as sanctioned by a rule of law. A fourth state, Brazil, has consistently regarded it as based solely upon local toleration, and a fifth, El Salvador, has done so on at least one occasion.

4. At least in recent years, four states have clearly asserted that the practice is sanctioned by a customary rule of law. Colombia, Cuba, Ecuador, and Guatemala must be included here, although the policy of Colombia has not been consistent in this regard.

5. Argentina, the Dominican Republic, and Bolivia cannot be classified on the basis of data presented in this chapter.

We may now measure this practice against the standards for a customary rule of law discussed in chapter three. These requirements are summarized in Article 38 of the Statute of the International Court of Justice and the Court's decision in the *Colombian-Peruvian Asylum Case*, respectively.

Inter-American Regional Law," *A.J.I.L.*, 48 (1954), p. 464, commented: "Lawyers may quarrel over the relative legal force of resolutions and treaties; but as a matter of fact the existing practice shows due respect for resolutions antecedent to the adoption of the Charter, treating them as if they had the full force of law." To say, however, that states such as Nicaragua, Venezuela, Paraguay or the Dominican Republic felt legally bound by all the provisions in the American Declaration of the Rights and Duties of Man would seem absurd. As to the resolutions of the Council, they are certainly not comparable to the resolutions of the International Conferences of American States. In "The Law of the Organization of American States," *op. cit.*, pp.259–260, Fenwick observes: "My own personal opinion is that the resolutions and declarations of conferences and consultative meetings do have juridical value, do create legal obligations for the parties to them. But it should be noted that they are as a rule phrased in very general terms, making it possible for the parties to qualify or limit or even evade the obligations in case it should be found to be too burdensome or difficult to carry out." This seems particularly applicable here.

The court shall apply ... international custom, as evidence of a general practice accepted as law;[1]

The Party which relies on a custom of this kind must prove ... that this usage is the expression of a right appertaining to the State granting asylum and a duty incumbent on the territorial State.[2]

When compared with these standards, the Latin American practice of diplomatic asylum is far more accurately described by the Peruvian assertion that "American governments permit, deny or discuss asylum according to political contingencies." [3] The most convincing single piece of evidence in this regard is the very fact that Latin American states insisted on applying this practice in Spain during the Civil War. In spite of the fact that they had clearly regarded asylum as a Latin American practice some of these states made no distinction in its application in Spain. This certainly indicates a policy of expediency with little regard for legal considerations. The chapter on conventions and treaties showed a similar reluctance to accept treaty obligations which would clearly establish a general right to grant asylum and a duty to respect it.

The legal significance of such a practice must also be measured in terms of a basic principle of international law, clearly put forth in the *Lotus Case* and the *Colombian-Peruvian Asylum Case*, respectively.

Now the first and foremost restriction imposed by international law upon a State is that – failing the existence of a permissive rule to the contrary – it may not exercise its power in any form in the territory of another State. In this sense jurisdiction is certainly territorial; it cannot be exercised by a state outside its territory except by virtue of a permissive rule derived from international custom or from a convention.[4]

In the case of diplomatic asylum, the refugee is within the territory of the state where the offence was committed. A decision to grant diplomatic asylum involves a derogation from the sovereignty of that State. It withdraws the offender from the jurisdiction of the territorial State and constitutes an intervention in matters which are exclusively within the competence of that State, Such a derogation from territorial sovereignty cannot be recognized unless its legal basis is established in each particular case.[5]

In summary, the general reluctance of Latin American States to claim or admit that the practice of diplomatic asylum is sanctioned by

---

[1] U. S. *Treaty Series*, p. 993.
[2] *Op. cit.*, p. 276.
[3] Perú, *Proceso*, p. 154. (My translation.)
[4] *Op. cit.*, p. 18.
[5] *Op. cit.*, pp. 274–275.

a rule of law, the statements asserting that it is not sanctioned by a rule of law, and the widespread contradictions in statements by each of a number of Latin American states make it impossible to say that such practice has ripened into a custom having the force of law.[1]

[1] The material available on the granting of asylum on public vessels is considerably less than that on diplomatic and consular asylum. In the first place the number of cases is considerably smaller. The reason offered in chap. VII in explanation of the smaller number of cases of consular asylum as compared with diplomatic asylum would also be applicable here. In addition to this, a vessel can leave territorial waters, the territorial state is presented with a *fait accompli* and the diplomatic exchanges which would normally present the position of the parties to the controversy are probably regarded as useless. In any event they seldom appear in the published diplomatic papers in Latin America. Thus there are very few statements clearly setting forth a government's views, either on a particular case or on the general principles regulating the practice.

Such evidence as is available clearly suggests that asylum on public ships is regarded as being subject to the same rules as are applied in the case of diplomatic asylum. The reader will note that all of the multilateral treaties on asylum signed by American states treat asylum on warships in exactly the same way that they treat asylum in embassies and legations: *supra*, chapter IV.

Instructions to commanders of public vessels of the United States show that our policy has been virtually the same as that regarding diplomatic asylum. "... While the rule governing such cases is that it is the duty of American men-of-war to protect American citizens, it is, as a general rule, against the policy of this Government to grant asylum in its ships to citizens of foreign countries engaged in political activity, especially when such asylum is for the purpose of furthering their political plans. Temporary shelter to such persons, when they are seeking to leave their country, has sometimes been conceded on grounds of humanity, but even this is done with great circumspection lest advantage be taken of it to further the political fortunes of individuals with the result of involving us in the domestic politics of foreign countries." Roosevelt, Acting Secretary of the Navy, to Bryan, Secretary of State, October 28, 1913, Hackworth, *op. cit.*, p. 640. For instruction in a similar vein see *ibid.*, pp. 639–641 and Moore, *op. cit.*, pp. 851, 853.

This writer is unaware of any case where objections have been raised by Latin American states *based upon a distinction between diplomatic asylum and asylum on a public vessel*. There are indeed cases where objections have been raised but they are generally based upon the contention that the refugees are common criminals rather than political refugees. See case of asylum granted on board a Portuguese man-of-war in Rio de Janeiro Bay in 1849, Moore, *op. cit.*, pp. 853–855. For a case involving a Chilean general on board a French vessel see Tocornal, Chilean Minister of Foreign Relations, to the Commandant to the French Station in the Pacific, February 15, 1838, Chile, *Jurisprudencia de la cancillería chilena*, pp. 145–146. For a case involving asylum on board an Argentine gunboat (and later, merchant vessels) in Paraguayan waters see exchange of notes in Argentina, *Memoria*, 1911–1912, pp. 87–99. In some cases it is not clear whether objections are raised because of the particular refugee involved, because of a refusal to recognize asylum generally or because of a refusal to recognize *some forms* of asylum (i.e. asylum on public ships) although willing to recognize other forms. See Tocornal, Chilean Minister of Foreign Relations, to the Foreign [Diplomatic?] Agents, February 17, 1938, Chile, *Jurisprudencia de la cancillería chilena*, p. 146.

CHAPTER VI

UNITED STATES PRACTICE IN LATIN AMERICA

... Not one of my predecessors has been able literally to carry out the instructions of the Department, and I am forced to add that it will be impossible for my successors to act differently from the course pursued by their predecessors as long as the other legations receive and protect those that come to them in such emergencies ... A refugee comes to us; asks protection; we refuse to extend it to him; in return he refuses to leave the premises. Are we to use force to compel him to leave? We can not ask the Government to aid us. That would violate the sanctity of our legation ... There is but one solution, I think, and that is for each legation absolutely to refuse to shelter any one but members of the Government in case of a revolution only.[1]

This note from a harassed United States minister to Haiti illustrates well the difficulty faced by a government in formulating a consistent policy under such conditions and the difficulty faced by a diplomatic representative in carrying out that policy. Mr. Powell, the minister quoted here, had weathered many difficult cases, including some where the refugee had dragged his would-be captors into the legation only to be dragged out again, returned after a protest and finally deported.[2] While he has taken an exaggerated position as to what would constitute a violation of the sanctity of the legation,[3] his

---

[1] Powell, U. S. Minister to Haiti, to Hay, Secretary of State, November 14, 1899, *For. Rel. of the U. S.*, 1899, p. 394.

[2] Powell to Hay, August 2, 1899, *ibid.*, p. 378. The consulate was located in the same building, directly below the legation.

[3] Minister Powell's views are apparently based upon an earlier instruction from the department which advised as follows: "... Even when the refugee criminal is pursued in regular course of law, with exhibition of a warrant of arrest by a qualified officer of the courts he may neither be formally arrested within the legation precincts nor formally surrendered by the minister to the agent of the law. The former would amount to an exercise of local jurisdiction within the envoy's domicile which is inconsistent with his diplomatic immunities and his representative dignity. The latter would virtually be an assumption by the envoy of a nonexistent function of surrender by way of quasi extradition, for which no warrant of international or statutory law can be adduced." Hay to Powell, August 3, 1899, *ibid.*, p. 281. But Oppenheim, *op. cit.*, pp. 795–796, says: "... No act of jurisdiction or administration of the receiving Governments can take place within these residences, *except by special permission of the envoys* ... If a crime is committed inside the house of an envoy by an indi-

difficulties go far in explaining the inconsistencies in the practice outlined in this and the previous chapter. It also emphasizes the fact that this is a practice which depends largely upon the existence of some other right rather than being regarded as a right in itself.

United States practice has consistently denied that a right of asylum is sanctioned by international law. Four communications of the Department of State selected at roughly equal intervals over the past 150 years are indicative of this. In 1851, the minister to Chile was instructed that "inasmuch . . . as the right itself is more than doubtful under the public law, and as a formal demand had been made upon you for the offender, if he should still be your guest when this reaches you, it is deemed advisable that you should inform him that your house can no longer screen him from prosecution." [1]

In 1875, the minister to Colombia was instructed as follows:

> The right of asylum is denied by public law, and though occasions for claiming it have been frequent in other countries in this hemisphere, it is believed that in no instance has asylum been granted with the approval of this government. [2]

..Recurrent disorders in Haiti have been the occasion for a number of instructions such as this one in 1902:

> There is not known to the law of Nations, nor does the Government of the United States, in practice, recognize any right of ayslum in the legations of refugees from the scenes and disorders of civil conflict. Any claim or assertion of such right, as such, is not to be conceded or recognized for a moment. [3]

A rash of revolutionary outbreaks throughout Latin America in 1930, led the Department to restate its general policy in a circular addressed to all its diplomatic representatives in this area.

> There is no law of asylum of general application in international law . . . While the practice is recognized in most Latin American countries . . . [it] has never been recognized [by the U. S.] as a right which could be claimed by refugees or granted by diplomatic missions. [4]

vidual who does not enjoy personally the privilege of exterritoriality, the criminal must be surrendered to the local Government." (My italics.) C. G. Fenwick, *International Law* (3rd. ed.; New York, Appleton–Century–Crofts, 1948), p. 472, says the domicile of the diplomatic envoy "may not be entered by the local police or other officers of justice or administration in the ordinary exercise of their duties."

[1] Webster, Secretary of State, to Peyton, U. S. Minister to Chile, July 12, 1851, William R. Manning, *Diplomatic Correspondence of the United States: Inter-American Affairs, 1831–1850* (Washington Carnegie Endowment for International Peace, 1935), V, p. 17.

[2] Hunter, Acting Secretary of State, to Scruggs, U. S. Minister to Colombia, Sept. 11, 1875, Moore, *op. cit.*, p. 800.

[3] Adee, Acting Secretary of State, to Powell, U. S. Minister to Haiti, August 6, 1902, *For. Rel. of the U. S.*, 1902, p. 682.

[4] Hackworth, *op. cit.*, p. 623.

The consistency in this respect is further emphasized by the fact that, in addition to these four, no less than 22 similar communications can be cited in the years 1867, 1868, 1869, 1873, 1875, 1883, 1885, 1888, 1892, 1893, 1895, 1896, 1899, 1908, 1911, 1912, 1913, 1925, 1931.[1]

The closest this country has come to claiming a legal basis for the practice of asylum, and this seems to be atypical, was in the position outlined in a sharp reprimand to our minister in Guatemala for having permitted the local authorities to board an American vessel and remove a refugee in 1890. In the course of the note the Secretary of State referred to asylum in legations as well as that granted on ships. He noted first that, as a general principle, a diplomatic representative is not permitted to grant asylum to offenders against the law in the country to which he is accredited. Then comes an important exception:

But an exception to the rule has been made in the case of political offenders and nowhere has it more generally prevailed than in Spain and in the countries of Spanish America. It is proper to say that the United States has never encouraged an extension of this exception for the reason that it is likely to lead to abuse. But at the same time it has on grounds of humanity frequently found itself obliged to maintain it ... Under these circumstances especially, no nation could acquiesce in the sudden disregard or heed a demand for the pre-emptory abandonment of a privilege sanctioned by so general a usage.[2]

---

[1] Seward, Secretary of State, to Hovey, U. S. Minister to Peru, February 25, 1867, *Dip. Cor. of the U. S.* ,1867, II, pp. 763–764; Seward, Secretary of State, to Hollister U.S. Minister to Haiti, May 28, 1868, *Dip. Cor. of the U. S.* ,1868, II, p. 258; Fish, Secretary of State, to Bassett, U. S. Minister to Haiti, December 16, 1869, *For. Rel. of the U. S.*, 1871, p. 695; Fish, to Bassett, March 26, 1873, *For. Rel. of the U. S.*, 1873, I, p. 459; Fish, to Bassett, June 4, 1875, *For. Rel. of the U.S.*, 1875, II, p. 701; Fish, to Reynolds, U. S. Minister to Bolivia, December 3, 1875, *For. Rel. of the U. S.*, 1876, p. 18; Frelinghuysen, Secretary of State, to Langston, U. S. Minister to Haiti, December 15, 1883, Moore, *op. cit.*, p. 818; Bayard, Secretary of State, to Scruggs, U. S. Minister to Colombia, June 16, 1885, *For. Rel. of the U. S.*, 1885, p. 214; Bayard, to Thompson, U. S. Minister to Haiti, November 7, 1885, *For. Rel. of the U. S.*, 1886, p. 530; Rives, Assistant Secretary of State, to Goutier, U. S. Consul at Cape Haitien, October 31, 1888, *For. Rel. of the U. S.*, 1888, I, p. 938; Blaine, Secretary of State, to Durham, U. S. Minister to Haiti, January 28, 1892, *For. Rel. of the U. S.*, 1892, p. 347; Gresham, Secretary to State, to Baker, U. S. Minister to Nicaragua, August 15, 1893, *For. Rel. of the U. S.*, 1893, p. 212; Olney, Secretary of State to Tillman, U. S. Minister to Ecuador, September 25, 1895, *For. Rel. of the U. S.*, 1895, I, p. 245; Olney, to Smythe, U. S. Minister to Haiti, February 18, 1896, *For. Rel. of the U. S.*, 1896, p. 381; Hay, Secretary of State, to Sampson, U.S. Minister to Ecuador, February 27, 1899, *For. Rel. of the U. S.*, 1899, p. 256; Root, Secretary of State, to Furniss, U. S. Minister to Haiti, April 11, 1908, Hackworth, *op. cit.*, p. 634; Knox, Secretary of State, to Fletcher, U. S. Minister to Chile, July 19, 1911, Hackworth, *op. cit.*, p. 637; Wilson, Acting Secretary of State, to the Secretary of the Navy, tel., October 23, 1912, *For. Rel. of the U. S.*, 1912, p. 860; Knox, Secretary of State, to the U. S. Minister in Ecuador, January 30, 1912, *For. Rel. of the U. S.*, 1912, p. 399; Carr, Director of the Consular Bureau, to Johnson, U. S. Consul at Matamoros, Meixco, April 24, 1913, Hackworth, *op. cit.*, pp. 638–639; Hughes, Sectetary of State, to Collier, U. S. Minister to Chile, tel., January 27, 1925, Hackworth, *op. cit.*, p. 630.

[2] Blain, Secretary of State, to Mizner, U. S. Minister to Guatemala, November 18, 1890, *For. Rel. of the U. S.*, 1890, p. 138.

There are scattered instances where a United States minister has attempted to give legal sanction to the granting of asylum by claiming exterritorial status for the legation. This writer is unaware of any cases where the Department of State has itself made such claims. On the contrary, it will be seen that it has specifically disapproved of them in a number of cases.

In 1892 the United States minister to Chile referred to asylum as "a principle which forms an integral part of the international practice of my country." [1] In this case it was based upon an extreme claim of extraterritorial status for the legation.

> The house of this legation is considered as an integral part of the United States, and without the will and permission of my Government your excellency could not consider as subject to the judicial action of Chile those persons who, from every point of view are beyond its jurisdiction. [2]

In 1875, the American minister to Haiti, restating the position taken by our legation there in 1870, asserted that "the persons who may have sought refuge under my flag are considered as being on the territory and under the protection of the United States." [3] A less extreme position was taken by the minister to Colombia in 1885. In reply to a Colombian note which raised some questions as to the future inviolability of embassies and legations should they in the future harbor refugees pursued by officers of the law he asserted that the house of the minister was "exempt from the operation of local law. And to make these exemptions the more complete, the fiction of exterritoriality has been invented, whereby though actually in a foreign country, he is supposed to remain within the territory of his own sovereign." [4]

In the first two cases there is no evidence that the Department either approved or disapproved of the minister's action. In the case of the minister to Colombia, the Department clearly disapproved of his course. It advised "that treating this figure of speech as a fact, and reasoning logically from it, have led to results of an unsatisfactory and

---

[1] Egan, U. S. Minister to Chile, to Matta, Chilean Minister of Foreign Relations, September 26, 1891 (inclosures in Egan to Blaine, Secretary of State, September 29, 1891) *For. Rel. of the U. S.*, 1891, p. 176.

[2] Egan to Matta (inclosure in Egan to Blain, October 26, 1891), *ibid.*, p. 176.

[3] Bassett, U. S. Minister to Haiti, to Excellent, Haitian Secretary of State for Foreign Affairs, May 4, 1875 (inclosure in Bassett to Fish, Secretary of State, May 8, 1875), *For. Rel. of the U. S.*, 1875, II, p. 694.

[4] Scruggs, U. S. Minister to Colombia, to Restrepo, Colombian Minister of Foreign Relations, February 21, 1885 (inclosure in Scruggs to Frelinghuysen, Secretary of State, February 23, 1885), *For. Rel. of the U. S.*, 1885, pp. 206–207.

not practical character; that the phrase should be treated as a figure of speech and not as a fact from which inferences can be drawn." [1]

A similar position was taken when in 1895 the Department instructed the minister to Ecuador that no disparagement of the authority of the state to which a minister is accredited can be countenanced "under the mistaken fiction of exterritoriality." [2] The 1930 circular addressed to the U. S. diplomatic representatives in Latin America made it very clear that no exterritorial status was to be claimed:

> Immunity from local jurisdiction is granted foreign embassies and legations to enable the foreign representatives and their suites to enjoy the fullest opportunity to represent the interests of their states. The fundamental principle of legation is that it should yield entire respect to the exclusive jurisdiction of the territorial government in all matters not within the purpose of the mission. The affording of asylum is not within the purpose of a diplomatic mission.[3]

Inasmuch as the United States has not claimed the granting of asylum in its embassies and legations as a right sanctioned by international law, either in its own right or as a consequence of any claims of exterritoriality of the diplomatic premises, on what grounds has it in fact based its action in granting such asylum?

In an early case it was justified simply on ground of the "barbarous or semi-barbarous" conditions in the Latin American countries:

> The right of a foreign legation to afford an asylum to political refugees is not recognized by the law of nations as applicable to civilized or constitutionally organized states, it is a practice, however, which, from the necessity of the case, is exercised to a greater of less extent by every civilized state in regard to barbarous or semi-barbarous countries. The revolutionary conditions seemed to become chronic in many of the South American nations after they had achieved their independence, and the United States, as well as the European nations, recognized and maintained the right of asylum in their intercourse with those republics.[4]

---

[1] Bayard, Secretary of State, to Scruggs, U. S. Minister to Colombia, June 16, 1885, *For. Rel. of the U. S.*, 1895, p. 216.

[2] Olney, Secretary of State, to Tillman, U. S. Minister to Ecuador, September 25, 1895, *For. Rel. of the U. S.*, 1895, I, p. 245.

[3] October 2, 1930, Hackworth, *op. cit.*, p. 623. This position was also implicit in the U. S. reply to the Argentine *Project of Convention on Asylum*, circulated in 1937: "My government feels that the recognition of the so-called right of asylum on such broad terms as those set forth on the draft convention would involve an extension of the traditional immunities and privileges enjoyed by diplomatic representatives transcending the original purposes for which such immunities and privileges were created namely, to accord full protection and freedom from interference to the diplomatic representatives of one state within the territorial jurisdiction of another, with a view to promoting peaceful and orderly relations between states." Draft Note from Wedell, U. S. Ambassador to Argentina, to Saavedra Lamas, Argentine Minister of Foreign Relations, undated, (inclosure in Wedell to Welles, Undersecretary of State, November 2, 1937), *For. Rel. of the U. S.*, 1937, V, p. 148.

[4] Seward, Secretary of State, to Hollister, U. S. Minister of Haiti, May 28, 1868, *Dip. Cor. of the U. S.*, 1868, II, p. 358.

The discussion in chapter three has already pointed out that in a great many cases the practice of asylum is not questioned and the matter of a basis for its exercise is not even discussed. But in the overwhelming majority of cases where the practice is questioned, either in instructions from our State Department or in exchanges between a foreign government and our diplomatic representative accredited there, its justification is claimed on the basis of local toleration.

In one of the earlier cases in the records of American diplomatic history the Department of State advised its minister to Chile that:

> The propriety of your granting asylum to Colonel Arteaga will depend upon circumstances which are at present unknown to the Department. If there should be any precedent showing that the Chilean Government had previously acquiesced in such a proceeding on the part of the diplomatic representative of any foreign nation at Santiago, it could not justly complain of our course, unless formal notice should have previously been given that it would not in the future tolerate the exercise of the right.[1]

Reprimands and solicited instructions to our diplomatic representatives in Haiti have been numerous on this score. "If as a custom, in any country, the practice of asylum prevails, and is tacitly or explicitly recognized by the local authorities . . . the exercise of the consuetudinary privilege by Americans could not be deemed exceptional" advised the Department in 1885.[2]

The American minister's claims of exterritorial status for the United States legation in Santiago seem to have gone unnoticed by the Department in the 1891 case referred to above. These claims were far more extreme than those of the Department. Regarding asylum granted to members of the deposed government of Balmaceda, the Department asserted that "the right of asylum having been tacitly, if not expressly, allowed to other foreign legations, and having been exercised by our minister with the old government . . . the President cannot but regard the application of another rule, accompanied by acts of disrespect to our legation, as the manifestation of a most unfriendly spirit." [3]

After noting that protection afforded to members of the deposed

---

[1] Webster, Secretary of State, to Peyton, U. S. Minister to Chile, July 2, 1851, Moore, *op. cit.*, pp. 787–788.

[2] Bayard, Secretary of State, to Thompson, U. S. Minister to Haiti, November 7, 1885, *For. Rel. of the U. S.*, 1886, p. 530.

[3] Warton, Acting Secretary of State, to Egan, U. S. Minister to Chile, October 1, 1891, *For. Rel. of the U. S.*, 1891, p. 177.

government and their families in Ecuador was not actually asylum inasmuch as there appeared not to have been any government in control at the time, the Department pointed out that "asylum is not a right derived from positive law or custom; it is not sanctioned by international law, and can only find excuse when tacitly invited and consented to by the state within whose jurisdiction it may be practiced." [1]

Reference has already been made to the 1930 circular sent to American diplomatic officers in Latin America, in which any right to grant asylum under international law was explicitly denied.[2] The circular did point out, however, that "where asylum is practiced, it is not a right of the legate state but rather a custom invoked or consented to by the territorial state in times of political instability." [3]

United States policy has not been entirely consistent in this regard, however. There have been cases where local toleration was not considered as a justification. In reply to a despatch from the United states minister to Haiti to the effect that he had granted asylum, *as had a number of other legations*, the Department insisted that "the course of the diplomatic representatives of other countries in receiving political refugees upon occasions is not deemed sufficient to warrant this government in sanctioning a similar step on the part of the representatives of the United States." [4] There is no evidence at the time these instructions were given that the Department had reason to distinguish this case from numerous others on grounds of the character of the refugee or conditions prevailing at that time. The minister in reporting this case to the Department, said: "I could not turn them out when I knew that within two minutes, if I should do so, and close my door behind them, they would be slaughtered without judgment or mercy." [5] Four months later the Department was itself using the arguments advanced by the minister.[6]

This, of course, merely shows that U. S. policy has not always held that the right to grant asylum in legations and consulates could be claimed on the basis of local toleration. But it does not alter the fact

---

[1] Olney, Secretary of State, to Tillman, U. S. Minister to Ecuador, September 25, 1895, *For. Rel. of the U. S.*, 1895, I, p. 245.

[2] *Supra*, p. 98.

[3] Hackworth, *op. cit.*, p. 623.

[4] Fish, Secretary of States, to Bassett, U. S. Minister to Haiti, June 4, 1875, *For. Rel. of the U. S.*, 1875, II, p. 701.

[5] Bassett to Fish, May 8, 1875, *ibid.*, pp. 688–689.

[6] Caldwalader, Acting Secretary of State, to Preston, Haitian Minister to the U. S., August 6, 1875, *ibid.*, p. 739.

that *where such a privilege has been claimed it has generally been on the basis of a local toleration*. But this last statement is subject to misinterpretation and the United States conception of "local toleration" must be further defined.

This toleration has not been looked upon as something which the territorial state could grant or deny in each individual case, purely on the basis of its own discretion. In 1867, the United States minister to Peru asserted that the latter was "entitled to all the rights and privileges of a Christian nation and as such should be placed precisely in the position of the United States, France, England and other Christian countries." Under these circumstances the doctrine of asylum could "not be properly claimed or enforced here unless it be to shield persons from the violence of a mob." But the qualification was added that if the doctrine were to be tolerated for others, in that case the United States would demand it too.

> Notwithstanding this view, if the Government of Peru should feel disposed to concede greater privileges to others, I, as the representative of my Government, would expect to be entitled to the same privileges granted to them.[1]

This position was "altogether approved" by the United States Department of State.[2]

This same position was taken in connection with cases in Haiti in 1868, 1875, 1885 and in 1908.[3] Thus Barry Gilbert concluded in 1909, after a study of United States practice, that while any right of asylum was disavowed in legal theory this country would "claim under certain conditions the quasi-right of being accorded the same privileges of asylum as have hitherto been granted in Central and South America."[4] The use of the term "quasi-right" here seems to mean that the United States will claim it as it would claim any right so long as it is granted to other states. But this leaves it subject to the toleration of the territorial state and if that state wishes to discontinue such toleration *and does so with regard to all nations alike*, presumably the United States would relinquish all its claims in this regard. Thus

---

[1] Hovey, United States Minister to Peru, to Pacheco, Minister of Foreign Relations of Peru, January 15, 1867 (inclosure in Hovey to Seward, Secretary of State, January 28, 1867), *Dip. Cor. of the U. S.*, 1867, II, pp. 738–739.

[2] Seward to Hovey, February 25, 1867, *ibid.*, pp. 763–764.

[3] Seward, to Hollister, U. S. Minister to Haiti, May 28, 1868, *Dip. Cor. of the U. S.*, 1868, II, p. 358; Fish, Secretary to State, to Preston, Haitian Minister to the U. S., December 11, 1875, *For. Rel. of the U. S.*, pp. 343–344; Thompson [office unknown], to Bayard, U. S. Minister to Haiti, November 7, 1885, *For. Rel. of the U. S.*, 1886, p. 530.

[4] "The Practice of Asylum in Legations and Consulates of the United States," *A.J.I.L.*, III, (1909), p. 585.

Gilbert asserts that "until an express renunciation by the particular state in question, as by Peru in 1867, or a general agreement among the powers to cease the practice, the question is liable to repeatedly reappear in diplomatic correspondence." [1]

But implicit in these instructions is the idea that it is not a question to be decided by the territorial state alone *even if it should decide to discontinue toleration of such a practice for all powers alike.* The powers represented in a particular country are also to have a part in the decision. Thus the 1868 instructions to the minister in Haiti said that the Department did not think it expedient that "it should be *renounced* by the United States legation any sooner or in any greater degree than it is *renounced* by the legations of the other important neutral powers."[2] In 1875 it instructed the minister to Haiti that the United States would like to see the practice abolished but would be willing to do it only if an accord could be reached with the other powers.[3]

Never-the-less, the United States has in some cases shown a willingness to renounce the practice unilaterally. It has already been noted that Peru, in 1867, declared that it would no longer tolerate the practice of asylum as it had existed there in the past and that, just prior to this declaration, the United States had said that it would be unwilling to renounce the practice unilaterally. But according to the Peruvian *Memoria* for 1867, the legation of the United States had "accepted in all its breadth, the conclusions of the Peruvian government." [4] While the American minister's despatches show no record of this, a copy of the *Memoria* was included in his despatch of February 22, 1867 with no disavowal on his part and no apparent response from the Department of State.[5] A year later the State Department pointed out to its minister to Haiti that "in the year 1867 we formally relinquished and renounced the right in the republic of Peru." [6]

In 1908, protection of the American legation and consulates was afforded to certain participants in a Haitian revolution. A few months later, however, the Department issued the following instructions:

[1] *Ibid.*

[2] Seward, Secretary of State, to Hollister, U. S. Minister to Haiti, May 28, 1868, *Dip. Cor. of the U. S.*, 1868, II, p. 358; Moore, *op. cit.*, p. 808. (My italics.)

[3] Fish, Secretary of State, to Preston, Haitian Minister to the United States, December 11, 1875, *For. Rel. of the U. S.*, 1876, pp. 343–344.

[4] Reprinted in *Dip. Cor. of the U. S.*, 1867, II, p. 759.

[5] *Ibid.*, p. 746.

[6] Seward, Secretary of State, to Hollister, U. S. Minister ot Haiti, May 28, 1868, *Dip. Cor. of the U. S.*, 1868, II, p. 358.

... Previous instructions have made it clear that this Government does not recognize the so-called right of asylum. Recent conditions prevented that policy from being carried out with regard to refugees who were then actually under shelter.

Now that the American legation and consulates have been cleared of refugees, you will make it distinctly known that no more Haitian refugees will be admitted to shelter by you or your subordinates and that no pretext will be afforded for reawakening the question of asylum so far as the Government of the United States is concerned.[1]

Not only was this unqualified renunciation made public but the American minister asked the Haitian Minister for Foreign Affairs to assist the legation in giving it publicity.[2] Shortly thereafter the Haitian government publicly declared that it would no longer tolerate the practice and expressed its thanks to the United States for "taking the initiative in abolishing this alleged right of asylum." [3]

This is indeed a curious position wherein the granting of asylum is both claimed and denied as a right. The reasons for it are understandable enough. The weak and unstable condition of Latin American governments means that a declaration that the practice will no longer be tolerated may not be enforceable in the face of legations who may insist on perpetuating it. Thus it has seemed safer to rely upon an agreement among the foreign diplomatic representatives in a particular country. It really amounts to saying that "we will *in fact* claim as a right that which we do not *in theory* claim as a right." This curious legal position has been referred to by the Department of State as "a quasi rule of public law."

If the so-called "right of asylum" (which this government has never been tenacious in claiming for its officers abroad) is to continue to exist as a quasi rule of public law, in communities where the conspirators of today may be the government of tomorrow, it should at least be so exercised as to afford no ground on the score of aiding and comforting rebellion ...[4]

More recent State Department communications published in the annual volumes of *Foreign Relations of the United States*, and in State Department manuscripts published in Hackworth's *Digest of Inter-*

[1] Root, Secretary of State, to Furniss, U. S. Minister to Haiti, April 11, 1908, *For. Rel. of the U. S.*, 1980, p. 435.

[2] Furniss, to Borno, Haitian Minister for Foreign Affairs, May 2, 1908 (inclosure in Furniss to Root, May 12, 1908), *ibid.*, p. 437.

[3] Borno to Furniss, May 20, 1908 (inclosure in Furniss to Root, May 22, 1908, translation) and Léger, Haitian Minister to the U. S., to the U. S. Acting Secretary of State, July 17, 1908, trans., *ibid.*, pp. 438–439.

[4] Evarts, Secretary of State, to Langston, U. S. Minister to Haiti, August 6, 1879, *For. Rel. of the U. S.*, 1879, p. 582.

national Law, as well as others available only in the National Archives, have shown a tendency toward abandoning the claim that a right of asylum can be claimed by the United States so long as such claims by other states are assented to by the territorial state. Emphasis has shifted toward justification purely on the basis of humanitarian considerations.[1]

This gradual shift away from the emphasis upon local practice as the grounds upon which asylum may be granted can also be noted in the standing instructions to diplomatic officers. A review of these instructions will necessitate quoting the relevant sections at some length.

The Instructions to Diplomatic Officers (1897) provided:

> 50. *Asylum.* – The privilege of immunity from local jurisdiction does not embrace the right of asylum for persons outside of a representative's diplomatic or personal household.
> 51. *Unsanctioned asylum.* – In some countries, where frequent insurrections occur and consequent instability of government exists, the practice of extraterritorial asylum has become so firmly established that it is often invoked by unsuccessful insurgents and is *practically recognized by the local government,* to the extent even of respecting the premises of a consulate in which such fugitives may take refuge. This Government does not sanction the usage and enjoins upon its representatives in such countries the avoidance of all pretext for its exercise. While indisposed to direct its representatives to deny temporary shelter to any person whose life may be threatened by mob violence it deems it proper to instruct them that it will not countenance them in any attempt knowingly to harbor offenders against the laws from the pursuit of the legitimate agents of justice.[2]

A significant difference appears in the 1930 circular sent to American diplomatic representatives in Latin America.

> The limited practice of legation asylum, which varies in the few states permitting it according to the nature of the emergency, the attitude of the government, the state of the public mind, the character of the fugitives, the nature of their offenses, and the legation in which asylum is sought, is in derogation of the local jurisdiction. It is but a permissive local custom practiced in a limited number of states where unstable political and social conditions are recurrent.[3]

This seems to indicate not only that the practice varies "in the few states permitting it," but that, among other grounds for permitting

---

[1] See, for example, Hughes, Secretary of State, to Collier, U. S. Minister to Chile, January 27, 1925, tel., Hackworth, *op. cit.,* pp. 628–629; Colby, Secretary of State, to Hanna, U. S. *Chargé d'Affaires* in Mexico, April 14, 1920, tel., *ibid.,* p. 627; Hull, Secretary of State, to the American Embassy in Madrid, August 25, 1936, *ibid.,* p. 632.

[2] U. S., Department of State, *Instructions to the Diplomatic Officers of the United States* (Washington, 1897), p. 20. (My italics.)

[3] Hackworth, *op. cit.,* p. 623.

it, these states may take into account the legation in which asylum is sought. Thus they would *not* be required to treat all legations equally in this respect. It should be noted at this point that the Havana convention of 1928 provided that:

> Asylum granted to political offenders ... shall be respected to the extent in which allowed, as a right or through humanitarian toleration, by the usages, the conventions or the laws of the country in which granted [country of refuge].[1]

The United States signed this convention with the express declaration that it did not recognize asylum as a part of international law.[2] Thus the United States as a state which does not recognize asylum in its usages, conventions or laws could hardly claim it in other states.

Executive Order 5956 of December 1, 1932 repeated in Instructions to Diplomatic Officers of June 1, 1938, provided:

> 97.31 *Asylum.* – The privilege of immunity from local jurisdiction does not embrace the right of asylum for persons outside of a representative's official personal household.
>
> 97.32 *Unsanctioned asylum.* – There is no asylum of general application in international law. Hence, where asylum is practiced, it is not a right of the legate state but rather a custom invoked or consented to by the territorial government in times of political instability. While the practice is recognized in most of the Latin American countries, and was the subject of a convention signed at Habana at the Sixth Pan American Conference in 1928, it has never existed in the United States and has never been recognized as a right which could be claimed by refugees or granted by diplomatic missions. The custom is justified publicly on humanitarian grounds, but in practice it is used primarily for the personal protection of conspirators planning a coup d'état or for the government fearing or experiencing one.[3]

Reference to local practice as a basis for the granting of asylum was completely abandoned in the Foreign Service Regulations of the United States of July 1939. In this case, the only ground suggested was that of humanitarian considerations.

> *Asylum.* A diplomatic representative or consular officer may not extend asylum to persons outside his official or personal household. (E.O. June 22, 1939).
>
> Note I. *Involuntary refuge.* The extension of refuge to persons outside the official or personal household of a diplomatic or consular officer can only be justified on humanitarian grounds. Diplomatic and consular officers may afford refuge to uninvited fugitives whose lives are in imminent danger from mob violence but only during the period active danger continues. Refuge must be refused to persons fleeing from pursuit of the legitimate agents of the local government. In case such persons have been admitted, they must be either surrendered or or dismissed from the mission or consulate.[4]

---

[1] *Supra*, p. 56.
[2] *Infra*, p. 122.
[3] *C.F.R.* (1939), Title 22, 97. 31, 97.32.
[4] Hackworth, *op. cit.*, p. 623.

This portion of the Foreign Service Regulations was amended in 1946 and, again, there is no reference to practice.

101.845 *Restrictions on extending asylum.* As a rule, a diplomatic representative or consular officer shall not extend asylum to persons outside of his official or personal household. Refuge may be afforded to uninvited fugitives whose lives are in imminent danger from mob violence but only for the period during which active danger continues. Refuge must be refused to persons fleeing from the pursuit of the legitimate agents of the local government. In case such persons have been admitted to the diplomatic or consular premises, they must be either surrendered or dismissed from the mission or consular office.[1]

The entire section (101.845) was excluded from the Code of Federal Regulations in December, 1948,[2] but appears with only slight changes in phraseology in the *Foreign Service Manual* for 1952, revalidated as of March 30, 1956.[3]

Within these assumptions concerning the basis upon which the practice of diplomatic asylum can be justified, the United States has attempted to lay down certain restrictions or limitations. The Department of State has been far more consistent in asserting them as generalizations than it has in adapting them to specific cases. A further inconsistency is added to United States practice by the fact that the diplomatic representative has not always followed the instructions, either through ignorance as to what such instructions were or through the difficulty of interpreting them as applied to a specific case. Three such limitations or restrictions have been consistently put forth.

1. *Diplomatic asylum may be granted only in case the life of the person seeking it is in immediate danger of mob violence or lawlessness.* Under these conditions the Department of State approved the action of its minister to Venezuela as early as 1848.

That your mansion, as well as the house of other foreign legations in Caracas, should have been employed during a period of popular excitement and alarm, as a temporary asylum for the weak or the timid who might have deemed their lives in jeopardy from lawless outrage, can nowhere be regarded with surprise or regret, and it is gratifying to perceive that its employment for this purpose is not complained of in either of the notes addressed to you by the minister of foreign affairs for the Government of Venezuela ...[4]

Although "deeply established" in Haiti, "this government does not sanction the usage" the Department advised in 1883. Nevertheless,

[1] 11 *F.R.* (1946), p. 13910.
[2] 13 *F.R.* (1948), p. 8738.
[3] 1 *FSM* I 225.2, issued under TL: A–66, Feb. 12, 1952, revalidated March 30, 1956.
[4] Buchanan, Secretary of State, to Shields, U. S. Minister to Venezuela, March 22, 1848, Moore, *op. cit.*, pp. 842–843.

it would be "indisposed for obvious motives of common humanity to direct its agents to deny temporary shelter to any unfortunate threatened with mob violence." This, however was not to include "any attempt to knowingly harbor offenders against the laws from the pursuit of the legitimate agents of justice." [1]

In 1905 two Haitian officials (members of the Auditing Committee) received asylum in the U. S. legation. They insisted that their lives were in danger because their records were unable to account for certain public funds and upon their refusal to change the records the President had declared them "in league with his enemies and conspirators ..." [2] For this action the minister was reprimanded by the Department of State in Washington.

> The Department has already ... been constrained to express its disapproval of the grant of shelter to Mr. Cameau. It appears that there was a controversy between the President and the Auditing Committee growing out of the report which the latter had made as Haitian officials to the Haitian Congress. There is not the slightest evidence that Mr. Cameau was in danger of mob violence or that he was even in imminent peril of his life. [3]

A Venezuelan subject whose father was in hiding as a result of the government's suspicion that he was connected with a recent revolutionary plot was informed that he would be imprisoned unless he produced his father. He asked for and received asylum in the home of the American Military Attaché in Caracas stating that "he could not again leave the Major's residence as he would be arrested and tortured if he fell into the hands of the police." [4] The Department advised that this could not be considered a case of immediate danger:

> It is contrary to the policy of this government to approve of granting asylum to political refugees, although in some cases the Department has approved of the action of diplomatic or consular officers in giving temporary shelter, for humanitarian reasons, in imminent peril of their lives. Under the circumstances the Department does not consider that the action ... in the case mentioned was warranted. [5]

A year later the United States minister to Chile was advised that "an individual fleeing before a mob might be given temporary refuge

---

[1] Frelinghuysen, Secretary of State, to Langston, U. S. Minister to Haiti, December 15, 1883, Moore, op. cit., p. 818.

[2] Powell, U. S. Minister to Haiti, to the Secretary of State, June 6, 1905, For. Rel. of the U. S., 1905, p. 551.

[3] Pierce, Acting Secretary of State, to Powell, June 29, 1905, ibid., p. 553.

[4] Cook [U. S. Minister to Venezuela], to Hughes, Secretary of State, March 15, 1924, Dept. of State file 831.00/1226.

[5] Hughes to Chabot, U. S. Chargé d'Affaires ad interim in Venezuela, April 19, 1924, Hackworth, op. cit., pp. 627-628.

in an American mission, if he entered the same in the course of flight, until the mob dispersed or until the mission could turn him over to the authorities of the country, *de facto* or otherwise, who were in a position to protect him from similar outbreaks of mob violence." [1] In 1930, the same legation was advised that granting asylum to members of the family of the President of Chile would be undesirable inasmuch as it did not appear that the persons concerned were in immediate danger of violence.[2]

The recent circulars and standing instructions to diplomatic officers have strongly emphasized this point. The 1930 circular, previously referred to, stated that "the United States can not countenance the affording of protection to other than uninvited fugitives whose lives are in imminent danger from mob violence." [3] The Foreign Service Manual of the United States, revalidated as of March 30, 1956, provides that refuge may be granted to uninvited fugitives "whose lives are in danger from mob violence but only for the period during which active danger continues." It further requires that protection must be refused "to persons fleeing from the pursuit of the legitimate agents of the local government." [4]

2. *Diplomatic asylum must be not promised when solicited in advance in anticipation of some future need.* This would seem to follow logically enough from the first requirement that asylum can only be granted under conditions of actual or imminent danger from mob violence or lawlessness.

In 1899, the American minister to Ecuador reported that the Minister of Foreign Relations had inquired if asylum might be granted to members of the present government "if the unexpected should happen and the Government should be defeated." [5] To this the Ame-

---

[1] Hughes, Secretary of State, to Collier, U. S. Minister to Chile, tel., January 27, 1925, *ibid.*, p. 629.

[2] Stimson, Secretary of State, to Culbertson, U. S. Ambassador to Chile, tel., June 7, 1932, *ibid.*, p. 630.

[3] Hackworth, *op. cit.*, pp. 623–624.

[4] 1 FSM I 225.2, issued under TL: A–66, Feb. 12, 1952, revalidated March 30, 1956. This appears somewhat weaker than the 1939 regulation: "A diplomatic representative or consular officer may not extend asylum to persons outside of his official or personal household." A note to this provides that "the extension of refuge to persons outside the official or personal household of a diplomatic or consular officer can only be justified on humanitarian grounds. Diplomatic and consular officers may afford refuge to uninvited fugitives whose lives are in imminent danger from mob violence but only during the period active danger continues. Refuge must be refused to persons fleeing from the pursuit of the legitimate agents of the local government. In case such persons have been admitted, they must be either surrendered or dismissed from the mission or the consulate." Hackworth, *op. cit.*, p. 623.

[5] Hay, Secretary of State, to Sampson, U. S. Minister to Ecuador, June 5, 1899, *For. Rel. of the U. S.*, 1899, p. 258. The minister's earlier note was quoted here.

rican minister had replied in the affirmative. On receiving this report the State Department informed him that it could not approve "the promise of shelter made ... to the members of the titular Government before the emergency had actually arisen for decision as to whether the circumstances then existing would justify or make it permissible." [1] The *chargé d'affaires* at the same legation reported in 1912, that he had refused to discuss a hypothetical case of future danger put to him by certain individuals. The Department approved of his course but referred him to an earlier instruction where a distinction was made between "asylum" and "temporary refuge." [2] This suggests the third limitation which, at least in theory, United States policy places upon the granting of asylum where such practice can be based upon local toleration.

3. *Diplomatic asylum may be granted only as a temporary expedient to preserve innocent human life.* This has certainly been the most difficult limitation to observe in practice. It may be noted that in the instructions discussed under limitation number one, above, the existence of immediate or imminent danger was given as a condition for *temporary* asylum.

In the 1912 instruction, referred to above, the Department said:

You are correct in assuming that what is technically known as "the right of asylum" in a strict sense is not claimed by this Government. However there is an evident distinction between this case and that where temporary refuge is given within the residence of a consular or diplomatic representative in order to preserve innocent human life.[3]

He was then referred to instructions which gave the Department's policy on temporary refuge. These instructions provided that temporary refuge could be granted at the discretion of the representative "where such is necessary to preserve innocent human life." [4]

This is essentially the same distinction which was made in chapter one between "temporary" and "definitive" asylum. The concept of temporary asylum was put forth much more clearly

[1] *Ibid.*

[2] Wilson, Acting Secretary of State, to Bingham, U. S. *Chargé d'Affaires ad interim* in Ecuador, May 6, 1912, Hackworth, *op. cit.*, p. 625. See also Olney, Secretary of State, to Tillman, U. S. Minister to Ecuador, September 25, 1895, *For. Rel. of the U. S.*, 1895, I, p. 246; Knox, Secretary of State, to Fuller, U. S. Minister to Haiti, tel., August 2, 1911, Hackworth, *op. cit.*, p. 624; Knox to the American Legation at Peking, tel., November 10, 1911, *ibid.*, pp. 624–625.

[3] Knox, Secretary of State, to Young, U. S. Minister to Ecuador, January 30, 1912, *For. Rel. of the U. S.*, 1912, p. 399.

[4] *Ibid.*

in instructions issued to the minister to Ecuador in 1895. These instructions pointed out that asylum "may be tolerated as an act of humanity when the hospitality afforded does not go beyond sheltering the individual from lawlessness. It may not be tolerated should it be sought to remove the subject beyond the reach of the law to the disparagement of the sovereign authority of the state." The meaning of "temporary" protection was then very clearly indicated:

> It seems to be very generally supposed that the case of a member of an overturned titular government is different; and so it may be until the empire of laws is restored and the successful revolution establishes itself in turn as the rightful government competent to administer laws and justice in orderly process. Until that happens the humane accordance of shelter from lawlessness may be justifiable; but when the authority of the state is reestablished upon an orderly footing, no disparagement of its powers under the mistaken fiction of extraterritoriality can be countenanced on the part of the representatives of this government.[1]

But it can easily be seen that this generalization creates as many problems as it solves. How does the minister determine when "the empire of laws is restored and the successful revolution establishes itself in turn as the rightful government competent to administer laws and justice in orderly process?" When one political faction has gained control of the government and wishes to gain revenge on their ousted political enemies is the minister to decide whether a fair trial will be given? If there is no chance of a fair trial, is this merely turning the refugee over to lawlessness? It is the difficulty in answering such questions as this that is responsible for the great difference between the theory put forth in general instructions and the actual United States practice.

In 1848 the Department seems to have at least recognized the possibility that the legation could be entered to apprehend a refugee under certain circumstances. Noting first that the point was really not an issue at present, it observed that "if it can be rightfully entered at all without the consent of its occupant, it can only be so entered in consequence of an order emanating from the supreme authority of the country in which the minister resides, and for which it will be held responsible by his Government." [2]

During the chaotic times which prevailed in Paraguay in the years

---

[1] Olney, Secretary of State, to Tillman, U. S. Minister to Ecuador, September 25, 1895, *For. Rel. of the U. S.*, 1895, I, p. 245; Moore, *op. cit.*, pp. 803–804.

[2] Buchanan, Secretary of State, to Shields, U. S. Minister to Venezuela, March 22, 1848, Moore, *op. cit.*, p. 843.

1867 and 1868, made worse by a war with Argentina, Brazil and Uruguay, the United States minister reported to the department that he had "not hesitated to report that this legation will give whatever protection it can to whosoever, save notorious criminals, may resort to it in time of danger." This, however, was in anticipation of an order by the Paraguayan ruler, López, that the city be evacuated, and the protection offered was against "the enemy" – presumably the invading forces from Argentina, Brazil or Uruguay.[1] This was approved by the Department.[2]

With the approach of the Brazilian fleet about thirty persons of various nationalities were given asylum.[3] When the fleet was withdrawn and Paraguayan authority was again extended over Asunción, the latter government demanded that asylum cease, "the ostensible motive of the asylum given by the American legation having ceased."[4] When this demand was made known to the refugees, all except two, whom the minister claimed as personnel of the legation, left.[5] A long correspondence followed concerning the latter but since the minister did not base his refusal to surrender them upon any right of asylum it need not be considered here.[6] The minister reported the case to Washington as follows:

> López ... demanded of me that I should deliver up to the tribunals those who had sought asylum in my house at the time the Brazilian fleet went to Asunción in February last. To defend these men and save them from the clutches of López, I had a correspondence with the Government long enough to make a volume of diplomatic despatches. It was all in vain, however. They all had to go; though none except Bliss and Masterman were taken by force.[7]

Nowhere in the numerous and lengthy exchanges connected with this case are objections raised on grounds that Paraguay in refusing to permit the refugees to remain in asylum was failing to respect any right or privilege due to the United States legation.

The Department noted that the legation in Haiti had granted protection to persons of property following a revolution in 1869. It informed the minister that he would not be required to expel those

---

[1] Washburn U. S., Minister to Paraguay, to Seward, Secretary of State, October 14, 1867, *Dip. Cor. of the U. S.*, 1868, II, pp. 647–648.

[2] Seward to Washburn, January 14, 1868, *ibid.*, p. 652.

[3] Washburn to Seward, April 7, 1868, *ibid.*, p. 656.

[4] Benítez, Paraguayan Minister of Foreign Relations, to Washburn, July 11, 1868, trans., *ibid.*, p. 734.

[5] Washburn to Benítez, July 12, 1868, *ibid.*, p. 736.

[6] See numerous exchanges, *ibid.*, pp. 723–838.

[7] Washburn to Seward, September 26, 1868, *ibid.*, p. 670.

who were there but was ordered to inform them that the government of the United States "can not on that account assume any responsibility for them, and especially can not sanction any resistance by ... [the minister] to their arrest by the authorities for the time being." [1]

Noting the request by the Haitian minister at Washington for the surrender of certain refugees in the U. S. legation, including Boisrand Canal and Associates, the Department informed its minister to Haiti that it had admitted that asylum had been improperly granted but had told the Haitian minister that they could not be surrendered in spite of this. It further advised the U. S. minister that

> I added that if his Government would apply to you for them in order that they might be tried, you would be authorized to give them up, provided the Government gives you its assurance that no punishment shall result from the trial, but that, if convicted, the parties will be allowed, without molestation, to leave the country. [2]

In the case of Boisrand Canal the decree placing him "beyond the pale of the law" for his continued resort to arms against the government in power had been issued and published the day before he took refuge in the United States legation. [3] Referring to this decree, the Acting Secretary of State noted that it may have been issued "pursuant to the constitution of Hayti" but that it could "scarcely ... be regarded as the result of any other than a military trial; and this in the absence of the accused, if, indeed, any trial, even of that character, took place." [4]

The controversy continued for nearly four months with the United States repeatedly refusing to surrender the refugees. In the meantime, the Haitian government had posted guards around the legation. The disorderly conduct of the soldiers, the insults and the inconvenience to the minister and personnel of the legation gave every indication of being intentional on the part of the Haitian government. [5] Repeated protests were of no avail and the Department finally informed its

---

[1] Fish, Secretary of State, to Bassett, U. S. Minister to Haiti, December 16, 1869, *For. Rel. of the U. S.*, 1871, p. 695; Moore, *op. cit.*, p. 809.

[2] Fish, Secretary of State, to Bassett, U. S. Minister to Haiti, June 4, 1875, *For. Rel. of the U. S.*, 1875, II, p. 701.

[3] Preston, Haitian Minister to the United States, to Cadwalader, Acting Secretary of State, August 26, 1875, *ibid.*, pp. 743–744.

[4] Hunter, Acting Secretary of State, to Preston, Haitian Minister to the United States, September 10, 1875, *ibid.*, p. 746.

[5] See numerous exchanges, *ibid.*, pp. 686–748; Moore, *op. cit.*, pp. 812–813.

minister that a man-of-war would be ordered to Port-au-Prince "with a view to your protection from insult." [1]

The United States took the curious position of insisting that it did not regard the granting of asylum as a legal right and yet would not agree to any compromise which seemed to suggest its abandonment. The Haitian government's proposal to grant a *pardon* was rejected, seemingly for this very reason. Noting that the United States minister to Haiti had been authorized to surrender the refugees only with guarantees that they would not be punished if tried and convicted, the Department observed:

> This condition did not imply any necessity for the exercise of the right of pardon, to which Mr. Preston refers in his note. Indeed, the proposition, as stated by that gentleman, would, it is conceived, involve not only the abandonment of the question of asylum, but practically an assent to its violation. [2]

It was then observed that the United States could not consent to this and that the proposition which had been made through the United States minister to Haiti "was based upon the principle of deferring to the dignity of Hayti by acknowledging her right to try the refugees, but also of maintaining the inviolability of the asylum so long as it should be generally tolerated." [3] Even with the Haitian guarantee of an amnesty for the refugees and a guarantee of safe conduct out of the country, the United States was unwilling to simply turn them over to the Haitian authorities. The final agreement provided that they would be escorted by Haitian military forces but that Mr. Bassett could also accompany them to the vessel. [4] The Department of State then noted that inasmuch as an acceptable arrangement had been made "the Navy Department will be appraised that at present there is no further occasion for a man of war to visit Hayti." [5]

In 1899, a Haitian, fleeing from soldiers sent to arrest him for implication in a plot to overthrow the government, entered and was removed from the U. S. legation. Upon demand of the U. S. minister he was returned. [6] The conditions under which asylum was sought and granted are well summed up in the U. S. minister's report:

---

[1] Hunter, Acting Secretary of State, to Bassett, U. S. Minister to Haiti, September 7, 1875, *For. Rel. of the U. S.*, 1875, II, p. 728.

[2] Cadwalader, Acting Secretary of State, to Preston, Haitian Minister to the United States, August 17, 1875, *ibid.*, pp. 741–742.

[3] *Ibid.*, p. 742.

[4] "Memorandum of Agreement," September 27, 1875, *ibid.*, p. 748.

[5] Fish, Secretary of State, to Preston, September 27, 1875, *ibid.*

[6] Powell, U. S. Minister to Haiti, to Hay, Secretary of State, August 2, 1899, *For. Rel. of the U. S.*, 1899, p. 378. Actually, the refugee entered the U. S. consulate which was di-

Duvivier, with others, was said to be implicated in a plot to overthrow the Government. An order was given for his arrest; if he resisted he was to be immediately shot. Happily for him the posse of soldiers, under the command of the general of La Place, charged with his arrest met him in front of our legation. From thence, as I have stated in a previous dispatch, he was taken by force. [But at this date had been returned] [1]

Earlier, the Department had indicated that a proper demand for him might not even require his surrender. The minister was told to decline judicial service upon the legation and say that it could only recognize a request made through the Minister of Foreign Relations. Even then the refugee would not be automatically surrendered: "If such a request be made, refer it to this Department for instructions." [2]

This case seems to be contrary to the general position maintained by the Department of State. The refugee was escaping from the officers of the government in power who had been sent to arrest him. The protection certainly could not be called "temporary" inasmuch as the United States was unwilling to surrender the refugee to the complete jurisdiction of the Haitian government. Here the Department got to the heart of its conception of "temporary" refuge.

... Upon adequate showing of the regularity of the judicial proceedings had against him, the right of the envoy to harbor him disappears ... [3]

In this case the U. S. minister was convinced that there would be no regularity of judicial proceeding. "Mr. Duvivier's life will not be safe so long as the present military chiefs are in power even though he should receive assurance of safety from the President" the minister reported.[4] Two weeks after the case was first reported the Haitian government decreed that all refugees were to be expelled from the country,[5] and the U. S. Department of State instructed its minister that he could not shelter the refugees against such an order.[6]

Thus it is clear that "temporary refuge" has not been construed to mean that the refugee must in all cases be surrendered to the officers of the government in power. The United States has, in fact, reserved for itself the right to decide whether or not the refugee will be given a

rectly below the legation. He was apparently returned to the legation, however, and in later dispatches the U. S. Minister refers to this as asylum in the U. S. legation. There is no evidence that the Department of State took any note of this.

[1] Powell to Hay, August 14, 1899, ibid., p. 384.
[2] Adee, Acting Secretary of State, to Powell, August 3, 1899, tel., ibid., p. 380.
[3] Adee to Powell, August 3, 1899, ibid., p. 381.
[4] Powell to Hay, August 14, 1899, ibid., p. 384.
[5] Powell to Hay, August 16, 1899, tel., ibid., p. 385.
[6] Adee to Powell, August 17, 1899, tel., ibid., p. 386.

proper trial. This position was summed up in unmistakable terms in a 1908 case. The United States minister to Haiti was first told to inform consular officers there that asylum was not to be granted and that if refugees were at that time being sheltered such protection was to be discontinued.[1] Upon receiving reports that refugees who left asylum were immediately shot or imprisoned by the government, the Department of State changed its instructions noting that the situation was now "entirely different."

> The United States denied sanctuary against due process of law, but will protect refugees against summary lawless slaughter, such as now appears to have been meted out to the refugees at St. Marc.[2]

That these instructions were to be equally applicable to the United States legation was obvious from the fact that the Department instructed the minister to have the refugees moved to the legation "until absolute guarantee from the President and Government of Haiti can be obtained for their trial according to the orderly operation of the Haitian law." [3] Since it was not possible to have the refugees removed, the minister informed the Haitian government that the refugees were to be considered under the legation's protection, a proposition to which the Haitian government agreed.[4]

In 1851 the American minister to Chile granted asylum to Colonel Arteaga who had been engaged in an unsuccessful attempt to overthrow the government. The prevailing conditions reported by the minister do not seem greatly different from those existing in other cases. He noted that Chile had for the past twenty years escaped the unhappy turmoil present in most Latin American countries. But he noted that this condition was changing: "Political clubs have been broken up, presses have been suppressed, processions of unarmed citizens have been prohibited." He also noted that a revolution had actually broken out in a neighboring province and that ,,martial law was proclaimed in the month of November last, followed by the late more serious affair, which I fear has not ended yet." Finally, he advised that if he were to let Arteaga go he would certainly be shot

---

[1] Root, Secretary of State, to Furniss, U. S. Minister to Haiti, January 28, 1908, tel. – paraphrase, *For. Rel. of the U.S.*, 1908, p. 429.

[2] The Acting Secretary of State, to Furniss, February 3, 1908, tel. – paraphrase, *ibid.*, p. 431.

[3] *Ibid.*

[4] Furniss to Root, February 5, 1908, tel. – paraphrase, *ibid.*

immediately and that this would no doubt set off a bloody revolution.[1]

The Department's reply seemed unconcerned with these circumstances or, in any event, took no particular note of them. It merely pointed out that inasmuch as "the right itself is more than doubtful under the public law" and since Chile had demanded the refugee "if he should still be your guest ... it is deemed advisable that your house can no longer screen him from prosecution." [2]

The American legation in Chile was again the scene of a prolonged controversy in 1891. The recognized government of Balmaceda had been deposed by revolution and a number of the officials of that government had been granted asylum in the U. S. legation. The revolutionary government had resolved to prosecute them and had asked for their surrender. To this the minister had replied that "to do so would be to sacrifice their lives" and that he had taken the stand that he would "permit them to go out of the legation *only under proper safe-conduct to neutral territory.*" [3] While the Department nowhere specifically approved of this position it likewise did not disavow it. It can certainly be said, however, that there was a tacit approval of his action in the instructions from the Department, sent six days after the receipt of the telegram mentioned above:

... The right of asylum having been tacitly, if not expressly, allowed to other foreign legations, and having been exercised by our minister with the old Government ... the President cannot but regard the application of another rule ... as a manifestation of a most unfriendly spirit.[4]

Even the minister's assertion that the refugees could not be affected by the impeachment against them in the Chilean Chamber of Deputies seems to have produced no comment by the Department.[5] In any event, the U. S. minister maintained his position for nearly five months until the Chilean Minister of Foreign Relations gave his *personal* assurance that they could leave unmolested.[6]

In 1893 the U. S. minister again granted asylum to two leaders of

[1] Peyton, U. S. Ministet to Chile, to Webster, Secretary of State, April 19, 1851, extract, Manning, *op. cit.*, V, pp. 188–189.

[2] Webster to Peyton, July 2, 1851, *ibid.*, p. 17.

[3] Egan, U. S. Minister to Chile, to Blaine, Secretary of State, September 25, 1891, tel., *For. Rel. of the U. S.*, 1891, p. 166. (My italics.)

[4] Wharton to Egan, October 1, 1891, tel., *ibid.*, pp. 177–178.

[5] Egan to Matta, Chilean Minister of Foreign Relations, December 7, 1891 (inclosure in Egan to Blain, December 7, 1891), *ibid.*, pp. 262–263.

[6] Egan to Blaine, January 13, 1892, *ibid.*, p. 268. See also memorandum of interview between Egan and Pereira, January 11, 1892 (inclosure in Egan to Blaine, January 19, 1892), *ibid.*, p. 305.

an unsuccessful insurrection.[1] Upon a claim by the Chilean government that they were wanted for common crimes the Department informed its minister in Chile –

> Mr. Egan is not authorized to protect Chileans against police officers whose duty it is to arrest them for violation of the laws of their country ... He instructs him to cease sheltering them if the Chilean Government demands the refugees on a criminal charge, and if such a charge was pending against them before they engaged in the disturbances of the 8th, or in insurrection.[2]

Upon being informed that the charges against them were for sedition, riot, mutiny and insurrection,[3] the Department nevertheless informed the minister that inasmuch as the Chilean *chargé d'affaires* had assured him that they would be tried by a civil court and that they would, on leaving the legation, "be protected against violence," he should "require them to leave the legation accordingly, but to give timely notice to the Chilean government that protection is expected to be afforded as promised before withdrawing the shelter theretofore accorded." [4] In his annual message to Congress, President Cleveland referred to "the unauthorized action of the late United States minister in receiving into his official residence two persons who had just failed in an attempt at revolution and against whom criminal charges were pending growing out of a former abortive disturbance." [5]

The long controversies over the surrender of the refugee do not appear in the volumes of *Foreign Relations of the United States* after about the first decade of this century. The discussion in chapter five shows that this cannot be attributed to any change in policy on the part of Latin American states. A number of extended controversies over a particular case of asylum have taken place there in recent years but the United States has not been a party to them.

The tendency of United States policy to justify asylum solely on the basis of humanitarian consideration rather than on local practice has already been noted. Along with this there has been a tendency to further emphasize the strictly temporary nature of the protection granted and to insist that it must not be protection against the legitimate authorities of the country. The following instructions were

---

[1] *For. Rel. of the U. S.*, 1893, pp. 217, 218, 219.

[2] Gresham, Secretary of State, to Egan, U. S. Minister to Chile, tel., April 15, 1893, *ibid.*, p. 219.

[3] *Ibid.*, p. 220.

[4] Gresham, Secretary of State, to Egan, U. S. Minister to Chile, April 18, 1893, *ibid.*, p. 221.

[5] December 4, 1894, *ibid.*, p. iv.

sent to the United States ambassador to Peru who had granted asylum to certain refugees there in 1930

When the provisional government is recognized by the Government of the United States on Thursday, September 18, it seems especially inappropriate that asylum should continue to be afforded in the American Embassy. Using your full discretion, you will please take appropriate steps at an early moment to terminate the asylum granted.[1]

It may be noted in the instructions discussed on pages 106–109 that although the 1897 instructions referred to "temporary shelter," the later instructions placed greater emphasis on this point. The 1930 circular asserted that "such protection may continue only so long as such imminent danger continues ... must be refused to persons fleeing from the pursuit of the legitimate agents of the local government, and in case such persons have been admitted they must be either surrendered or dismissed from the embassy or legation." These same words were used in the 1939, 1946 regulations and the same idea was conveyed in those of 1956.[2]

The policy of the United States during the Spanish Civil War shows a similar, cautious position. The Department of State instructed its *chargé d'affaires* in Chile to inform that government "that inasmuch as the Government of the United States has consistently refused to adopt the policy with regard to the giving of refuge to political refugees in diplomatic missions which has been followed by many of the other American republics, and was officially made known by the Government of the United States at both the Habana and Montevideo Conferences, this Government is unable, much to its regret, to comply with the request made by the Chilean Government that it support the initiative of the latter through the missions of the United States in the other American republics." [3]

This writer has found no case of asylum in the embassies, legations or consulates of the United States in Latin America after 1931, nor does Hackworth cite any cases after that date.[4] Reports from two of

---

[1] Stimson, Secretary of State, to Dearing, U. S. minister to Peru, September 17, 1930, paraphrase, *For. Rel. of the U. S.*, 1930, III, p. 757. It should be pointed out that the U. S. minister had earlier informed the Department that "Lima is orderly and quiet, and the new authorities make an increasingly good impression by their acts." Dearing to Stimson, *For. Rel.of the U. S.*, 1930, III, pp. 747–748.

[2] *Supra*, 106–109.

[3] Hull, Secretary of State, to Trueblood, U. S. *Chargé d'Affaires* in Chile, June 20, 1939, tel., *For. Rel. of the U. S.*, 1939, II, pp. 781–782.

[4] For what appears to be the last reported case see Dawson, U. S. *Chargé d'Affaires* in Ecuador, to the Acting Secretary of State, August 24, 1931, tel., *For. Rel. of the U. S.*, 1931, II, p. 138. See also Hackworth, *op. cit.*, pp. 624–639.

our ministers in Latin America (1931 and 1932) are perhaps indicative of an emphasis on extreme caution in this regard.

> President resigned and is still in Moneda. Already he has requested asylum for his son-in-law and family and I have replied that I cannot admit them to the Embassy unless they are threatened with physical violence and then only temporarily.[1]

> "I have also been asked in several instances to shelter persons in my home or in the Chancery. I have consistently refused to grant such requests."[2]

The United States attitude toward conventions and other attempts to provide a juridical basis for the practice of diplomatic asylum has been in keeping with the practice outlined above. Of the three inter-American conventions discussed in chapter four, it has signed only the Havana Convention of 1928. Mr. Hughes, speaking for the United States delegation to the Sixth Inter-American Conference, said that it would not participate in the discussion on this project "inasmuch as asylum was contrary to the practice of the United States, and, in the opinion of the Government of the United States, was not a part of general international law." [3] Although it signed (but has not ratified)[4] this convention, it did so with the following reservation:

> The delegation of the United States of America, in signing the present convention, establishes an explicit reservation, placing on record that the United States does not recognize or subscribe to as a part of international law, the so called doctrine of asylum.[5]

---

[1] Culbertson, U. S. Ambassador to Chile, to the Acting Secretary of State, July 26, 1931, tel., *ibid.*, I, p. 905.

[2] Reed, U. S. *Chargé d'Affaires* in Cuba, to the Secretary of State, October 7, 1932, *For. Rel. of the U. S.*, 1932, V, p. 559. This course was approved by the Department in White, Secretary of State, to Reed, October 19, 1932, *ibid.*, p. 560.

[3] International Conference of American States, Sixth, *Report of the Delegates of the United States of America to the Sixth International Conference of American States Held at Habana, Cuba, January 16 to February 20, With Appendices* (Washington: U. S. G. P. O., 1928), p. 19. The project on Asylum of the International Commission of Jurists, Rio de Janeiro, 1927, served as the basis for this treaty. The report of the U. S. delegates shows a similar position: "The delegates of the United States deemed it to be their duty to interpose a general reserve to the entire project on the express ground that it was not only contrary to the long-established and well-known policy of the United States, but also, in this opinion, opposed to the generally recognized modern practice of the world at large in such matters.

As, however, it appeared that all of the countries represented in the commission, with the exception of the U. S., were desirous of recognizing the right of asylum for political refugees, as stated in the convention, the American delegates did not oppose its discussion and adoption by the commission. Their desire was in this case as in all other ways, to advance the work of the Commission without interposing objections to the desires of the other delegations." *For. Rel. of the U. S.*, 1927, I, p. 387.

[4] See Appendix I.

[5] International Conference of American States, Sixth, *Report of the Delegates of the United States of America to the Sixth International Conference of American States Held at Habana Cuba, January 16 to February 20, 1928, With Appendices* (Washington: U. S. G. P. O., 1928), p. 227.

Not only did the United States delegation refrain from signing the Convention on Political Asylum at the Seventh Inter-American Conference at Montevideo, 1933, but it apparently wished to emphasize its position by affixing the following declaration to the convention:

Since the United States does not recognize or subscribe to, as a part of international law, the doctrine of asylum, the delegation of the United States of America refrains from signing the present Convention on Political Asylum.[1]

No such declaration was made with regard to the Convention on Diplomatic Asylum signed at the Tenth Inter-American Conference held at Caracas, 1954. While the United States did not sign this convention[2] and while the report of the delegates points to the usual position of this government, this report, unlike previous ones, takes note of the fact that the United States does in fact grant asylum:

With respect to diplomatic asylum it was pointed out that the United States does not recognize or subscribe to the doctrine of asylum as part of international law and does not, in practice, grant asylum except in a very limited sense, a traditional position which is well understood by other countries of the hemisphere.[3]

The following summary is offered in order to trace the main course of the policy described above.

1. United States policy has consistently denied that a right of asylum is sanctioned by general international law or by a regional rule of law.

2. The United States has *in fact* granted diplomatic asylum in its embassies, legations and consulates throughout Latin America and has insisted that it be respected.

3. The practice has been justified primarily on grounds of local toleration.

4. This has not meant "local toleration" in the sense that the territorial state could respect it or refuse to do so depending upon its feelings in a particular case. The United States not only has insisted that it would demand the "right" so long as other states engaged in the practice in a particular Latin American country but has at times

---

[1] International Conference of American States, Seventh, *Report of the Delegates of the United States of America to the Seventh International Conference of American States, Montevideo, Uruguay, December 3–26, 1933*, p. 144.

[2] [Pan American Union, Division of Law and Treaties], *Status of the Pan American Treaties and Conventions*, Law and Treaty Series (revised to September 1, 1954; Washington: Pan American Union), p. 9.

[3] International Conference of American States, Tenth, *Report of the Delegation of the United States of America with Related Documents*(Washington, U. S. G. P. O., 1955), p. 12.

asserted that the dis-continuance (even if applied to all diplomatic missions accredited there) must come from an agreement among the major powers rather than from a unilateral declaration by the territorial state.

5. More recent policy (very roughly, since 1920) has emphasized humanitarian considerations rather than local toleration (as described in point four) in justification of its practice.

6. Insofar as it has been justified on the grounds stated above, it has, in theory, placed three limitations upon its practice. But these limitations seem to have been intended more as a guide or an "ideal" for the diplomatic representatives than a precise set of limitations by which the Department has felt bound.

a. Diplomatic asylum may be granted only in case the life of the person seeking it is in immediate danger of mob violence or lawnessness.

b. Diplomatic asylum must not be offered in advance in anticipation of some future need.

c. Diplomatic asylum may be granted only as a temporary expedient to preserve innocent human life.

7. There have been numerous exceptions and deviations from these observations but the latter do show the main course of United States policy.

CHAPTER VII

ASYLUM IN CONSULATES

The discussion thus far has pointed out that practice shows a great deal of disagreement as to whether the institution of diplomatic asylum is sanctioned by a rule of law in Latin America. It has also concluded that the undeniable existence of such a widespread practice must be explained largely in terms of extra-legal factors – political expediency and humanitarian considerations, and by the fact that international law affords to ambassadors, ministers and other accredited diplomatic officers certain well recognized immunities from local jurisdiction including immunity of their offices and official residences from invasion by local authorities.

Nowhere is the extra-legal basis of the practice of asylum more clearly demonstrated than in its application to consulates. Again, we must start with the immunities granted to consular officers. Hackworth points out that, while such officers are not under international law entitled to the diplomatic immunity alluded to above, they are, nevertheless, "as representatives of their governments bearing commissions from their own government and recognized as such officials by the government of the state in which they serve, entitled to special respect and consideration by the local authorities." [1] Both Hackworth and Oppenheim assert that most states recognize, as a rule of law, the inviolability of consular archives, although the latter points to some disagreement in this respect.[2] While international law cannot be said to exempt the consular buildings or offices themselves from invasion by local authorities,[3] such exemption has in fact been widespread in Latin American practice and treaties.

Multilateral and bilateral treaties strongly support this observation.

---

[1] *Op. cit.*, p. 621.
[2] *Ibid.*; Oppenheim, *op. cit.*, pp. 841–842.
[3] *Ibid.*

Article 18 of the Convention on Consular Agents Signed at the Sixth International Conference of American States provides:

The official residence of the consuls and places used for the consulate's office and archives are inviolable and in no case may the local authorities enter them without the permission of the consular agents . . . [1]

All twenty-one of the American Republics signed this convention and thirteen had ratified as of June, 1957.[2]

A number of bilateral conventions have included similar provisions. Article 21 of the Consular Convention of 1879, between Peru and El Salvador provides a typical example.

In order to guarantee compliance with the stipulations in article XVIII, the archives, the consular chancellery and its papers are declared inviolable, so that, in no case and under no pretext, will the local authorities take possession of them or submit them to examination.[3]

On the other hand, a number of conventions have specifically limited inviolability to the archives and official property. Article 1

---

[1] Hudson, *International Legislation*, IV, p. 2389; International Conference of American States, Sixth, *Final Act; Motions, Agreements, Resolutions and Conventions* (Habana: Imprenta de Rambla, Boya y Cía., 1928), p. 150; *League of Nations Treaty Series*, CLV, p. 289; Martens, *Nouveau recueil* . . ., XL (3e série par Triepel; Greifswald: Librairie Julius Abel, 1943), p. 358; U. S. Congress, Senate, *Treaties, Conventions, International Acts, Protocols, and Agreement between the United States of America and Other Powers: 1923–1937*, IV (Washington: G. P. O., 1938), p. 4338.

[2] Pan American Union, Legal Division, Department of International Law, *Inter-American Treaties and Conventions: Signatures, Ratifications and Deposits with Explanatory Notes*, (Washington: 1957), p. 25. Dates of deposit of instrument of ratification with the Pan American Union are as follows: Brazil, Sept. 3, 1929; Colombia, Dec. 26, 1935; Cuba, April 5, 1933; Dominican Republic, April 23, 1932; Ecuador, Sept. 4, 1936; El Salvador, Sept., 11, 1956; Haiti, April 30, 1953; Mexico, Dec. 26, 1929; Nicaragua, March 20, 1930; Panama, May 21, 1929; Peru, June 21, 1945; United States, February 8, 1932; Uruguay, Sept. 16, 1933.

[3] Convención consular [Perú-El Salvador], 3 de agosto de 1879, Perú, *Colección de los tratados*, 11, (1907), p. 29. (My translation.) For similar provisions see Consular Convention between the United States of America and the Republic of Costa Rica, Signed at San José, on 12 January 1948, Article 6, United States Department of State, *Treaties and Other International Acts Series 2045] United Nations Treaty Series*, 70, p. 40; Treaty of Friendship, Commerce and Consular Rights between the United States of America and Honduras, Signed at Tegucigalpa, December 7, 1927, Article 19, *U. N. Treaty Series*, 88, p. 434; Martens, *op. cit.*, XXI (3e série par Triepel, 1930), p. 664; U. S. Senate, *Treaties Convention, Int'l. Acts, Protocols and Agreements between the U. S. A. and Other Powers: 1923–1937*, IV, (Wash: G. P. O., 1938), p. 3360. Consular Convention Between the Republic of Cuba and the United States of America, Signed at Havana, April 22, 1926, Article 7, *U. N. Treaty Series*, 60, p. 375; Martens, *op. cit.*, XVI (3e série par Triepel 1927), p. 875; U. S., Senate, *Treaties Conventions Int'l. Acts, Protocols, Agreements between the U. S. A. and Other Powers: 1923–1937*, IV (Wash: G. P. O., 1938), p. 4048; Treaty of Friendship, Commerce and Consular Rights Between the United States of America and Salvador, Signed at San Salvador, February 22, 1926, Article 18, *League of Nations Treaty Series*, 134, p. 221; U. S. Senate, *Treaties, Conventions, Int'l. Acts, Protocols, and Agreements between the U. S. A. and other Powers: 1923–1937*, IV (Washington: G. P. O., 1938), p. 4615.

of the Agreement on Consuls, signed at the Bolivarian Congress at Caracas, June 18, 1911, provides:

The archives, emblem and flag of the consulates will be inviolable. The emblem and flag do not make the domicile of the consul inviolable when the authority may enter it according to law.[1]

More frequently the convention will merely provide for the inviolability of the archives without reference to the building itself although in some cases exception of the building may be implied as in an 1883 convention signed by Bolivia and Venezuela.

Article 6. The consular archives are inviolable at all times, and the territorial authorities cannot under any pretext examine nor take possession of the papers pertaining to them. Therefore, said archives will be totally separated from the personal papers of the consuls, vice consuls and consular agents.[2]

It was suggested earlier in this discussion that the respect for asylum granted in diplomatic premises was more a result of certain well recognized immunities which these premises enjoyed than of any feeling of legal obligation to respect the practice of asylum in its own right. This suggests that the more limited immunities which consulates have in fact enjoyed in Latin America provide a similar basis for the exercise of consular asylum. This in fact seems to be the case. But a very important difference must be emphasized here because, in this writer's view, it provides further evidence that the whole practice of asylum stems largely from extralegal factors.

[1] Venezuela, Ministerio de Relaciones Exteriores, *Tratados públicos y acuerdos internacionales de Venezuela* (Caracas: Tipografía Americana, 1925), II, p. 431. (My translation.) See also Tratado sobre derecho internacional, entre el Ecuador, Chile y Bolivia, 17 de mayo de 1877, Artículo 4, Ecuador, *Colección de tratados* (Guayaquil: Imprenta de A. Noboa, 1920), p. 93.

[2] Convención consular [Venezuela-Bolivia], Firmada en Caracas el 27 de setiembre de 1883, Venezuela, Ministerio de Relaciones Exteriores, *Tratados públicos y acuerdos internacionales de Venezuela* (Caracas; Tipografía Americana, 1924), I, p. 410. (My translation.) See also Convención consular [Argentina-Perú], 5 de mayo de 1874, Artículo 8, Perú, Ministerio de Relaciones Exteriores, *Colección de los tratados, convenciones capitulaciones, armisticios y otros actos diplomáticos y políticos* (Lima: Imprenta del Estado, 1890), II, p. 24; Tratado de paz, amistad y servicio consular [Mexico-Paraguay], 25 de enero, 1902, Artículo 15, Paraguay, Ministro de Relaciones Exteriores y Culto, *Colección de tratados: históricos y vigentes* (Asunción: Imprenta Nacional, 1934), I, p. 579; Convención consular [Argentina-Paraguay], 14 de marzo, 1877, Artículo 11, *ibid.*, p. 127; Convención consular entre la República de la Nueva Granada y la República de Chile, 30 de agosto de 1853, Artículo 6, Antonio José Uribe, *Anales diplomáticos y consulares de Colombia* (edición oficial; Bogotá: Imprenta Nacional, 1920), VI, p. 182; Convención consular [Perú-Colombia], January 20, 1870, *ibid.*, Artículo 6, pp. 261–262; Convención consular entre Los Estados Unidos Mexicanos y La República de Panamá, firmada en Mexico, el 9 de junio de 1928, *League of Nations Treaty Series*, CXLI, p. 194; Convenio consular entre Chile y los Paises Bajos, firmada en la Haya el 4 de noviembre de 1913, Artículo 5, *ibid.*, LXXXIV, p. 83; Martens, *op. cit.*, XX (3e série par Triepel, 1929), p. 185.

In the first place it should be noted that numerous bilateral treaties signed by Latin American states *have clearly stipulated that consulates should not be used as a place of asylum.* It must also be emphasized that these are *not qualified prohibitions* against asylum for common criminals but, rather, *unqualified prohibitions against "asylum."* Typical of this kind of agreement is the Consular Convention of 1883, between Venezuela and El Salvador. After providing that consular officers may place the flag or emblem of their country above the entrance to the premises, article 9 provides:

> It is understood, that neither the emblem nor the flag signifies the right to asylum, exemption, or privilege which removes the consul, the house or those in it from the ordinary law [derecho común] and territorial jurisdiction.[1]

The following list shows that such conventions have been widespread in Latin America and that they have not been confined to any one period.

Ecuador-New Granada [Colombia] (1858) [2]
New Granada-United States (1840) [3]
Colombia-Netherlands (1881) [4]
Guatemala-Costa Rica-Honduras-Nicaragua-El Salvador
(1887) [5]
Venezuela-El Salvador (1883) [6]
Guatemala-Netherlands (1914) [7]

---

[1] Venezuela, Ministerio de Relaciones Exteriores, *Tratados públicos y acuerdos internacionales de Venezuela* (Caracas: Tipografía Americana, 1924), p. 386. (My translation.)

[2] Convención consular entre el Ecuador y Nueva Granada, 12 de abril de 1858, Artículo 7, Ecuador, [Ministerio de Relaciones Exteriores], *colección de tratados* (Guayaquil: Imprenta de Noboa, 1902), 11, p. 160. See also Convención consular entre la Nueva Granada y el Ecuador, 1 de agosto de 1854, Artículo 7, Antonio José Uribe, *Anales diplomáticos y consulares de Colombia* (edición oficial; Bogotá: Imprenta Nacional, 1920), VI, p. 198.

[3] Consular Convention, signed at Washington May 4, 1840, Article 5, Hunter Miller, ed., *Treaties and Other International Acts of the United States of America* (Washington: U. S. G. P. O., 1937), p. 812.

[4] Convención consular entre los Estados Unidos de Colombia y Su Majestad, el Rey de los Paises Bajos, 20 de julio de 1881, Artículo 4, *ibid.*, p. 306; Martens, *op. cit.*, X (2me série par Hopf, 1859), p. 159.

[5] Convención consular entre Guatemala, Costa Rica, Honduras, Nicaragua y El Salvador, 16 de Febrero 1887, Artículo 3, Guatemala, [Ministerio de Relaciones Exteriores], *Derecho internacional guatemalteco* (Guatemala: Tipografia y Encuadernación Nacional, 1894), I, p. 459.

[6] Convención consular entre Guatemala y los Paises Bajos, 7 de marzo de 1914, Artículo 4, *ibid.*, (1919), III, p. 17; Martens, *op. cit.*, XII (3e série par Triepel, 1924), p. 124.

[7] Convención consular [Venezuela-El Salvador] 27 de agosto de 1883, Artículo 9, Venezuela, Ministerio de Relaciones Exteriores, *Tratados públicos y acuerdos internacionales de Venezuela* (Caracas: Tipografía Americana, 1924), p. 386; Martens, *op. cit.*, XIV (2me série par Stoerk, 1888), p. 224.

Venezuela-Bolivia (1888) [1]
Peru-Venezuela (1859) [2]
Peru-El Salvador (1879) [3]
Peru-Bolivia (1870) [4]
Peru-Chile (1870) [5]
Mexico-Panama (1928) [6]
Cuba-United States (1926) [7]
Cuba-Netherlands (1913) [8]
Chile-Netherlands (1913) [9]
Honduras-United States (1927) [10]
El Salvador-United States (1926) [11]
Argentina-Netherlands (1938) [12]

[1] Convención consular [Venezuela-Bolivia], firmada en Caracas el 27 de setiembre de 1888, Artículo 8, Venezuela, Ministerio de Relaciones Exteriores, *Tratados públicos y acuerdos internacionales de Venezuela* (Caracas: Tipografía Americana, 1924), I, p. 411.

[2] Tratado de amistad, comercio y navegación, [Perú-Venezuela], 1 de abril de 1859, Artículo 27, Perú, *Colección de los tratados*, 12 (1907), p. 617.

[3] Convención consular [Perú-El Salvador], 3 agosto de 1879, Artículo 20, Perú, *Colección de tratados*, 11, (1907), p. 29.

[4] Convención consular [Perú-Bolivia], 26 de julio de 1870, Artículo 4, Perú, Ministerio de Relaciones Exteriores, *Colección de los tratados, convenciones, capitulaciones, armisticios y otros actos diplomáticos y políticos* (Lima: Imprenta del Estado, 1890), II, p. 418.

[5] Convención consular [Perú-Chile], 21 de febrero de 1870 Artículo 4, *ibid.*, (1892), IV. p. 97.

[6] Convención consular entre los Estados Unidos Mexicanos y La República de Panamá, firmada de México, el 9 de junio de 1928, *League of Nations Treaty Series*, CXLI, p. 194.

[7] Consular Convention Between the Republic of Cuba and the United States of America, Signed at Havana, April 22, 1926, Article 8, *ibid.*, LX, p. 375; Martens, *op. cit.*, XVI (3e Série par Triepel, 1927), p. 875; U. S. Senate, *Treaties, Conventions, Int'l. Acts, Protocols, and Agreements between the U. S. A. and Other Powers: 1923-1937*, IV (Washington, G. P. O., 1938), p. 4048.

[8] Convenio consular celebrado entre la República de Cuba y el Reino de los Paises Bajos, 31 de diciembre de 1913, Artículo 4, Cuba [Ministerio de Relaciones Exteriores?], *Tratados, convenios, y convenciones celebrados por la República de Cuba desde 1916* (Habana: Imprenta y Papelería de Rambia, Bouza y Cía., 1929), p. 76; Martens, *op. cit.*, XIV (3e série par Triepel, 1926), p. 460.

[9] Convenio consular entre Chile y los Paises Bajos, firmada en la Haya el 4 de noviembre de 1913, Artículo 4, *ibid.*, LXXXIV, p. 83; Martens, *op. cit.*, XX(3e série par Triepel, 1929), p. 185.

[10] Treaty of Friendship, Commerce and Consular Rights Between the United States of America and Honduras, Signed at Tegucigalpa, December 7, 1927, Article 19, *ibid.*, LXXXVII, p. 434; Martens, *op. cit.*, XXI (3e série par Triepel, 1930), p. 664; U. S. Senate, *Treaties, Conventions, Int'l. Acts, Protocols, and Agreements between the U. S. A. and Other Powers: 1923-1937* IV (Washington: G. P. O., 1938), p. 3360.

[11] Treaty of Friendship, Commerce and Consular Rights Between the United States of America and Salvador, Signed at San Salvador, February 22, 1926, Article 18, *League of Nations Treaty Series*, CXXXIV, p. 221; U. S., Senate, *Treaties, Convention, Int'l. Acts, Protocols, and Agreements between the U. S. A. and Other Powers: 1923-1937*, IV, (Washington: G. P. O., 1938), p. 4615.

[12] Convención consular entre la República Argentina y los Paises Bajos, 8 de setiembre de 1938, artículo 7, *Revista Argentina de derecho internacional*, I (Buenos Aires, octubre-diciembre 1938, p. 190.

Mexico-United States (1942) [1]

In a few cases there is an implicit admission that strictly temporary protection may be afforded. Thus the 1928 Consular Convention between Mexico and El Salvador provides:

> The consular offices and residences will not be used as places of asylum. Consular functionaries are obligated to surrender to the competent authorities of the receiving nation, when they demand it, individuals pursued as delinquents according to the laws of the country who have found refuge in the house occupied as such office or residence.[2]

This would seem to imply protection against mob violence and lawlessness but the important point is that the "refugee" must be surrendered to the local authorities without any distinction being made as to the type of crime for which he is pursued. The convention on Consular Agents, signed at the Sixth International Conference of American States contains a similar provision but without the initial prohibition on asylum. Article 19 of this convention provides that:

> Consuls are obliged to deliver, upon the simple request of the local authorities, persons accused or condemned for crimes who may have sought refuge in the consulate.[3]

In this case, as in the treaties specifically prohibiting "asylum," the word "refuge" is used where it is implied that some kind of protection may be granted. But again, the important point would seem to be that the "refugee" must be surrendered "upon the simple request of the local authorities" when he is "accused or condemned for crimes" with no distinction being made as to the type of crime involved. The antecedents to this convention in fact suggest that this was specifically intended to eliminate the possibility that questions as to the nature of the offence or the charges against the refugee might serve as a pretext for continuing the protection against the demands of the territorial state. The article originated in Project 23 of the American Institute of International Law which provided:

---

[1] Consular Officers: Convention between the United States of America and Mexico, Signed at Mexico City, August 12, 1942, U. S. *Treaty Series*, 985, p. 10.

[2] Convención consular entre los Estados Unidos Mexicanos y la República de Panamá, firmada en México, el 9 de junio de 1928, *League of Nations Treaty Series*, CXLI, p. 194. (My translation.)

[3] Pan American Union, Division of Law and Treaties, Department of International Law, *Documents and Notes on Privileges and Immunities with Special Reference to the Organization of American States*, Law and Treaty Series (Washington: Pan American Union, 1953), p. 18. Martens, *op. cit.*, XL (3e Série, 1930), p. 358; *League of Nations Treaty Series*, CLV, p. 289.

If a fugitive from justice takes refuge in a consulate the consul is bound to hand him over on the simple demand of the authorities.[1]

This was modified by the 1927 meeting of the International Commission of American Jurists.

Article 22

A consul is obliged to give up, on the simple requisition of the local authorities all persons suspected of, or condemned for crimes and who have taken refuge in the consulate.[2]

In spite of numerous implicit and explicit treaty provisions prohibiting the use of consulates as places of asylum, Latin American practice shows no significant difference between consular and diplomatic asylum. The following considerations are offered in support of this position.

1. *The granting of asylum in consulates in Latin America has in fact been widely practiced and generally respected.* The following list of cases is offered *as evidence of a widespread practice.*

1843 – United States consulate in Ecuador [3]

1849 – French consulate in the Dominican Republic [4]

1850 – Consulate of New Granada (Colombia) and later the consulate of the United States in Ecuador.[5]

1855 – United States consulate in Nicaragua [6]

1873 – British consulate in the Dominican Republic [7]

1877 – United States consulate in Mexico [8]

1891 – Mexican and Liberian consulates in Haiti [9]

1904 – United States consulate in the Dominican Republic [10]

---

[1] *A.J.I.L.*, Supplement, XX (1926), p. 357.

[2] Brazil, Ministry of State for Foreign Affairs, *International Commission of American Jurists, 1927 Meeting* (English edition; Rio de Janeiro: Imprensa Nacional, 1927), IV, p. 45.

[3] Perú, *Proceso*, p. 383.

[4] Jimenes, President of the Dominican Republic, to the French Consul at Santo Domingo, May 14, 1849, Dominican Republic, Archivo General de la Nación, *Correspondencia del consul de Francia en Santo Domingo*, II (Ciudad Trujillo, Editoria Motalvo, 1944), p. 155.

[5] Perú, *Proceso*, p. 378.

[6] Argentine Republic, Ministry of Foreign Affairs and Worship, *Project of Convention of the Right of Asylum* (Buenos Aires, 1937), p. 47.

[7] Perú, *Proceso*, p. 385.

[8] *Ibid.*, p. 383.

[9] Flesch, French Minister to Haiti and Dean of the Diplomatic Corps, to the Haitian Minister of Foreign Relations, May 30, 1891; Lechaud, Haitian Minister of Foreign Relations, to the Diplomatic Corps, June 1, 1891, Raoul Rouzier, *Le droit d'asile en Haiti* (Port-au-Prince: "La Nation," 1943), pp. 21–22.

[10] Powell to Hay, February 9, 1904, *For. Rel. of the U. S.*, 1904, p. 286.

1904 – Italian consulate in the Dominican Republic [1]

1908 – Mexican, British, German, French and United States consulates in Haiti [2]

1911 – United States consulate in Chile [3]

1911 – United States consulate in Mexico [4]

1913 – United States consulate in Mexico [5]

1914 – United States consulate in Nicaragua [6]

1919 – United States consulate in Costa Rica [7]

1930 – French consulate in Mexico [8]

1936 – Peruvian consulate in Spain [9]

Later discussion will show that in some of these cases objections were raised on grounds that consuls do not possess the right of asylum and that in some cases the refugees were forcibly removed from the consulate or voluntarily surrendered. In most cases, however, it appears that asylum was in fact respected or at least there is no evidence that it was not. We of course do not know why it was respected in these cases but they are cited only as evidence of the fact that the practice of granting asylum in consulates is widespread *in spite* of numerous implicit and explicit treaty prohibitions.

2. *Whether Latin American governments have drawn a distinction between consular and diplomatic asylum or have failed to do so seems to have depended upon the needs of the moment.*

On March 12, 1866, a report of the British government stated:

That it appears from the answers of the foreign Consuls to Her Majesty's *Chargé d'Affaires* in Hayti, that the Government of that country has been in

---

[1] Villain, U. S. Commercial Agent in Samana, to Powell, February 9, 1904 (inclosure in Powell to Hay, February 12, 1904), *For. Rel. of the U. S.*, 1904, p. 286.

[2] Furniss, U. S. Minister to Haiti to the Secretary of State, February 5, 1908, *For. Rel. of the U. S.*, 1908, pp. 431–432; Furniss to the Secretary of State, January 17, 1908, *ibid.*, pp. 425–426; Furniss to the Secretary of State, January 28, 1908, *ibid.*, p. 429. See also exchange of notes between Haitian Minister of Foreign Affairs and French Minister to Haiti in Rouzier, *op. cit.*, pp. 12–15.

[3] Hackworth, *op. cit.*, p. 637.

[4] Edwards, U. S. Consul in [Juarez?] Mexico, to the Secretary of State, May 13, 1911, *For. Rel. of the U. S.*, 1911, pp. 483–484.

[5] Johnson, U. S. Consul at Matamoros, Mexico, to Bryan, Secretary of State, April 7, 1913, Hackworth, *op. cit.*, p. 639.

[6] Bryan, Secretary of State, to Clare, U. S. Consul at Bluefields, Nicaragua, July 19, 1914, *For. Rel. of the U. S.*, 1914, p. 940.

[7] Chase, U. S. Consul at San José, Costa Rica, to Polk, Acting Secretary of State, June 16, 1919, *For. Rel. of the U. S.* 1930, II, p. 703.

[8] Yepis, U. S. Vice-Consul at Guaymas, Mexico, to the Secretary of State, November 8, 1930, *For. Rel. of the U. S.*, 1930, II, p. 703.

[9] Perú, *Boletín* (2°. trimestre de 1937), p. 209.

the habit of granting to Consular houses the privilege of protecting refugees. This, as the American Consul justly observes, is an exceptional privilege not in accordance with the general law of nations.[1]

In 1873 the British vice-consul at Puerto Plata, Haiti, gave asylum in his private dwelling to three refugees whom the latter government described as "political offenders for the last month." [2] The British vice-consul refused all demands for the surrender of the refugees stating that his house was the British vice-consulate and that they were under the protection of the British flag.[3] The Haitian authorities did not deny the existence of a right of asylum in consulates but insisted that the consul's dwelling could not be considered a part of the consulate which was located in another place. The refugees were removed by Haitian authorities but British demands for the return of the refugees and proper apologies were finally met.[4]

In 1875, the United States minister to Haiti pointed to a policy which was even more extreme.

...Each successive administration has clung to the right, and practically, once or twice formally, refused to assent to its discontinuance. Only lately, as I had the honor of stating to you personally, when I was at the Department in November last, the work of completing our consular treaty with this government was arrested because the Haytian plenipotentiary would not agree to having the exercise of this right taken away from *even our consulates in the inferior ports*.[5]

Nevertheless, in the following year, we find the government of Haiti announcing its intention to abolish the practice even in legations.[6] In 1908 it again announced such an intention.

I have the honor to inform your excellency that the Haitian Government has decided to put an end to the custom of asylum *in legations and consulates* established in this country.[7]

In 1837 the government of Chile informed the French consul general that "the right of asylum, which you assume, does not appertain to

[1] Report of Phillimore, cited in McNair, *op. cit.*, p. 75.
[2] Hamburger, British Vice-Consul at Puerto Plata, to St. John, British *Chargé d'Affaires* in Haiti, February 25, 1873, (inclosure in Bassett, U. S. Minister to Haiti, to Fish, Secretary of State, March 26, 1873), *For. Rel. of the U. S.*, 1873, I, p. 462.
[3] *Ibid.*
[4] González, Governor of the District of Puerto Plata, to the Governor of Turks Island, February 25, 1873, *ibid.*, pp. 462–463. These views were supported by the Haitian Foreign Ministry, see Bassett to Fish, April 16, 1873, *ibid.*, p. 464.
[5] Bassett, U. S. Minister to Haiti, to Fish, Secretary of State, May 19, 1875, *For. Rel. of the U. S.*, 1875, II, p. 697. (My italics.)
[6] "Memorandum," October 25, 1875, trans., *For. Rel. of the U. S.*, 1876, pp. 341–342.
[7] Borno, Haitian Minister of State for Foreign Affairs, to Furniss, U. S. Minister to Haiti, May 20. 1908, trans., *For. Rel. of the U. S.*, 1908, p. 438. (My italics.)

consuls, and in a case such as the present, diplomatic agents of the highest rank would scarcely assume it." [1] The following year, again in connection with a case of asylum in that consulate, it asserted that asylum was a privilege which "is not granted to consuls in any part of Christendom." [2]

Replying to a British note of 1859, which asserted that Latin American custom gave consuls a right to grant asylum, the government of Chile asserted "that if such a custom has come to prevail in other states, Chile has never incorporated it as a rule of conduct among the principles which have determined, until now, her international relations with other powers." [3]

That same year the government of Chile withdrew the exequatur of the United States consul at Valparaíso on the grounds that he had refused to surrender certain refugees who had been engaged in a revolutionary movement. While there was considerable disagreement as to the facts, the United States minister insisting that the consul had not refused to surrender the refugees but had only protested against the entry of an armed force into his dwelling,[4] the important point is that these were the grounds upon which the Chilean government based its action. This is clear from its note addressed to the United States minister.

> This refusal of the consul to surrender the accused whom authority demanded, amounts to a disregard of the local jurisdiction, with a tendency, on his part, to consider his house as a place of asylum for those persons who may take refuge within its walls. You cannot but agree that such a pretension, besides being rejected by international law, would be a cause of frequent embarrassments for the free exercise of the local jurisdiction . . . [3]

For these reasons it had resolved to withdraw the exequatur of the consul.[6] The representations of the United States minister were of no avail and the United States finally decided to acquiesce and replace the officer [7] even though it had noted earlier "that the practice on the part of Consuls of extending asylum to political refugees is almost

---

[1] Tocornal, Chilean Minister of Foreign Relations, to the Consul General of France, December 26, 1937, *Jurisprudencia de la cancilleria chilena*, p. 147. (My translation.)

[2] *Ibid.*, p. 148.

[3] Urmeneta, Chilean Minister of Foreign Relations, to the British *Chargé d'Affaires*, May 21, 1859, *ibid.*, p. 490. (My translation.)

[4] Biger, U. S. Minister to Chile, to Urmeneta, Chilean Minister of Foreign Relations, March 15, 1859, extracts, Manning, *op. cit.*, pp. 249–258.

[5] Urmeneta to Bigler, March 12, 1859, *Jurisprudencia de la cancilleria chilena*, p. 488. (My translation.)

[6] *Ibid.*

[7] Cass, Secretary of State, to Bigler, May 1, 1860, Moore, *op. cit.*, pp. 790–791.

generally permitted in the Pacific republics and in none more frequently than in Chile." [1]

During the early stages of the Spanish Civil War the Peruvian
consulate in Madrid granted asylum to more than 300 refugees.[2]
While the claims made by Peru were phrased in vague and ambiguous
legal language it is clear that they made no distinction between asylum
granted in their consulate and that granted in the legation. The *Memoria* for the period from April 13 to October 22, 1936, referred to "the
problem of the Spanish refugees who sought protection under our
flag, in the locale of the legation and consulate in Madrid and to whom
we owed, in conformity with a juridical tradition and through motives
of humanity, a protection which in most cases represented the defense
of their lives." [3] Safe coduct was granted and the refugees left Spanish
territory without grave incident.[4]

In 1937, asylum was again granted to Spanish nationals in the
Peruvian consulate in Madrid and in May of that year Spanish police
broke into the consulate and removed them.[5] In protesting this act
the Peruvian government at one point declared that there was no
point in discussing "the basis of consular asylum in international law
when it is a reality ... [and when] such has in fact been recognized by
the government of ... [Spain] with respect to other countries and
even ours." [6] Spain insisted that her consideration in recognizing
asylum had only extended to embassies and legations.[7]

Nevertheless, Peru continued to press for the return of the refugees
and it seems clear that it was the refusal of Spain to return them which
ultimately led to the break in relations between Spain and Peru. The
Memoria covering the period from November 20, 1937 to April 20,
1939 reported that Spain had returned all except eighteen men of
military age whom the latter insisted were to be tried in Spanish

---

[1] Case to Bigler, June 17, 1859, Moore, *op. cit.*, p. 789.

[2] Perú, *Boletin* 2°. trimestre de 1937), p. 209.

[3] Pp. LXX-LXXI. (My translation.)

[4] *Ibid.*, p. LXXII.

[5] Perú, *Boletin* (2°. trimestre de 1973), p. 208. There is disagreement as to the nature of
the entry. The Spanish government insisted that the consulate "was not assaulted or broken
into but courteously occupied by police after notification to the honorary consul and in
legitimate defense [of the] Spanish Republic." Reyes, Mexican *Chargé d'Affaires* in Lima
[acting Spanish Representative in Lima], to de la Fuente, Peruvian Minister of Foreign
Relations, May 16, 1937, tel., Perú, *Boletin* (2°. trimestre de 1937), p. 213. (My translation.)

[6] De la Fuente, Peruvian Minister of Foreign Relations, to the Spanish Minister of State,
June 2, 1937, *ibid.*, pp. 216–217. (My translation.)

[7] Reyes, Mexican *Chargé d'Affaires* in Lima [acting Spanish representative in Lima],
to de la Fuente, Peruvian Minister of Foreign Relations, May 16, 1937, tel., *ibid.*, p. 213.
(My translation.)

courts. Peru had already recalled her minister to Madrid "because of affronts to our diplomatic and consular representatives." Spain finally agreed to negotiate the return of the eighteen young men but only if Peru would "reestablish a legation of permanent character." When Spain refused to permit the government of Chile to take over the responsibility, the *Memoria* notes that "all avenues to a settlement being closed, Peru decided to break relations, May 17, 1938." [1]

On August 5, 1876, the Colombian government observed in a circular to the members of the diplomatic corps that the local function-aries of some states had in the past consented to grant to consuls a type of right of asylum which did not legitimately belong to them under the law of nations. In the future, it asserted that "the government of the union has determined to put a stop to the practice which was not acceptable in foreign relations and which impaired the true status [condición] of consuls and gave a false idea of their attributes and immunities." [2] Apparently this declaration had little success inasmuch as the *Memoria* for the following year points out that "this purely doctrinary measure was badly interpreted" and that the President, not wishing to inflame the existing discord, chose to ignore it.[3] With calm restored, however, the government again directed a circular to the foreign governments in order to put the previous declaration into force. This lengthy circular asserted that neither authorities on inter-national law nor existing treaties recognized any right of asylum as pertaining to consuls.[4]

In spite of all this the Colombian government cited cases of consular asylum (including some where the refugees had been forcibly removed) and cases of diplomatic asylum without distinction as evidence of a customary rule of law in the *Colombian-Peruvian Asylum Case*.[5] Likewise, the Argentine government in supporting its 1937 *Project of Convention on the Right of Asylum* cited cases of consular asylum along with the cases on diplomatic asylum as evidence of a widespread practice.[6]

3. *Instructions to United States consular officers in Latin America have not generally differed from those despatched to diplomatic officers.*

---

[1] Pp. LXX–LXXXIII. (My translation.)

[2] Antonio José Uribe, *Anales diplomáticos y consulares de Colombia* (edición oficial; Bogotá: Imprenta Nacional, 1914), p. 799. (My translation.)

[3] *Ibid.*, pp. 813–814. (My translation.)

[4] *Ibid.*, pp. 814–818.

[5] Perú, *Proceso*, pp. 376–386.

[6] Pp. 36–51.

On occasion, United States consular officers have been flatly instructed that they have no right to grant asylum but this has been equally true of instructions issued to diplomatic officers. The similarity in instructions would seem logical enough in view of the fact that the United States has claimed no legal grounds for granting asylum in either case, basing its action on local practice or humanitarian considerations instead.

Some defeated Peruvian revolutionaries received protection in the consulate of the United States at Tumbez, in 1854. The governor of the province made three different demands for their surrender, each one rejected by the American consul, and finally sent police in to remove the refugees.[1] In this case the State Department asserted that the consul could not grant asylum and suggested that the case might be different had it involved the legation.

Neither the law of nations nor the stipulations of our treaty with Peru recognizes the right of consuls to afford protection to those who have rendered themselves obnoxious to the authority of the government under which they dwell. And in a case so flagrant as that now under consideration *it may be doubted whether even a high diplomatic functionary would be justified* in casting the protection around those who were engaged in the commission of the highest crime recognized among civilized nations.[2]

This distinction seems to be the exception rather than the rule and, even in this case, the Department implied that temporary refuge might be given but declared that it would be the duty of the consul "to deliver them to the Peruvian authorities upon demand."[3] Since the consul had been unwilling to do this there were no grounds for complaint.

The subsequent course of the governor, in sending to the consulate and arresting the insurgents, can not be condemned by this Government. The national flag was not insulted, nor the national dignity affected by this proceeding. The former had been unwarrantably used; under the treaty it would and should have protected the property of American citizens, but in this case no such plea for its use can be presented.[4]

The conduct of the consul was thus regarded by the Department as "censurable in the highest degree" and the minister was directed so to inform the Peruvian government.[5]

---

[1] Moore, *op. cit.*, pp. 831–832.
[2] Marcy, Secretary of State, to Clay, U.S. Minister to Peru, January 24, 1854, *ibid.*, p. 833. (My italics.)
[3] *Ibid.*, p. 834.
[4] *Ibid.*
[5] *Ibid.*, p. 835.

In 1872 the United States vice-consul at St. Marc, Haiti, granted protection to a Haitian subject who apparently was under arrest and entered the consulate with or without permission of the officer in whose custody he was. The vice-consul refused to surrender said refugee until he had had time to consult the legation whereupon he (the consul) was dragged through the streets and generally mistreated. A short time later, Haitian police returned, searched the consulate and removed the refugee.[1] In the exchanges which followed this event the United States did not complain of violation of any right of asylum or even of the violation of the consulate and no demand was made for the return of the refugee. It was the treatment accorded to the vice-consul personally which brought objections.[2]

In 1899, the Haitian government notified the United States legation there that it proposed to search, among other buildings, the dwelling of the United States vice-consul. Before any reply was made to this notice, the search was carried out.[3] In this case the Department of State raised no objections to the fact that the dwelling had been searched but objected to the fact that it had been done before a reasonable time had elapsed in which a reply might have been given. It specifically stated that "no objection could be seen to effecting the proposed search after notification, and with the sanction and, if necessary, the full assistance of the officers of the legation." [4] It is not clear from this, however, whether such permission might have been refused.

But the discussion in the previous chapter pointed out that United States policy has asserted that even legations can grant only temporary protection and cannot shelter refugees from the pursuit of the legitimate authorities. It was also pointed out that this has not always been put into practice when it has been felt that the local authorities themselves would use arbitrary and summary procedures. In this respect the practice with regard to consulates has not differed greatly from that of legations.

When, in 1908, the Department of State instructed its minister to Haiti that asylum was not to be granted in consulates to anyone

---

[1] Bassett, U. S. Minister to Haiti, to Fish, Secretary of State, March 25, 1872, extract, *For. Rel. of the U. S.*, 1872, pp. 264–266.

[2] Bassett to Etheart, Haitian Secretary of State for Foreign Affairs, March 25, 1872, *ibid.*, p. 270.

[3] See inclosures in Powell, U. S. Minister to Haiti, to Hay, Secretary of State, November 11, 1899, *For. Rel. of the U. S.*, 1899, pp. 406–407. "Deputy consul" is used in these exchanges.

[4] Hay to Powell, November 27, 1899, *ibid.*, p. 407.

participating in the revolution then under way, there was no indication that such instructions were given because a consulate rather than a legation was involved.[1] On the contrary, when the minister informed the Department that refugees who had been surrendered by the consul were summarily shot, the former was instructed to inform the Haitian government that "the United States denies sanctuary against due process of law, but will protect refugees against summary lawlessness and slaughter as now appears to have been meted out to the refugees at St. Marc."[2] That respect for asylum rests more upon the immunity of the premises than upon any recognized right of asylum is shown by the fact that the Department suggested the transfer of the refugees to the legation.[3] This could hardly change the legality of the original grant of asylum and, in view of our traditonal policy of denying any right of asylum in either case, was in all probability based upon the feeling that Haitian police would be less likely to invade the legation than the consulate. When the refugees had left, the Department's new instructions prohibiting asylum applied to legation and consulates alike.[4]

Aside from any question of legal right, as regards the practice of asylum in its own right, it may be said that United States policy has generally been more cautious in permitting its consuls to engage in the practice simply because the immunity of the consulate is less well established than that of the legation. In 1865 it advised that:

> Consuls may harbor political refugees, but the law of nations confers upon them no right to do this, and as the treaty between the United States and Hayti is silent upon the subject, no sufficient cause of complaint would arise if refugees so harbored were to be taken by the local authorities from the consular abode.[5]

The *Instructions to Diplomatic Officers of the United States* (1927) point this out even more clearly.

> The quality of inviolability is inherent only in diplomatic missions, but is possessed by non-diplomatic missions, e. g., consulates, to the degree essential for the proper exercise of their function. In the one case the obligation, which rests upon the local authorities to respect the inviolability of the premises is absolute, whereas in the other it is contingent. The distinction is important in

---

[1] Root, Secretary of State, to Furniss, U. S. Minister to Haiti, January 28, 1908, tel.-paraphase, *For. Rel. of the U. S.*, 1908, p. 429.

[2] The Acting Secretary of State, to Furniss, February 3, 1908, tel.-paraphrase, *ibid.*, p. 431.

[3] *Ibid.*

[4] Root to Furniss, April 11, 1908, *ibid.*, p. 435.

[5] Hunter, Acting Secretary of State, to Peck, October 4, 1865, Moore, *op. cit.*, p. 807.

determining the attitude to be assumed toward the authorities of the local government.[1]

The diplomatic instructions given in anticipation of solicitations of asylum in the consulate at Guayaquil are typical.

> You are correct in assuming that what is technically known as "the right of asylum" in a strict sense is not claimed by this Government. However there is an evident distinction between this case and that where temporary refuge is given within the residence of a consular or diplomatic representative in order to preserve innocent human life . . .
>
> In the case of temporary refuge, the Department finds it expedient to give a certain latitude to the judgment of the official who is called upon to determine, within his discretion, the course recommended by broad considerations of humanity in each individual case.[2]

In 1888, the United States consul at Cape Haitien had instructed his consular agents that they were not to grant asylum to political refugees and that, if they did, they could expect no support from their government. The consul was corrected in the Department's reply as not having expressed correctly the policy of the United States.

> We do not regard extraterritorial asylum either in a legation or a consulate, as a right to be claimed under international law. We do not sanction or invite the exercise of asylum in those countries where it actually exists as a usage, but in such cases we recognize and admit its existence, and should circumstances bring about the uninvited resort of a political refugee for shelter to a consulate or legation of the United States, we should expect equal toleration and privilege in this regard with that allowed by such local usage to any other consulate or legation.[3]

Perhaps the best indication that United States practice has not regarded the granting of asylum in consulates as having a different legal basis from asylum in legations is the numerous instructions such as this where both are referred to without distinction.[4]

At the beginning of this chapter it was stated that, in practice, consular asylum did not differ *significantly* from diplomatic asylum.

---

[1] *A.J.I.L.*, Special Supplement, XXVI (April, 1932), p. 64.

[2] Knox, Secretary of State, to Young, U. S. Minister to Ecuador, January 30, 1912, *For. Rel. of the U. S.*, 1912, p. 399.

[3] Rives, Assistant Secretary of State, to Goutier, U. S. Consul at Cape Haitien, October 31, 1888, *For. Rel. of the U. S.*, 1888, I, p. 938.

[4] Bayard, Secretary of State, to Thompson, U. S. Minister to Haiti, November 7, 1885, *For Rel. of the U. S.*, 1886, p. 530; Blaine, Secretary of State, to Durham, U. S. Minister to Haiti, January 28, 1892, *For. Rel. of the U. S.*, 1892, p. 347; Olney, Secretary of State, to Tellman, U. S. Minister to Ecuador, September 25, 1895, *For. Rel. of the U. S.*, 1895, p. 245; Root, Secretary of State, to Furniss, U. S. Minister to Haiti, April 11, 1908, Hackworth, *op. cit.*, p. 634. See also similar provisions in the Foreign Service Regulations of the United States, 1939, Hackworth, *op. cit.*, p. 623; 1946, 11 *F.R.* (1946) and the latest regulations, revalidated as of March 30, 1956, 1 FSM I 225.2, issued under TL: A–66.

A word of explanation on this point is now in order. The reader has no doubt noted by now that differences do exist. But this writer regards them as differences in degree. First of all, it must be admitted that cases of consular asylum, while numerous, are less numerous than cases of diplomatic asylum. There are a number of reasons for this. The members of a deposed government will naturally seek refuge in the capital city and this, of course, accounts for a large portion of the asylum seekers. Latin American revolutions are very often small-scale affairs involving only the nation's capital and, thus, embassies and legations are conveniently available. But there are also consulates available in the capital cities so this does not explain entirely why legations are chosen rather than consulates. On this score it is very likely that the better-established immunities of the embassies and legations account for the difference. This brings us to the second difference between diplomatic and consular asylum.

There can be no doubt that refugees are more often removed from consulates than from embassies and legations. This writer can only offer a hypothesis in explanation of this fact. It seems likely that this arises *less* from any difference regarding a rule of law so far as asylum is concerned than it does from the fact that consular immunities are not nearly so well established and thus a remedy is more readily available in the former case than in the latter. Although the removal of refugees is not unknown even in the case of embassies and legations, this writer has found no case where its propriety has been admitted.[1]

What conclusions can be drawn from a situation such as this where numerous treaty provisions lay down one rule of conduct and practice shows quite another? The most obvious conclusion would seem to be a reaffirmation of the principle put forth earlier in this discussion, namely, that practice alone is not a sufficient basis for the establishment of a customary rule of law. Secondly, it would seem to suggest that we must also avoid *overemphasizing* the existence of a number of treaties on a particular subject as evidence of a customary rule of law. Finally, and most important for our main problem – that of *diplomatic* asylum, it provides another piece of evidence that the whole practice of one nation granting asylum within the territorial jurisdiction of another has owed its development primarily to extra-legal factors.

[1] See for example the removal of a refugee from the Mexican legation in Guatemala in 1904, Guatemala, *Memoria*, 1904, pp. 181–191.

PART II

INTRODUCTION

The *Colombian-Peruvian Asylum Case* has emphasized the fact that even where states have, by treaty or otherwise, declared that they regard themselves as legally or morally bound to respect the practice of diplomatic asylum this constitutes only an extremely vague sort of obligation. What does a government mean when it declares that it recognizes or respects the practice of asylum – either as a legal or humanitarian obligation?

It was pointed out in chapter I, and treaties and practice substantiate this, that asylum in this sense means "asylum for political offences." At least in treaties and practice asylum for common criminals has never been claimed as such. But what constitutes a political offence? The practice which has developed in the case of territorial asylum and extradition presents many of the same questions which we find in diplomatic asylum. A brief look at some of these questions will help to crystallize the questions to be investigated in this part of the present discussion.

In an article appearing in the *American Journal of International Law* in 1933, Lora L. Deere noted some 350 extradition conventions which had been signed since the middle of the 18th century.[1] This, she suggested, should make it relatively easy to ascertain the relationship between political offences and the extradition process. That this has *not* been the case, however, is attributed to the fact "that the conventions and laws refer to political offences without defining the term, so that what would otherwise be a clear cut statement of policy concerning the treatment to be afforded political offenders, becomes instead a matter of uncertainty and doubt because of the lack of

---

[1] "Political Offences in the Law and Practice of Extradition," *A.J.I.L.*, XXVII (April, 1933), p. 247.

agreement as to what constitutes a political offence." [1] The problem is well put by M. de Visscher in his observations on the Brierly report on extradition, presented to the League of Nations Committee of Experts for the Progressive Codification of International Law.

> The difficulty connected with political offences arises mainly from the fact that, in connection with extradition an exceptional extension is given to the conception of "political offence." Ordinarily by political offence is meant a purely political offence, i.e., one not accompanied by an offence against the ordinary law; but in connection with extradition the conception is frequently extended to cover *ancillary* offences, i. e., offences against the ordinary law connected with political acts or events. [2]

Charles Cheney Hyde does not attempt to define "political offences," so far as U. S. practice is concerned, but lists instead the *circumstances* under which a fugitive has been regarded as a political offender within the terms of relevant treaties. In all of the cases reviewed, he has found the following elements present:

> (1) There has been an uprising of revolutionary origin and purpose against the demanding government. In some cases the uprising has been of vast dimensions ... In others it has been of insignificant proportions ... It has been regarded as sufficient if there were in fact a party seeking governmental control however lacking in military or civil organization.
> (2) The accused has been connected with the movement. In no case has there been serious question as to his relation to the uprising.
> (3) Either the acts charged against the accused have been deemed incidental to the movement, or the evidence has failed to show that acts committed in the course of the uprising which might possibly not be justly regarded as incidental thereto, were in fact committed by the accused. [3]

As for general international practice, Deere, in the above mentioned article, concludes that "the question as to where the line shall be drawn when an act contains both political and common crime elements is closely linked with the problem of defining a relative political offence, and there has been no progress in evolving a general definition to cover all cases." [4] But if there is no agreement upon a definition of "a relative political offence," the author finds agreement on one point at least: "the rule, now universally accepted, that the decision concerning the character of an offense shall be vested in the state of refuge." [5]

---

[1] *Ibid.*

[2] *Ibid.*, p. 248.

[3] *International Law: Chiefly as Interpreted and Applied by the United States* (2d ed. rev.; Boston: Little, Brown and Company, 1945), pp. 1021–1022.

[4] *Op. cit.*, p. 269.

[5] *Ibid.*

This clearly points to the fact that it is not simply the offence itself which is the controlling factor. The circumstances under which the offence was committed are of equal or perhaps even greater significance. Thus we have the question often referred to as that of "ancillary offences." This problem is literally "written into" the Havana Convention of 1928, insofar as it prohibits the granting of asylum to deserters from the army or navy. In a part of the world where the military are notoriously engaged in politics it is obvious that they will very often be forced to seek asylum for their political activities and in doing so will be deserting their post. Are they then political refugees or deserters? Closely related to this has been the problem of defining a state of "urgency." The Caracas Convention of 1954 attempted for the first time to define this condition but only succeeded in demonstrating that it was perhaps undefinable.

Urgent cases are understood to be those, among others, in which the individual is being sought by persons or mobs over whom the authorities have lost control, or by the authorities themselves, and is in danger of being deprived of his life or liberty because of political persecution and cannot, without risk, ensure his safety in any other way.[1]

This part of the discussion will attempt to ascertain to what extent treaties and practice offer a definition of "political offences" and the *circumstances* under which otherwise common offences can be regarded as "political" for purposes of diplomatic asylum. It will next attempt to ascertain whether these sources show any agreement as to which party to a controversy is considered competent to qualify the nature of the offence and the circumstances.

[1] *Infra.*

CHAPTER VIII

QUALIFICATION OF THE OFFENCE: TREATIES

In the *Colombian-Peruvian Asylum Case,* Colombia maintained that the right of unilateral qualification of the offence by the state granting asylum was understood in Article 2 of the Havana Convention.[1] This was based first of all on the provision that "asylum ... shall be respected to the extent in which allowed as a right or through humanitarian toleration, by the usages, the conventions or the laws of the country in which granted ..." Since Colombia, through conventions and usages, had recognized the right of the granting state to qualify the nature of the offence this was the rule which should prevail under the Havana Convention.[2] The Court flatly rejected this argument saying that "nothing ... can be deduced from this provision so far as qualification is concerned." [3]

Since Colombia asserted that this had been the intention of the framers of the Havana Convention [4] (without offering any proof thereof) it will be necessary to investigate the antecedents of the Sixth International Conference of American States. There is nothing in the records of that conference to indicate that such was the intention. On the contrary, chapter IV of this thesis has already pointed out that Article 2 assumed its final form largely to meet the objections of those states not recognizing the practice of asylum. It seems unlikely, then, that the objection of these states would have been met by placing the right to qualify the nature of the offence in the hands of the state

---

[1] Perú, *Proceso,* p. 115.

[2] *Colombian-Peruvian Asylum Case, Judgment of November 20th, 1950:* I.C.J. *Reports* 1950, p. 275-276.

[3] *Ibid.,* p. 276. The Court's ruling seems much closer to the position taken by Peru. According to this position the governments signing the convention merely intended to say: "You can adopt whatever policy on asylum you please, we cannot impose one upon you, but at least that policy must conform with your own juridical system and must be constant." Perú, *Proceso,* p. 426. (My translation.)

[4] Perú, *Proceso,* p. 260.

granting asylum. Surely the states which raised objections did not do so in anticipation of their role as the state *granting* asylum. The only possible explanation would be that they were considering their role as the territorial state.

But if, as the Court ruled, the state granting asylum is not, under this convention, competent to qualify unilaterally the nature of the offence, is it then left to the territorial state? The second paragraph of Article 1 suggests that this might be the case.

> Persons accused or condemned for common crimes taking refuge in any of the places mentioned in the preceding paragraph, shall be surrendered upon the request of the local government.[1]

Does the mere fact that the territorial state considers the crime for which the refugee is accused as a "common crime" mean that the refugee must be surrendered? The Court implied that this was not the case. It would be necessary for the territorial state to *prove* that the accusation was for a common crime.

> The onus of proving that Haya de la Torre had been accused or condemned for common crimes before the grant of asylum rested upon Peru...
> On the other hand, the Court considers that the Government of Peru has not proved that the acts of which the refugee was accused ... constitute common crimes.[2]

It must be emphasized that this statement was made with reference to the Peruvian counter claim that Colombia had granted and maintained asylum contrary to the treaty.[3] Nothing is said concerning who shall decide whether or not such proof has been provided. In the absence of "some impartial agency, judicial or other, for resolving any disagreement on the question," such as Lauterpacht says they must resort to,[4] the state of refuge must decide this for itself. Thus the Court really said that neither party is authorized to determine unilaterally the nature of the offence.

The Convention on Diplomatic Officers signed at the same conference contains a similar provision.

> Article 17. Diplomatic officers are obliged to deliver to the competent local authority that requests it any person accused or condemned for ordinary crimes, who may have taken refuge in the mission.[5]

---

[1] Hudson, *International Legislation*, IV, p. 2414. All multilateral treaties on asylum discussed in this chapter were discussed in chapter IV in a different connection. For respective citations in standard treaty sources see chapter IV.

[2] *Op. cit.*, p. 281.

[3] *Ibid.*, pp. 280–281.

[4] *Op. cit.*, p. 798.

[5] Hudson, *International Legislation*, IV, p. 2391; *League of Nations Treaty Series*, CLV, p. 259; Martens, *op. cit.*, (3e série par Triepel), p. 362.

There is a significant difference between this provision and that originally suggested by the American Institute of International Law.[1] Article 22 of its Project 21 provided that:

> The diplomatic agent is obliged to surrender to the competent local authority any individual pursued for crime or misdemeanor under the law of the country to which he is accredited who may have taken refuge in the house occupied by the agent or in that of the legation. Should the agent refuse to surrender him, the local authority has the right to guard the house of the agent or the legation until the government of the agent decides upon the attitude which he will take.[2]

First of all, no attempt is made to distinguish between "political" and "ordinary" crimes. Secondly, it clearly contemplates a situation where the agent may not surrender the refugee even though he is obliged to do so. The form given to this provision in Article 22 of Project 7, which the International Commission of American Jurists submitted to the Sixth International Conference of American States, omitted both of these features and is nearly identical to the form used in the convention.[3]

A comparison of the Convention on Asylum and the Convention on Diplomatic Officers with the Convention on Consular Agents, all signed at this same conference, sheds some light on interpretation. Article 19 of the latter convention provides that:

> Consuls are obliged to deliver, upon the simple request of the local authorities, persons accused or condemned for crimes who may have sought refuge in the consulate.[4]

In the case the words "simple request of the local authorities" plus the fact that no distinction is made between types of crimes certainly indicates an attempt to remove any discretion on the part of the consul so far as the surrender of the refugee is concerned. But the same Conference, in referring to *diplomatic* representatives, provided in one convention that "persons accused of or condemned for common crimes ... shall be surrendered upon the request of the local government."[5] In another convention it provided that such officers were "obliged to

---

[1] The reader will recall that the American Institute of International Law submitted a number of projects to the 1927 meeting of the International Commission of American Jurists which in turn submitted its projects to the Sixth International Conference of American States at Havana, 1928.

[2] *A.J.I.L.*, Special Supplement, XX (July and October, 1926), p. 353.

[3] *A.J.I.L.*, Special Supplement, XXII (January, 1928), p. 252.

[4] Hudson, *International Legislation*, IV, p. 2399. For a complete documentation see chapter IV.

[5] Convention on Asylum.

deliver to the competent authority that requests it any person accused or condemned for ordinary crimes." [1]

The discussion in chapter IX will show that there has in fact been a great deal of disagreement on the question of *who* shall qualify the nature of the offence among Latin American states which have in one way or another agreed to recognize "a right of asylum for political refugees." The report of the Fourth Sub-Committee on Political Asylum at the Seventh International Conference of American States clearly recognized that the question was by no means settled in the Havana Convention.

> The Havana Convention did not clearly specify who should judge the political character of the delinquency, which omission has given rise to lamentable incidents. [2]

The Convention on Political Asylum signed at Montevideo, 1933, was an attempt to establish which party to such a controversy should qualify the nature of the offence. Article 1 of this convention replaces Article 1 of the Havana Convention:

> It shall not be lawful for the States to grant asylum in legations, warships, military camps, or airships to those accused of common offenses who may have been sentenced by ordinary courts of justice, nor to deserters of land or sea forces. The persons referred to in the preceding paragraph who find refuge in some of the above mentioned places shall be surrendered as soon as requested by the local government. [3]

In this case, however, the state of refuge would decide whether or not the refugee falls within this category. Article 2 provides that "the judgment of political delinquency concerns the state which offers asylum." [4]

M. M. L. Savelberg in *Le problème du droit international américain*, has pointed out that this convention did not, however, fill the gaps

---

[1] Convention on Diplomatic Officers.

[2] International Conference of American States, Seventh, *Minutes and Antecedents* (Montevideo, 1933), p. 171. A report of the Advisory Committee of the Ministry of Foreign Relations of Colombia also noted this: "... In its application, the Convention of Havana has produced annoying controversies, especially as a result of the fact that is contains a gap concerning the point as to which state shall qualify the offence as political ..." Perú, *Proceso*, p. 291. (My translation.) Project X of the American Institute of International Law, submitted to the Seventh International Conference of American States noted the same difficulty. See International Conference of American States, Seventh, *Projects Submitted by the Executive Committee of the American Institute of International Law Pursuant to a Resolution of the Governing Board of the Pan American Union*, No. 4 (Washington, 1933), pp. 22–23.

[3] Hudson, *International Legislation*, VI. pp. 609–910.

[4] *Ibid.*, p. 610. A better translation would seem to be "the judgment of political delinquency appertains to the state which offers (or gives) asylum," the Spanish version being: "La calificación de la delincuencia corresponde al Estado que presta el asilo."

left by the Havana Convention, these gaps being the qualification of political offences and the guarantees necessary for the safety of the refugees.[1] In the *Colombian-Peruvian Asylum Case* Peru raised a very fundamental question concerning Article 2. Does the treaty provide for provisional or definitive qualification? "That is, is it a case of a qualification susceptible of being discussed before an impartial organ, whatever that may be, especially before a tribunal, or of a qualification against which no objection may be presented?"[2] Peru argued that it provided only for a provisional qualification. In support of this it pointed to Article 4 which provides as follows.

> When the withdrawal of a diplomatic agent is requested because of discussions that may have arisen in some case of political asylum, the diplomatic agent shall be replaced by his government, and his withdrawal shall not determine a breach of diplomatic relations between two states.[3]

This, Peru argued, "evidently supposes that there will be discussions concerning a case of asylum, consequently, that the qualification will not be peremptory." [4]

This is the interpretation given to this convention by the Dominican Republic, according to Peña Batlle, ex-Secretary of Foreign Relations. Speaking of the period when he was Secretary of Foreign Relations he says:

> In 1945 the Dominican Chancellery established a definitive criterion in the matter in dealing with various cases of asylum which then occupied its attention. The conventions of Montevideo do not permit qualification by the state of refuge except provisionally and as a point of departure for the study of the case by the interested governments.[5]

In the light of our discussion thus far concerning Latin American practice, and, more clearly, the discussion to follow in chapter X, this thesis can hardly be supported. In none of the cases discussed in these chapters is there any evidence that Latin American states have objected to a *provisional* qualification of the offence by the state of refuge. It is only when this qualification becomes definitive by a refusal to surrender the refugee that objections are raised. It could of course be

---

[1] (La Haye: A. A. M. Stols, 1946), pp. 282.

[2] Perú, *Proceso*, p. 649. (My translation.)

[3] "Shall not determine a breach of diplomatic relations" is the official translation given for the Spanish "sin que ello pueda determinar la interrupción de las relaciones diplomáticas." Perhaps "shall not produce a breach of diplomatic relations" would be an easier translation.

[4] *Ibid.* For a similar interpretation see Savelberg, *op. cit.*, p. 283.

[5] "Una sentencia de la Corte Internacional de Justicia," *El Caribe*, 8 de abril de 1951. (My translation.)

argued that, if the Montevideo Convention of 1933 was intended as a declaration of an already existing rule of law, this is precisely what was meant. But the evidence presented above indicates that the convention was clearly intended to settle certain questions about which there had been considerable disagreement and which had "given rise to lamentable incidents." This could only have referrred to the question of definitive qualification of the offence.

Another avenue of disagreement was shown in a recent case involving asylum granted in the Guatemalan legation in Nicaragua. Among the refugees was a Nicaraguan army officer. A Nicaraguan *Corte de Investigación* "named by His Excellency the President of the Republic and Commandant General, in accord with the military laws and in conformity with Article 319 of the Constitution" ruled that he had deserted the service. The Nicaraguan government asked that he be surrendered.[1] The Guatemalan government asserted that "the fact of abandoning his post does not necessarily imply a manifest intention of abandonment of duty ... It is simply the consequential result of other acts of a political character which impelled him to take refuge although to do so he would have to abandon the performance of his charge." [2] Thus the Guatemalan *Diario oficial* summarized the case as follows.

> Here arose a disagreement between our government and that of the government of Managua. Concretely, in the personal case of Lieutenant Duarte, whom the Nicaraguan authorities consider a subject of common crime and who, consequently, ought to be surrendered to the military authorities who demand him for judgment. Of what is Lieutenant Duarte accused? The Nicaraguan government accuses him of the crime of desertion. On this it bases the request that the protection of our flag be withdrawn and that he be surrendered to his prosecutors.[3]

The provisions of the Treaty on Political Asylum and Refuge, signed at the Second Congress on Private Internationl Law on August 4, 1939, are very similar to those of the 1933 convention with regard to the qualification of the offence. Article 2 provides that asylum may be granted "exclusively to persons pursued for political reasons or offences, or under circumstances involving concurrent political offences, which do not legally permit of extradition." [4] Article 3 further defines this.

---

[1] Santizo Román, Guatemalan Ambassador to Nicaragua, to the Nicaraguan Minister of Foreign Relations, May 17, 1954, *Diario de Centro América*, 24 de mayo de 1954, p. 1. (My translation.)

[2] *Ibid.*

[3] *Ibid.*, 25 de mayo de 1954, p. 1. (My translation.)

[4] Hudson, *International Legislation*, VIII, p. 406.

Asylum shall not be granted to persons accused of polititical offenses, who shall have been indicted or condemned previously for common offenses, by the ordinary tribunals.

The determination of the causes which induce the asylum appertains to the state which grants it.[1]

This provision is obviously open to the same questions of interpretation as those discussed in connection with the 1933 convention. There is one important difference here, however: nowhere does it provide for the surrender of refugees, political or otherwise, except where the refugee has himself abused the privileges of asylum granted in which case "the diplomatic agent or commander shall immediately terminate asylum." [2]

The Convention on Diplomatic Asylum signed at the Tenth Inter-American Conference at Caracas, on March 28, 1954, returned to the form of the Montevideo Convention of 1933. Article 1 contains the usual stipulation that asylum granted "to persons being sought for political reasons or for political offences shall be respected by the territorial state in accordance with the provisions of this convention." [3] Article 3 then lists the conditions under which asylum *may not* be granted and provides for the surrender of the refugees in these cases.

It is not lawful to grant asylum to persons who, at the time of requesting it, are under indictment or on trial for common offenses or have been convicted by competent regular courts and have not served the respective sentence, nor to deserters from land, sea and air forces, save when the acts giving rise to the request for asylum, whatever the case may be, are clearly of a political nature.

Persons included in the foregoing paragraph who *de facto* enter a place that is suitable as an asylum shall be invited to leave or, as the case may be, shall be surrendered to the local authorities, who may not try them for political offenses committed prior to the time of the surrender.[4]

Paragraph 1 attempts to provide for cases such as the Nicaragua-Guatemala case just referred to where a military deserter had apparently left his charge due to political circumstances. The scope of Article 4 is somewhat broader than its counterpart in other treaties and would seemingly leave it up to the state of refuge to decide whether or not this is the case. Article 4 provides that "it shall rest with the state granting asylum to determine the nature of the offence or the motives

---

[1] *Ibid.*, pp. 406–407.

[2] *Ibid.*, p. 407.

[3] Pan American Union, *Convention on Diplomatic Asylum Signed at the Tenth Inter-American Conference, Caracas, March 1–28, 1954*, Law and Treaty Series (Washington: Pan American Union, 1954), p. 1.

[4] *Ibid.*

for the persecution." [1] Nothing is said, however, as to whether this shall be a provisional or definitive qualification.

The related problem which this discussion has referred to as "qualification of the circumstances" has also been the subject of more recent treaty arrangements. The Montevideo Treaty of 1889 did not refer to the question of "urgency." [2] The Havana Convention of 1928 provided that "asylum may not be granted except in urgent cases and for the period of time strictly indispensable for the person who has sought asylum to ensure in some other way his safety." [3] This, of course, only restates something upon which there has been a tacit but vague agreement. It is of of slight value, however, in the absence of agreement as to what constitutes a case of "urgency." Nothing is said concerning the party authorized to pass upon this question in case of disagreement.

The question of *who* shall determine whether or not conditions warrant the granting of asylum was not directly considered in the Court's decision in the *Colombian-Peruvian Asylum Case*. It may be said, however, that the absence of any right of unilateral qualification by either party was implicit in the discussion inasmuch as it carefully considered the merits of the arguments of each party as to whether or not this was a case of "urgency." [4] If a right to decide this unilaterally had existed for one or the other of the parties this would have been unnecessary.

The Montevideo Convention of 1933 makes no reference to the question of urgency.[5] The provisions of the 1939 convention, also signed at Montevideo, seem broad enough to cover this. "The determination of the *causes which induce asylum appertains* to the state which grants it." [6] No reference is made to any prerequisite of "urgency."

The Caracas Convention of 1954, no doubt as a result of the *Colombian-Peruvian Asylum Case*, is very explicit on this matter.

Article V

Asylum may not be granted except in urgent cases and for the period of time strictly necessary for the asylee to depart from the country with the guarantees granted by the government of the territorial state, to the end that his life, liberty, or personal integrity may not be endangered, or that the asylee's safety is ensured in some other way.

---

[1] *Ibid.*
[2] Martens, *op. cit.*, XVIII (2me série par Stoerb, 1893), p. 432.
[3] Hudson, *International Legislation*, IV, p. 2414.
[4] *Op. cit.*, pp. 282–286.
[5] Hudson, *International Legislation*, VI, pp. 609–611.
[6] *Ibid.*, VIII, p. 407. (My italics.)

Article VI

Urgent cases are understood to be those, among others, in which the individual is being sought by persons or mobs over whom authorities have lost control, or by the authorities themselves, and is in danger of being deprived of his life or liberty because of political persecution and cannot, without risk, ensure his safety in any other way.

Article VII

If a case of urgency is involved, it shall rest with the state granting asylum to determine the degree of urgency of the case.[1]

Only the Caracas Convention of 1954 clearly provides for unilateral qualification of both the nature of the offence and the existence of "urgency." But only eleven Latin American states have ratified this convention,[2] probably a reflection of the explicitness of the rights and obligations set forth in it. In view of the small number of states that had ratified, a number of proposals which would make it more acceptable to a larger number of states were submitted for consideration by the Inter-American Juridical Committee. Two of the proposals called for a committee of investigation to qualify the nature of the offense when there might be disagreement between the two parties. Another would set up a simple procedure whereby the territorial state, after the safe-conduct had been granted to the refugee, might request the Supreme Court of the state granting asylum to review the decision of the diplomatic agent or of the Foreign Ministry of that country.[3]

The Juridical Committee did not feel that the proposals for committees of investigation or an authority to qualify the nature of the offense would offer any advantage over the present treaty provisions. It felt that this would amount to a system of arbitration which, under the circumstances, would have disadvantages. Under the present system, the Committee observed, "there is neither victor nor vanquished, as there is in the case of arbitration, where one of the parties is defeated when its theses are found to be without basis. This undoubtedly affects the prestige of the state for which the award is unfavorable, and may bring about unexpected reactions in the public opinion of that state." [4]

[1] Pan American Union, *Convention on Diplomatic Asylum Signed at the Tenth Inter-American Conference, Caracas, March 1–28, 1954* (Washington, 1954), p. 2. The word "asylee" appears here for the first time in an official translation. This discussion and previous official translations have used the word "refugee" in translating the Spanish word "asilado."

[2] Pan American Union, *Status of Inter-American Conventions*, Treaty Series No. 5, Revised to September 1, 1963 (Washington, 1963), p. 9.

[3] Inter-American Juridical Committee, *New Articles on Diplomatic Asylum* (Washington 1960), pp. 1–5.

[4] *Ibid.*, pp. 10–11.

The proposal that would authorize the territorial state to request the Supreme Court of the state granting asylum to review the qualification of the offense was also questioned by the Committee, since it noted that this would be complicated by constitutional provisions in some of the states. It recommended, instead, that an attempt be made to improve the provisions under which the territorial state could request extradition after the refugee had left the country. This, it felt, would accomplish the same thing since the Supreme Court in each of the countries would be in a position to review these cases, a procedure which the Committee felt would be beneficial. It would provide the opportunity whereby a case could be reviewed by persons of outstanding moral and professional character after the immediate tensions are lessened and after passions have lost much of their violence. In order to improve these provisions of the 1954 Convention, it recommended that the refugee be required to remain in the country granting him asylum (to which he would have been granted safe conduct) "for a period of 60 days with a view to the possible presentation of a request for extradition." Thus the territorial state would not have to indicate in advance of the safe conduct whether or not it intended to request extradition.[1]

No action has yet been taken on these proposals but they will undoubtedly come up for consideration at the next Inter-American Conference which is now overdue.

[1] *Ibid.*, pp. 12–14.

CHAPTER IX

THE PROBLEM OF "POLITICAL" OFFENCES

Chile, 1851. After a military uprising in 1851, one of the persons involved received asylum in the United States legation in Santiago. The Chilean definition of a political offence was extremely interesting in this case. It depends as much upon the conditions of the society in which it occurred as the nature of the offence itself. Under certain conditions the minister would be justified in sheltering persons implicated in revolutionary movements. These conditions were described as follows.

> [When] ... all idea of legality and respect for authority is lost and it becomes impossible to characterize the acts of the persons who are involved ... the vanquished frequently exchange places with the victors, without it being possible to consider the one more guilty or more innocent than the other: the laws scorned, the legal authority upset, there is no way of judging anyone ... In these sad periods of a society, when the laws are able to offer it little or no protection and when everything yields to the storm of domestic agitations, the diplomatic agent who expands the scope of his immunity as much as possible in order to save some victims from partisan vengeance, [victims who are] perhaps innocent of all crime except that of an opinion fallen into disgrace, it cannot be said that he is offending either an authority which lacks the character of legality or laws which are no longer respected.[1]

But, needless to say, the conditions in Chile were reputed to be quite different from this. There had not been any contending parties there, "but a permanent, legal and recognized authority, punishing a military insurrection plotted by some leaders who rebelled against the laws and against the constitution." [1]

Any one familiar with Latin American history can see how it would be impossible to reach any agreement on a criterion as subjective as this. According to the government in power, all revolutionary

---

[1] Varas, Chilean Minister of Foreign Relations, to the Minister from the United States, May 15, 1851, Chile, *Jurisprudencia de la cancillería chilena*, pp. 262–263. (My translation.)
[2] *Ibid.*, p. 263.

attempts are nothing more than criminal agitations of a very few which will be extinguished as soon as the unanimous will of the people can rally behind their legally constituted leaders. Thus quite a different picture of events was given by the United States minister. He pointed out that Chile had indeed, for the last 20 years, escaped the turbulence of other Latin American countries. But events had recently changed and for the last several months Chile had tended toward the very conditions which were described in the previous note. "A revolution actually broke out in the neighboring province, and martial law was proclaimed in the month of November last, followed by the late more serious affair" which the minister feared had not ended.[1] Finally, he observed:

I am well assured that if I permit Col. Arteaga to be arrested, he will be shot, and that his execution would be the signal for a sanguinary civil war, marked by the most inveterate feelings of revenge. I consider that it would alike be impolitic and unjust to shoot him. He was not a leader, but on the contrary, must have acted a very subordinate part.[2]

The Chilean historian, Galdámes, gives a similar description of the years 1850–1851. Scattered revolutions broke out, individual guarantees were suspended, by the fall of 1851 President Bulnes "was leaving his high office involved in the vortex of a revolution." [3]

Venezuela, 1858. In 1858, the Venezuelan dictator, General Monagas, having been forced to resign in the face of a successful revolution, was granted asylum by the French *chargé d'affaires*. Gutiérrez, a cabinet minister and Guiseppi, apparently not a former office holder, were also given asylum. The numerous demands made for the refugees offer little toward a definition of the term "political offence" inasmuch as the Venezuelan notes strongly imply that *all* persons pursued by authorities of the country must be surrendered on the demand of the latter regardless of the nature of the charges.[4] Whatever might have been its policy with regard to refugees charged with other offences, it is very clear that the Venezuelan government did not regard the nature of the offences charged against these particular refugees as qualifying them for any kind of definitive protection in a foreign

---

[1] Peyton, U. S. Minister to Chile, to Webster, Secretary of State, April 19, 1851, extracts, Manning, *op. cit.*, V, p. 189.

[2] *Ibid.*

[3] Luis Galdámes, *A History of Chile*, trans, I. J. Cox (Chapel Hill: University of North Carolina Press, 1941), p. 288. See also *ibid.*, pp. 285–288.

[4] Toro, Venezuelan Secretary of Foreign Relations, to Bingham and Levraud, *Chargés d'Affaires* of Britain and France, April 30, 1858, Venezuela, *Cuestión promovida a Venezuela por los agentes de Francia y de la Gran Bretaña*, pp. 28–43.

legation (i.e., protection which would withdraw them from Venezuelan jurisdiction either by granting them safe conduct out of the country or by guarantees that they would not be prosecuted for the charges against them).

While the charges against the refugees were given only in very general terms they dealt with misconduct in public office in the case of Monagas and Gutiérrez. They were charged with "all kinds of unlawful acts against the nation which charged them with loyally administering their interests." [1] "On what sane principle," the Venezuelan Secretary of Foreign Relations asked, "could the claim be supported of exempting from submission to the nation those who took an oath to govern it according to its laws, and not only made a mockery of their principles, but transgressed in snatching from Venezuelans their most sacred rights?" [2]

The United States minister to Venezuela reported that Gutiérrez was charged with maladministration and peculation of public funds. Guiseppi, he reported, had held no government post but the present government alleged that his general conduct had amounted to a common crime, a charge which the minister felt would be difficult to prove legally. [3]

A protocol finally was signed by the Secretary of Foreign Relations and the members of the diplomatic corps whereby General Monagas would be placed at the disposition of the Venezuelan government but, at the same time, the latter guaranteed that he would not be submitted to justice and that he would be permitted to leave the country in safety. [4] Later, however, the Secretary denied that this constituted a binding agreement. [5] The Secretary was himself dismissed for his action and his successor insisted that the protocol had been no more than a promise made to General Monagas by the Secretary of Foreign Relations to which the members of the diplomatic corps had added their signature in testimony thereof. [6]

As for the other two refugees, the Venezuelan government demanded

[1] *Ibid.*, (My translation.)

[2] *Ibid.*

[3] Eames, U. S. Minister to Venezuela, to Cass, Secretary of State, April 22, 1858, Manning, *op. cit.*, XII, p. 808.

[4] March 26, 1858, Venezuela, *Cuestión promovida a Venezuela por los agentes de Francia y de la Gran Bretaña*, pp. 3–5.

[5] Urrutia, Venezuelan Secretary of Foreign Relations, to Levraud and Bingham, March 29, 1858, quoted in Planas–Suárez, *op. cit.*, pp. 423–424.

[6] Toro to the Members of the Diplomatic Corps, april 21, 1858, Venzuela, *Cuestión promovida a Venezuela por los agentes de Francia y de la Gran Bretaña*, p. 8.

their immediate surrender, making clear that at least in this case there
was no right of asylum.

> The government insists on demanding ... the acceptance of the judicial
> findings for the persons of Mssrs. Gutiérrez and Guiseppi; and for that reason,
> the undersigned has special orders to deny to Your Excellency the right of
> asylum which he claims in favor of two individuals accused and submitted to
> justice for theft and peculation.[1]

The United States Minister to Venezuela reported that the government "went into permanent session and intimated that if they were
not delivered within business hours of that day, Mr. Levraud would
receive his passport at once." [2] Both were "surrendered" within the
next day but there was disagreement as to whether they gave themselves up voluntarily or whether they were arrested in violation of the
immunity of the legation.[3] Charges and countercharges were made
regarding the violation of the diplomatic premises but Venezuela
refused to make any concessions even in the face of threats from
French and British warships in the harbor of La Guaira.[4]

A settlement was finally reached in a convention signed at la
Guaira. Though in some respects a compromise, it clearly recognized
Venezuela's right to submit Gutiérrez and Guiseppi to Venezuelan
authorities after proper amends for the violation of the diplomatic
premises. It appears that Britain and France were recognizing the
right of Venezuela to demand the refugee and their own obligation to
surrender him in return for Venezuela's recognition of the absolute
inviolability of the diplomatic premises. Gutiérrez was to be returned
to the French and English legation "and placed at the dispositon of
the Venezuelan government as soon as it may demand it, unless before
the solicitation is made he may be pardoned by the executive power of
the Chief of State, using the extraordinary powers that have been
conceded to him." [5] As for Guiseppi, "if the charges against ... him
should not permit him to be placed at liberty, a judgment by the
competent tribunals will follow in the shortest possible time." [6] The

---

[1] Urrutia to Levraud, March 30, 1858, quoted in Planas-Suárez, op. cit., pp. 429–30.
(My translation.)

[2] Eames to Cass, April 22, 1858, Manning, op. cit., XII, pp. 808–809.

[3] Toro to Levraud, April 30, 1858, Venezuela, Cuestión promovida a Venezuela por los
agentes de Francia y de la Gran Bretaña, pp. 40–43.

[4] Joint Note Signed by de Gueydon and Dunlop, French and British Commandants in
the Port of La Guaira, May 5, 1858, ibid., pp. 43–44.

[5] Convention Signed at La Guaira, August 27, 1858, reprinted in Planas-Suárez, op. cit.,
pp. 482–483. (My translation.)

[6] Ibid.

original promise made to General Monagas was to be carried out.[1]

While the date of the charges was not discussed in this case, it is obvious from the facts that charges were not brought against the refugees until *after* asylum had been granted. The former President and the cabinet minister had taken refuge immediately after the President had resigned his post as the head of the recognized government of Venezuela,[2] Guiseppi took refuge at the same time so charges brought against him by the new government could have occurred only after asylum was granted.

Peru, 1865–66. After what was considered a humiliating settlement of Peru's controversy with Spain, the government of General Pezet was overthrown in 1865 in a revolution led by General Prado. The former left the country on board a British man-of-war and four of his cabinet ministers received asylum in the French legation. In its note to the French minister, the Peruvian government raised no objection to the original grant of asylum but solicited the surrender of said refugees in order that their guilt could be ascertained in Peruvian courts.[3] The precise nature of the charges was not indicated in the notes published by the Peruvian government but it was clearly for misconduct in public office. The contents of a note from the *Corte Central*, annexed to a note to the French minister, merely read:

> The President of the *Corte Central*, on petition from the public prosecutors [los fiscales], has decreed the arrest of ex-General Manuel Ignacio Vivanco, Dr. D. Pedro José Calderón, Dr. D. Jorge Loayza and D. Pedro José Carrillo for serious accusations against them.[4]

A note from the United States minister reported that they were charged with "peculation, conspiracy, and treason." [5]

The Peruvian government gave scant attention to the nature of the charges, i.e., whether or not they were "political." It merely insisted throughout that Peru had every right to try these particular individuals. At one point, however, it did insist that "this is not a political persecution, the only object being that of freeing the government

---

[1] *Ibid.*

[2] Planas-Suárez, *op. cit.*, pp. 384–385; Bingham and Levraud to the Venezuelan Minister of Foreign Relations, April 15, 1858, *ibid.*, pp. 404–405.

[3] Pacheco, Peruvian Secretary of State for Foreign Relations, to Vion, French Envoy to Peru, December 20, 1865, Perú, *Correspondencia diplomática relativa a la cuestión sobre asilo*, pp. 3–4.

[4] *Ibid.*, p. 4.

[5] Hovey, U. S. Minister to Peru, to Seward, Secretary of State, January 28, 1867, extracts, *Dip. Cor. of the U. S.*, 1867, p. 737.

from enemies which harm it." [1] But in a note to the Peruvian diplomatic representatives in Chile, Bolivia and Ecuador it implied that, regardless of the nature of the charges, refugees were to be surrendered when properly demanded by the local government. Referring to the controversy with France, the Peruvian Minister of State for Foreign Relations said: "Verbally first, and in writing afterwards, I interposed a demand for extradition, taking the position that the right of asylum did not exist when the refugee was demanded by a judicial authority." [2]

As to conditions prevailing at the time, Peru denied that the revolutionary events which had taken place affected this case or that the fact of a special court having been created after the acts giving rise to the charges was of any significance. "Your Excellency knows perfectly well that if it is not legal to prosecute and punish for actions which previously have not been qualified as crimes, it is permitted, at any time, to vary the form of the proceedings, in full or in part," the Peruvian minister asserted in a note to the French envoy. "The circumstance of having proceeded thus, in consequence of political events, in no way influences the legal force of its determinations, as it would not alter, either, the circumstance of the crime for which some individuals might be accused being merely political; because it is not certain, not even admissible, that political crimes ought to remain unpunished, nor that it may be lawful for a diplomatic agent to remove from the action of justice, delinquents of that kind when a tribunal formally demands them." [3]

The precise disposition of the refugees is not indicated except for notes from the French envoy informing the Peruvian government that the refugees had left the legation, in one case for a foreign country.[4] The Peruvian position on the outcome of the case was made known in the *Memoria* for 1867.

The government repelled with energy, as was its duty, such exaggerated pretensions. It would not, however, provoke a conflict which under the circumstances in which we were placed, it was at any rate expedient to avoid, and therefore limited itself to protesting against the proceedings of the chief *ad interim* of the legation.[5]

Haiti, 1875. On March 5, 1875, the National Constitutional Assembly of Haiti brought charges against General Lamothe, a former

---

[1] Pacheco, to Vion, December 20, 1865, *op. cit.*, p. 3. (My translation.)
[2] May 19, 1866, *ibid.*, pp. 21–22.
[3] January 2, 1866, *ibid.*, pp. 8–13.
[4] *Ibid.*, pp. 7, 13, 14.
[5] Translation, reprinted in *Dip. Cor. of the U. S.*, 1867, II, p. 758.

office holder for "unfaithfulness in the discharge of his functions as Minister of Interior and Foreign Affairs, under President Saget's administration." [1] General Lamothe sought and obtained refuge in the British legation. The Haitian government asserted that the charges were not of a political character and that, consequently, the refugee had no claim to the protection which had been afforded him. The British minister refused to surrender him, asserting that in Haiti it was not always easy to distinguish between administrative acts and those of a political character.[2]

By the end of the month it was agreed that General Lamothe could return to his home although it is by no means clear that he was given any absolute guarantees as to the charges against him. The United States minister to Haiti at that time has recorded the interview which he and his British colleague had with the Haitian Minister of Foreign Relations. This interview shows that Haiti maintained its position that this was not a case involving political charges. Furthermore, it gives no indication that concessions made by that government were motivated by a willingness to regard them as such.

In the interview it was stated, as the view of both the British and United States ministers, "that it [asylum] is generally regarded as an exceptional but humane measure, which, if continued at all, ought to be open alike to citizens of all parties in the country, and that once a person has been received as a refugee in a foreign legation, the rule seemed to be not to deliver him up on requests or demands such as had been made for General Lamothe, without a guarantee for his personal security from irregular proceedings against him." [3] It was also intimated to the Haitian minister "that if his government would formally express its desire and purpose to renounce the so-called right without reference or prejudice to any case actually at hand, it is possible that our governments, in conjunction with any others having legations here, might acquiesce in an understanding to that end." [4] The Haitian minister did not appear favorable to this suggestion and "with some warmth," reiterated his view "that the case of General Lamothe was not a political one, and that, therefore, the general was not entitled to the refuge he had obtained." [5] The British and Ameri-

---

[1] Bassett, U. S. Minister to Haiti, to Fish, Secretary of State, March 11, 1875, *For. Rel. of the U. S.*, II, p. 682.

[2] *Ibid.*

[3] Bassett to Fish, April 9, 1875, *ibid.*, p. 683.

[4] *Ibid.*

[5] *Ibid.*

can representatives then put forth a compromise proposal. It was suggested that "if the government wished merely, as ... inferred from ... [the Haitian minister's] remarks, to place General Lamothe on trial for a misappropriation of public moneys, he might be relieved from further refuge in the British legation by entering on his part into security sufficient for the sums alleged to have been misappropriated, and the government, on its part, giving my colleague a guarantee that no irregular proceedings or persecutions [prosecutions?] should be taken against the ex-minister." [1] In accordance with this proposal, the refugee left the British legation although the American minister expressed doubt that he would ever be brought to trial. [2]

Since it is most unlikely that the Haitian government would have admitted that it ever had any intentions of bringing any *irregular* proceedings against the refugee it does not seem that it was offering much in this case. Yet it was forced at least to offer the guarantee to the British minister before it could effectively establish its right to try the refugee. General Lamothe was granted asylum after charges had been initiated against him but there is no indication here as to whether or not either side to the controversy regarded this as being of any significance. [3]

Haiti, 1875. On May 2, 1875, General Boisrand Canal, accused by the Haitian government of conspiracy, was by decree placed beyond the pale of the law. The following morning he and some of his associates were granted asylum in the residence of the United States minister. [4] The Haitian government insisted that he could not be regarded as a political refugee.

> ...It is impossible for it to admit with you that General Boisrand Canal should be considered as a political refugee ... a general officer legally summoned to deliver himself up to the call of superior authority. He failed in all the duties that honor and military subordination commended to him, in order to give himself over voluntarily and without cause (sans raison) to criminal acts which laws reprobate ...
>
> This is why it still insists [calls?] upon you for the delivery of those who find themselves under your protection ... [5]

Two of the refugees were permitted to leave but this raised no

---

[1] *Ibid.*

[2] *Ibid.*

[3] *Ibid.*

[4] Bassett, U. S. Minister to Haiti, to Fish, Secretary of State, May 8, 1875, *For. Rel. of the U. S.*, 1875, II, pp. 686–693.

[5] Excellent, Haitian Secretary of State for Foreign Affairs, to Bassett, July 8, 1875 (inclosure in Bassett to Fish, July 22, 1875), *ibid.*, p. 720.

problems inasmuch as decrees of banishment from the country had been issued against them before they were granted asylum.[1] The controversy over General Canal and his brother continued more than five months. On August 26, the Haitian minister to Washington informed the Department of State that an arrangement could be made whereby the President would grant a pardon to the refugees. But this proposal seemed to make a distinction between a *pardon* which would remove the pronouncement of guilt and an *amnesty* which would merely mean that punishment would not be inflicted.[2] The United States Undersecretary of State had previously objected to the idea of a pardon, asserting that the only condition under which a surrender would be authorized was "that the Haytian government should stipulate not to punish the refugees if after trial they should be convicted of any offense, but should, of its own accord, allow them to leave the country, and should furnish them with passports for that purpose." In his opinion, "this condition did not imply any necessity for the exercise of the right of pardon." [3] The Haitian minister said that he was "unable to see how the Honorable Mr. Cadwalader explains that it is possible for the President to put individuals at liberty, or to put them in a position to leave Haytian territory without exercising his pardoning power." [4] He then quoted article 125 of the Haitian Constitution as the only article "which can even allow the President to act in a circumstance similar to the one which occupies us, namely, that which gives him the right of pardon." [5]

The President of Hayti has the right to pardon and that of commuting punishment; the exercise of this right will be regulated by law. He can also exercise the privilege of granting amnesty only for political delinquencies.[6]

Thus, since the constitution permitted the president to exercise his power of amnesty only in the case of *political delinquencies*, and since he did not regard this as a political offence, a pardon rather than an amnesty would be necessary.

The United States Department of State objected for this very reason, asserting that "the proposition as stated ... would, it is conceived, involve not only an abandonment of the question of asylum,

---

[1] Bassett to Fish, May 19, 1875 and Bassett to Fish, May 8, 1875, *ibid.*, pp. 686–699.
[2] Preston to Cadwalader, Acting Secretary of State, August 26, 1875, *ibid.*, pp. 742–744.
[3] Cadwalader to Preston, August 17, 1875, *ibid.*, p. 741.
[4] Preston to Cadwalader, August 26, 1875, *ibid.*, p. 744.
[5] *Ibid.*
[6] *Ibid.*

but practically an assent to its violation." [1] This objection is difficult to understand in view of the Department's earlier note to its minister asserting that "such a practice [asylum] has no basis in public law, and, so far as this Government is concerned, is believed to be contrary to all sound policy." The Department also told him that in answer to the Haitian minister's request for the surrender of refugees in the legation the Department answered that "though it might have been preferable that you should not have received those persons, it is not deemed expedient to comply with his request." [2]

By the end of September the Haitian minister in Washington was willing to concede that the refugees were "political." An agreement signed September 27 with the United States Acting Secretary of State provided that "certain political refugees who, for some time past, have had an asylum in the residence of Mr .Bassett . . . shall receive from the Haitian government a full amnesty for all offences up to the time of their departure from the island." [3] It is impossible to tell, however, whether or not it was on the basis of a willingness to regard the offence as political that the grant of safe conduct was finally made. Previous to this the United States had sent a very thinly veiled threat of the possibility of a use of force should the controversy not be settled satisfactorily. It notified the minister to Haiti as follows.

This Department is informed by that of the Navy that pursuant to our request for a man-of war at Port au Prince the United States Steamer Powhatan, Captain James E. Jouett, which is the bearer of this communication, will proceed thither. We have no further despatches from you. It is hoped, however, that before the arrival of the Powhatan the question of the refugees will be satisfactorily settled. We are aware of no sufficient reason for the Haitian government to take offense at the visit of that vessel or to suppose that it has been occasioned by any hostile purpose or by any intention unduly to influence its decision upon that delicate subject.[4]

It does not appear that the agreement referred to above was known to the Haitian government when it finally permitted the refugees to leave the country. The day after the agreement was signed in Washington, the United States minister to Haiti informed that government of the intention of the Department in Washington to send a man-of-war as indicated above and of its hope that the controversy might be

---

[1] Cadwalader to Preston, August 17, 1875, *ibid.*, p. 742.
[2] Fish to Bassett, June 4, 1875, *ibid.*, p. 701.
[3] "Memorandum of Agreement," September 27, 1875, *ibid.*, p. 748.
[4] Fish to Bassett, September 21, 1875, *ibid.*, p. 729.

settled before this happened. Apparently the Haitian government had no desire to wait for this to occur.

> The Minister seemed cordially to accept my arguments and views. And I was afterwards authentically informed that he dispatched a courier the same evening to His Excellency President Domingue, who was then at Miragone ... His Excellency thereafter immediately returned to the capital without fulfilling his contemplated visits in the south.[1]

On October 2, the United States minister had an interview with the President in which the former repeated his "friendly arguments in favor of the immediate termination of the embarrassing case of the Messieurs Canal." To this the President replied: "Well, you are probably right. I will see what I can do. I will call together my cabinet at once." Later that evening the United States minister was informed that the government had "decided to embark Boisrand Canal and his brother." [2]

Did the Government of Haiti agree to permit the departure of the refugees in this case because it eventually concurred in the opinion that this was a political offence? Or did it do so out of a feeling of legal obligation to accept the qualification of the offence by the United States? The facts as discussed above would seem to indicate that neither played a very important part in the decision. The vague and contradictory position of the United States and the apparent desire on the part of the Haitian government to settle the matter in the face of the United States threats indicate that considerations of legality played a minor role at best. It would indeed be difficult to maintain that Haiti recognized a legal obligation to meet the demands of the United States when the latter had not clearly asserted that its demands could be legally justified or, at best, had taken two different positions in this regard. This is clearly indicated in a note dated near the end of the controversy which clearly shows that the United States was only interested in getting out of a difficult position *and that it did not even give much consideration to the nature of the charges or the circumstances surrounding the grant of asylum.* What is more, it clearly abandoned its former objection to a pardon rather than an amnesty.

> Still the impression here is strong that in receiving Mr. Boisrand Canal, you allowed your partialities for that individual, as well as your general feelings of humanity, to overcome that discretion which, pursuant to the instruction to you, ... you were expected to exercise ... The Department will not take into

---

[1] Bassett to Fish, October 12, 1875, *ibid.*, p. 734.
[2] *Ibid.*

consideration the antecedents of Mr. Boisrand Canal. It is also bound to disregard the complaints of the existing Haytian administration against him, or
the reason therefor. If, however, as is understood to be the case, that person
had actually been tried and sentenced for conspiracy before he sought refuge in
your abode, he must have gone thither to escape punishment and arrest . . .
These circumstances certainly present a case in which it would be unreasonable
to expect the government to acquiesce in the privilege of sanctuary granted by
you to Boisrand Canal. Consequently that step on your part cannot be approved.
*Still there is no disposition to change the conditions upon which you have been
authorized to surrender the refugees*, except so far as this may be made necessary
by the fact that Boisrand Canal had actually been tried and sentenced before he
sought asylum . . .
   It is presumed that the embarkation might take place by the convenience
of the government without any change in the sentence, *or that, if necessary, the
sentence might be repealed or so modified that the embarkation might be carried into
effect* . . . [1]

The Department's assertion that a sentence prior to the granting of
asylum should alter the course of its minister in Haiti, was greatly
qualified two weeks later in a note to the Haitian minister in Washington. Referring to the decree which had placed the general "beyond
the pale of the law" because he had "answered the legal requisition
which has been made of him by the government, by recourse to arms,"
and to the Haitian assertion that this had been issued *before* he had
taken asylum, the note said:

   The decree averted to may, as Mr. Preston says, have been issued pursuant
to the constitution of Hayti. It can scarcely, however, be regarded as the result
of any other than a military trial; and this in the absence of the accused, if,
indeed, any trial, even of that character, took place. [2]

Colombia, 1885. In 1885, during a Civil War in Colombia, the
Argentine minister granted asylum to Señor Uribe, a wealthy Colombian citizen who refused to pay a war contribution which had been
levied by the Colombian government upon certain citizens. [3] Apparently the diplomatic corps regarded this as improper and dangerous to the future immunity of the diplomatic missions. The American
minister to Colombia reported that, following a circular in which the
Colombian government implied that it might even enter an embassy
or legation if necessary under such circumstances, the diplomatic
corps tried to induce the Argentine minister to surrender the refugee. [4]

[1] Hunter, Acting Secretary of State, to Bassett, August 26, 1875, *ibid.*, p. 727. (My
italics.)
   [2] Hunter, to Preston, September 10, 1875, *ibid.*, p. 746.
   [3] Scruggs, U. S. Minister to Colombia, to Frelinghuysen, Secretary of State, February 23,
1885, *For. Rel. of the U. S.*, 1885, p. 205.
   [4] *Ibid.*

Chile, 1891. The events leading up to the revolution of 1891 entered into the long United States-Chilean dispute over the granting of asylum to President Balmaceda. The points in question in this case will necessitate a brief reference to these events.

A heated controversy had existed between the President and the Congress as to the former's powers. As a consequence of this controversy, the Congress closed its session without approving the appropriation bill for 1891. Rather than convening Congress in extraordinary session, President Balmaceda issued a decree declaring that the previous year's appropriation bill would be in force for the next year. In the words of the Chilean historian, Galdámes, "The Constitutional conflict came to an end. The President concluded by violating the constitution and assuming actual dictatorship." [1] Congress answered with revolution and published an act by a majority of its members deposing President Balmaceda for having violated the constitution. On August 30, Balmaceda abdicated and in the last days of the revolution a large number of persons "both Government supporters and oppositionists" came into the United States Legation "fearing an outbreak of city mobs." [2]

Of about 80 persons who sought shelter in the legation, all but about 15 had left by the end of September.[3] It appears from the minister's notes, however, that those who left did so on a purely informal basis. "No one has been granted a safe conduct to leave the country," he said on October 8.[4] About a week later, he summarized the events as follows.

> When the first excitement settled down, many of those persons went out of the legations, some who had but slight responsibility giving bonds to appear before the tribunals when required and others seeking concealment in the house of the supporters of the successful party. In this legation there remain now fourteen, one having gone out since the date of my latest telegram, five in the Spanish legation and one in the German legation.[5]

The Chilean government at no time objected to the granting of asylum but it appears that it had in mind only temporary or provisional protection. While it did not demand the surrender of the refugees, it seemed to imply that they would remain in the legation until the minister was ready to surrender them.

[1] *Op. cit.*, p. 346.
[2] Egan, U. S. Minister to Chile, to Blaine, Secretary of State, August 24, 1891, *For. Rel. of the U. S.*, 1891, pp. 153–154.
[3] Egan to Blaine, September 29, 1891, *ibid.*, p. 168.
[4] Egan to Blaine, October 8, 1891, *ibid.*, p. 184.
[5] Egan to Blaine, October 17, 1891, *ibid.*, p. 186.

It is those who took upon themselves the responsibility who should know what steps are necessary to adopt, and not the undersigned who should under—take to point out the way or the means by which they or the refugees can succeed in getting out of the difficult position in which they are placed ...

As the undersigned has not considered, for reasons which it is not necessary to explain, but which his excellency the minister plenipotentiary can well under-stand, that it was his duty to ask for the extradition of the refugees in the legation, he believes also that his Government has no obligation to grant, and certainly is by no means willing to grant, a safe conduct to these persons, to whom the legation can generously give a place of refuge, but to whom it cannot give the right or privilege to conspire against the laws, the authorities or the interests of Chile.[1]

But the government did not explain whether it was because of the particular nature of the offences that it was unwilling to grant a safe conduct or whether it was not obliged to grant a safe conduct re-gardless of the nature of the offence. In any event, it would be safe to say that Chile did not feel obliged to recognize anything more than provisional refuge for persons accused of the offences involved here – whatever it might have been willing to do in other cases. The nature of the offences was described in a decree of the Governmental Junta (promulgated after asylum had been granted).

Whereas public justice requires that all persons who have taken part in the acts of the Dictator Balmaceda since the 1st day of January last be immediately held responsible, not only that the injury done to the country may be repaired, but also that the offenders may be punished;

Whereas among those persons are Don José Balmaceda ex-President of the Republic, ministers and counselors of state, the members of the bodies which styled themselves the National Congress; ...

Whereas the action that may be taken by the judicial authorities is no bar to the exercise of the power which the constitution grants to Congress to indict and try the officers designated by the constitution;

The Governmental Junta decrees;

Art. 1. The public prosecutors of Santiago shall, with as little delay as possible institute such action as is sanctioned by law against the persons above mention-ed.[2]

Thus, the United States minister explained that the government would prosecute criminally "all of the ministers, senators, deputies, judges, municipal authorities, and all other civil officers, and all of the army officers of the late Government from the grade of Captain up-ward." This was to be done "on the grounds that since 1st January last they had been acting in violation of the constitution of the

---

[1] Matta, Chilean Minister of Foreign Relations, to Egan, September 29, 1891, trans. (inclosure in Egan to Blaine, October 6, 1891), *ibid.*, p. 181.

[2] "Decree of the Governmental Junta of September 14, 1891" (inclosure in Egan to Blaine, October 17, 1891), *ibid.*, pp. 193-194.

country." [1] Other refugees in the legation were charged with treason and with "having made arrangements to blow up with dynamite some of the ships of the Government." [2]

On October 26, the Minister of Foreign Relations informed the United States minister that he considered the discussion closed and that any further discussion would be useless.[3] Here the matter rested until January 12 of the next year when assurances were given that the refugees could depart in safety. It is clear, however, that the Chilean government wanted to avoid an implication of legal obligation in its action. The Minister of Foreign Relations refused to give any more than a verbal promise for their safety [4]; while unable to give "formal safe-conducts," he was willing to give "the strongest personal assurance that the refugees could go out of the country, whenever they pleased, without molestation or inconvenience." [5] When it became known that the American, Italian and Spanish ministers had accompanied the refugees on board ship, the Chilean Minister of Foreign Relations expressed "considerable annoyance." In an interview with the American minister he pointed out "that he had given no official permission, and in fact, no permission to the refugees to go out; but had acted with *vista gorda*, or with closed eyes ..." [6]

It appears from this case, then, that the government of Chile regarded itself as legally bound to respect no more than provisional asylum for former office holders accused of governing unconstitutionally.

Haiti, 1899. In the Duvivier case in Haiti, 1899, a number of refugees were protected in the United States legation in *Port-au-Prince* in consequence of numerous uprisings by revolutionary elements and harsh reprisals by the government. Among the refugees was one named Duvivier who was forceably removed from the legation but later returned by the government.[7] According to the American minister, the principal crime imputed to Duvivier was the writing of an article

[1] Egan to Blaine, September 29, 1891, *ibid.*, p. 170.

[2] *Ibid.*

[3] Egan to Blaine, October 26, 1891, tel., *ibid.*, p. 197.

[4] Egan to Blaine, January 12, 1892, *ibid.*, p. 285.

[5] "Memorandum of Interview between Mr. Egan and Señor Pereira," January 15, 1892 (inclosure in Egan to Blaine, January 19, 1892), *ibid.*, pp. 305–306.

[6] *Ibid.*

[7] Powell. U. S. Minister to Haiti, to Hay, Secretary of State, August 2, 1899, *For. Rel. of the U. S.*, 1899, p. 378.

in one of the papers in which he was severely critical of certain military officers of the Government.[1]

While the Department of State instructed its minister that the refugee could not be protected against regular Haitian justice, it reserved for itself the right to decide if proceedings were regular and if he was truly demanded as a common criminal or if he was in fact a political refugee.

> ... Upon sufficient allegation of the criminality of the refugee, and upon adequate showing of the regularity of the judicial proceedings against him, the right of the envoy to harbor him disappears, and ... the evidence of criminality and of the regularity of the legal process against the accused should be made known to the envoy through the diplomatic channel and not by the invasion of his domicile by attempted arrests therein.
>
> Should a demand be diplomatically made upon you for the person of Duvivier, or any other person similarly situated, you will report it to the Department, with the evidence of criminality and the regularity of the proceedings, in order that the matter may be determined with full knowledge of all pertinent facts.[2]

The conclusion of the case tells little concerning Haiti's views. A decree ordered the *expulsion* of all refugees from the country. The United States Secretary of State noted that in the past American ministers had exceeded their legitimate rights and had asked permission in order that the refugees leave the country. In this instance, he noted, "the Haitian Government seems to have anticipated some such demand on part of the foreign representatives, and to have either ordered or permitted – it is not clear which – the departure of the refugees.[3]

Haiti, 1908. Revolutionaries who took refuge in the French consulate in Haiti in 1908 were clearly regarded as common criminals by the Haitian government. Even in the note which indicated that the government would permit them to leave the country the view was again reiterated that they were nothing more than this.[4] While there is no way of knowing whether or not the published notes on this case constitute all of those exchanged, in none of the notes did the Haitian government indicate why it regarded the refugees as common criminals. No specific charges were made and no attempt was made to show that refugees of this sort had been generally regarded as such. Likewise,

---

[1] Powell to Hay ,August 14, 1899, *ibid.*, p. 388.

[2] Adee, Acting Secretary of State, to Powell, U. S. Minister to Haiti, August 3, 1899, *For. Rel. of the U. S.*, 1899, p. 381.

[3] Hay to Powell, September 2, 1899, *ibid.*, p. 390.

[4] Haitian Minister of Foreign Relations, to the French Minister to Haiti, March 17, 1908, Raoul Rouzier, *Le droit d'asile en Haiti* (Port-au-Prince: "La Nation," 1943), p. 15.

the French notes did not indicate the criteria by which it had qualified them as "political." [1]

Paraguay, 1911. In 1911, a number of Paraguayan citizens who had been involved in an unsuccessful revolution in that country were given refuge on board the Argentine gunboat *Paraná.* Throughout the exchange of notes both governments treated the case as though it were a matter of diplomatic asylum. The Paraguayan government at no time raised any objections on the grounds that asylum had been given on board a warship rather than in a legation or embassy. Upon receiving notice of the grant of asylum from the Argentine Minister, the Paraguayan Minister of Foreign Relations asserted that "neither legations nor warships may give asylum to citizens such as the refugees on the gunboat *Paraná,* without detracting from their object and nature." [2]

The Argentine government likewise treated the case as though the legation had granted the asylum.

This legation, or what is the same, warships anchored in territorial waters, has accorded asylum to Paraguayan citizens without considering them guilty by reason of their political opinions, conforming in all proceedings to those established by the treaty of Montevideo. [3]

The case followed the usual pattern with the Argentine government declaring that they were political offenders while the Paraguayan government insisted that they were not.

I fulfill the duty of informing you that none of the persons sheltered on the gunboat *Paraná* are pursued for political reasons [perseguidos políticos].

Most of them are citizens who are trying to evade military service and are devoted to armed subversion ...

The right of asylum, inspired by high sentiments of humanity, has no more scope and purpose than to safeguard the life of those pursued for political reasons, but it can never serve as a means of fomenting sedition, of gathering together elements in order to support disturbance of the public peace; proceedings at variance with the very purpose of the diplomatic missions ...[4]

The Argentine government invoked the Treaty on International Penal Law signed at Montevideo in 1889, which both governments had signed and ratified.[5] This treaty merely recognized the right of asylum

---

[1] See various notes and author's comments, *ibid.,* pp. 1–15.

[2] Irala, Paraguayan Minister of Foreign Relations, to Martínez Campos, Argentine Minister to Paraguay, December 19, 1911, Argentine Republic, *Memoria,* 1911–1912, pp. 87–88. (My translation.)

[3] Martínez Campos to Irala, December 10, 1911, *ibid.,* p. 88. (My translation.)

[4] Irala to Martínez Campos, December 19, 1911, *ibid.,* pp. 87–88. (My translation.)

[5] Congreso Sudamericano, 2d Montevideo, Antecedentes, p. 5.

for political offenders without further defining "political offences." [1]
The Paraguayan government asserted "that neither precedents nor
the principles of international law, nor the Treaty on Penal Law of
Montevideo justifies and authorizes asylum in the conditions under
which the refugees are on board the gunboat *Paraná*." [2]

The term "political offenders" did not include deserters from the
armed forces.

> I have the honor of informing Your Excellency that on board the ships *Holanda*
> and *Lambara*, under Argentine flag, many deserters with arms have been shelter-
> ed.
> One of these ships, according to information that the Government has, came to
> rest along side one of the Argentine warships.
> Therefore, since the Government does not wish to exercise any violent act
> against a ship with Argentine flag, this Chancellery asks Your Excellency for
> the disarming and surrender of the deserters and the arms of the Government.[3]

The commander of the Argentine ship clearly admitted that some
of the refugees had belonged to the Paraguayan army. In a note to
the Argentine legation he stated:

> ... I can guarantee personally that by the politeness of manners and by
> the education revealed, many, most of the refugees, show that they belong to
> the cultured classes of Paraguay, the rest being artisans and common people
> who had fought for their political ideals. And although undoubtedly there may
> have been officials of the Paraguayan army, I ought to call attention to the
> erroneous application of the word *deserter*, which is used in the notes whose
> affirmations I am refuting.[4]

Nevertheless, the Argentine minister informed the Paraguayan government that "tomorrow they will leave this port, duly guarded, in order
to be interned in Argentine territory." [5] This was precisely what
happened and the government of Paraguay was faced with a *fait
accompli*. Nevertheless, the strong protest which followed two days
later made it clear that at no time had the latter accepted Argentina's
qualification of the nature of the offence as "political." Referring to
article 17 of the Treaty of Montevideo, it asserted,

> That the chief of the legation is obliged to submit the list of refugees so that
> it can be determined if they are pursued for political reasons [perseguidos
> políticos], deserters from the army or navy or common delinquents, since only
> those of the first category can take advantage of the right of asylum.

[1] Martens, *op. cit.*, XVIII (2me série par Stoerb, 1893), p. 432.
[2] Irala to Martínez Campos, December 22, 1911, *ibid.*, p. 90. (My translation.)
[3] Irala to Martínez Campos, January 17, 1912, *ibid.*, p. 94. (My translation.)
[4] January 22, 1912, *ibid.*, pp. 101–110. (My translation.)
[5] Martínez Campos to Irala, January 17, 1912, *ibid.*, pp. 94–95. (My translation.)

In the present case the Argentine ships have conceded refuge and asylum to more than two hundred citizens and embarking for a destination unknown by my government, without the previous remittance of the names of same, in this way making impossible all verification of the identity of the persons ...

Permit me to ask Your Excellency, how has Rear Admiral O'Connor proceeded to identify the persons who asked for asylum? Are rebels from the Corps of Prison Guards, Artillery Regiments and Civil Guards, who with arms and uniforms of the national army have taken refuge on board Argentine ships, citizens without military character?

Besides, my government has reliable information that among those transported on board the *Lambare* are common criminals who have escaped from the public prison, taking advantage of the confusion of the first moments.

In the presence of so grave an incident, this chancellery formulates the most energetic and formal protest against the proceeding adopted, which conflicts with international precedents and practice and is contrary to the spirit and letter of the treaty of Montevideo.[1]

In this case no charges had been instituted against the refugees prior to the grant of asylum.[2]

Peru, 1930. Following the overthrow of the Leguía government in Peru in 1930, former officials and supporters of the deposed regime took refuge in a number of the embassies and legations in Lima. One such refugee was Dr. Alberto Salomon, ex-government minister who was granted asylum in the Bolivian legation. An extract from the notes exchanged, published by the Bolivian foreign office, shows that the Bolivian minister had done so "in compliance with Article 17, paragraph 2, of the Treaty of International Penal Law, signed in Montevideo November 23, 1889." [3] The part of the treaty referred to merely provides that asylum will be respected for political refugees.

In response to this, Peru asserted that "Dr. Salomon, not being pursued for political reasons but for common crimes of embezzlement and misuse of fiscal funds, his status [condición] was that foreseen in the first part of the mentioned article 17, that is to say, that which corresponds to one accused of common crimes." [4]

[1] Irala to Martínez Campos, January 19, 1912, *ibid.*, pp. 98–99. (My translation.)

[2] Irala to Martínez Campos, December 22, 1911, *ibid.*, pp. 90–92. In 1954 a Nicaraguan military officer was granted asylum in the Guatemalan embassy in Managua. The Nicaraguan government insisted that military personnel who desert their posts cannot be considered "political" refugees. The Guatemalan government insisted that the officer had left his post because of his politican activities and could not for this reason be considered a deserter. When the two governments broke diplomatic relations (it is not known if the controversy over asylum was responsible for the break) the refugees were transferred to the embassy of El Salvador. See notes published in *Diario de Centro-America*, 24 de mayo de 1954, pp. 1,7. See also *ibid.*, 25 de mayo de 1954, p. 1; *La Noticia*, 3 de junio de 1954, pp. 1, 6. Both countries had ratified the Montevideo Convention of 1933 but the Nicaraguan position, though not clearly stated, seemed to be that the right to qualify the offence would not apply in the case of military deserters.

[3] Bolivia, *Boletín* (abril-diciembre, 1930), p. 38.

[4] *Ibid.*

Spain, 1936–40. The question as to what constitutes an offence for which asylum may be granted was not explicitly discussed during the earlier part of the controversy arising out of the Spanish Civil War. In the first place Spain was unable to provide specific charges against particular individuals. The following is typical of the charges provided:

> ...Those who have sought protection in the localities of the embassies and legations have not done it so much to protect themselves from the possible and natural risks which citizens always face in movements like these in which the people struggle against the rebellious army ... but in order, upon protection of the exterritoriality of the diplomatic buildings, to elude the laws, to evade the authorities and to cooperate from a safe refuge with the fascist movement and to incorporate themselves in it as quickly as it may be possible for the embassy or legation which protected them to obtain their exit from the country.[1]

It can easily be understood, however, why Spain was unable to make more specific charges. Spain simply did not know precisely who the refugees were inasmuch as the Chilean ambassador, as spokesman for (and apparently with the concurrence of) the diplomatic corps, refused to provide the names of the refugees. It actually refused to discuss the nature of the Spanish charges by merely stating that the refugees were not guilty. "The persons enjoying refuge in the foreign establishment are principally women and children, and other persons having no connection with the government ... and there is no obligation on the part of the diplomatic corps to submit their names to the government." [2]

But even this was an admission that at least *some* of the refugees fell within the scope of the Spanish charges. And in at least one category the Spanish demands were quite precise. It insisted that military personnel and persons of military age who were evading their duties or expecting later to cooperate with the enemy were not to be permitted to leave. Thus the Spanish Minister of State pointed out that "it is natural that the government of the Republic put definite and fixed conditions on the exit of the refugees and thus refused the authorization for all military [personnel] regardless of their status [situación]." [3] The offer was again repeated in unambiguous terms:

---

[1] Giral for the Spanish Ministry of State, to Lynch, Chilean *Chargé d'Affaires* in Spain, July 7, 1937, Chile, *Memoria*, 1937, pp. 265–266. (My translation.)
[2] Núñez Morgado, Chilean Ambassador to Spain, to del Vayo, Spanish Minister of State, October 19, 1936, Helfant, *op. cit.*, p. 194.
[3] Giral to Lynch, July 7, 1937, Chile, *Memoria*, 1937, pp. 265–266. (My translation.)

... And not wishing to continue this controversy ... I have the honor of repeating to you that the evacuation of persons who are not males between the ages of 18 and 45 years and soldiers or marines by profession, whatever may be their status in the army or the marine, will find the maximum facilities, without renouncing for the government of the Republic the right to impede the exit from national territory of those persons, whatever their age or sex, whose exit from Spain it may judge contrary to law.[1]

That there were persons of military age and military personnel under the protection of the Chilean flag is beyond doubt. The Chilean *Memoria* for 1937 gave the following tabulation of refugees as of September of that year:

> 612 women and children
> 31 men over 45 years – non military
> 620 men of military age and military personnel. [2]

This was further indicated by the fact that Chile at one point agreed to sanction an exchange of loyal Spanish subjects found in territory controlled by revolutionaries for "a number equal to that of the refugees of military age who may be evacuated." [3] By the end of the year nearly all the women and children had been evacuated leaving only the males in question. Chile continued to press for their evacuation until the fall of the Republican Government.[4]

While the government of Chile nowhere stated explicitly that members of the armed forces who apparently refused to discharge their duties could be granted asylum, this is in fact what that government insisted upon doing. The same may be said of men of military age whom the government feared would leave the country only to cooperate with the enemy.[5] It cannot be said that Chile took the position that the nature of the charges against an individual were of no importance inasmuch as it insisted instead that these individuals were not guilty of such charges. This matter will be further pursued in the following chapter in connection with the question as to the party possessing the right of qualification. There is considerable evidence, however, that little consideration was given to the matter of what type of individual was granted asylum. The Proceedings of the Diplomatic Corps in Madrid, October 28, 1936, show that "the ambassador from Chile spoke to say that he had persons in his embassy

---

[1] *Ibid.*
[2] Chile, *Memoria*, 1937, p. 268. (My translation.)
[3] Lynch to Giral, July 3, 1937, *ibid.*, pp. 263–265. (My translation.)
[4] Chile, *Memoria*, 1938, pp. 263–265, 436.
[5] Giral to Lynch, July 7, 1937, Chile, *Memoria*, 1937, pp. 265–266.

whom he considered undesirable." [1] The Proceedings of the same corps held on May 8, 1937 reveal the existence of widespread conspiracies among the refugees in several of the legations.[2] A flagrant case of abuse involved the legation of Finland. Bombs were thrown from windows and when the Spanish authorities attemped a search of the premises they were greeted with heavy rifle fire. The authorities, according to the Spanish government, "found 525 Spanish subjects, many affiliated with the Spanish Falange." In addition there were "active and retired soldiers and some discharged police personnel" as well as rifles, pistols, machine guns, and bombs.[3]

Bolivia, 1946. In July 1946, a successful uprising overthrew the Villaroel government in Bolivia and a large number of officials and supporters of the deposed regime took refuge in many of the legations in La Paz. The diplomatic corps met in the residence of the Venezuelan ambassador and unanimously agreed to empower him to present a list of refugees in the various legations and "to solicit for all of them, without exception, the respective safe conduct in order that, in conformity with the international conventions signed by Bolovia, the principles of international law and of Customary Latin American Law, they may leave the country with due security and protection." [4] In a memorandum to the diplomatic corps, the Minister of Foreign Relations affirmed Bolivia's "loyal adherence to the principles consecrated by the right of asylum" but he did not feel that the present case was covered by these principles. He asserted that "according to the spirit and the letter of the international agreements in force and the practice of Latin American Customary Law, ... the right of asylum, not being unlimited, does not protect individuals notoriously stamped as authors, accomplices and concealers of common crimes, whose sanction is known in advance by the penal legislation of all civilized countries." [5] It is clear from what follows that these were "common crimes" growing out of their conduct in public office.

Against many of them the regular Bolivian tribunals of justice are bringing proceedings based upon the perpetration of nefarious common crimes which demand the sanctions determined by the private laws of the country; crimes which amount to serious transgressions against constitutional guarantees per-

---

[1] Helfant, *op. cit.*, p. 199.

[2] *Ibid.*, p. 219.

[3] Del Vayo to the Ambassador from Chile, December 6, 1936, tel., *ibid.*, p. 223.

[4] Memorandum of the Diplomatic Corps, July 30, 1946, Chile, *Memoria*, 1946, p. 51. (My translation.)

[5] *Ibid.*, pp. 52–54.

sistently violated by agents of the deposed regime. These delinquencies embody today in free America a new crime not foreseen by the old agreements on penal law but which the post-war juridical instruments now consider the crime of perverted civilization which is called Nazism and of which the Villaroel government was an authentic satellite . . .[1]

More specifically, charges included assassination, homicide, multiple assassination, torture, and falsification of death certificates.[2]

The diplomatic corps gave scant attention to the question as to whether or not these were political crimes. It was asserted instead that even where criminal charges exist, so long as these charges were instituted *after* asylum was granted, the refugee can be surrendered only after he has left the country and then according to the rules of extradition.[3] This argument was ignored by the Bolivian government, stating that it would "comply with the conventional obligation of conceding safe conduct to the refugees of a purely political character, but reserves the right of not granting it to those comprehended within the penal sanctions applicable to the perpetration of common crimes." [4] Nowhere in the published exchanges was the diplomatic corps willing to declare that it regarded all the refugees as political.

Safe conduct out of the country was finally granted but it appears that this was done out of a willingness to recognize a right of unilateral qualification of the offence by the state of refuge rather than out of any change in Bolivia's qualification of the offence. This aspect of the case will be discussed in the next chapter but it may be observed here that the Bolivian press release following the close of the case (after all refugees had left the country) stated that extradition proceedings would be instituted.[5] This indicates that they were still regarded as guilty of common crimes so far as Bolivia was concerned.

Since communications in this case were addressed in the name of the diplomatic corps, a word should be said concerning its composition at

---

[1] *Ibid.*

[2] Memorandum of the Bolivian Minister of Foreign Relations and Worship, August 9, 1946, *ibid.*, pp. 56–57. (My translation.)

[3] "The circumstances under which, after the grant of asylum, criminal proceedings are initiated against some of the refugees, cannot invalidate the plenitude of the right of asylum which protects those pursued for political reasons. In accord with all the precepts, including those defended by Bolivia in identical cases, the refugee against whom criminal justice is instituted, can only be made the object of extradition once he abandons the country . . ." Memorandum of the Diplomatic Corps, August 19, 1946, Bolivia, *Boletín*, (julio-diciembre, 1946), p. 51. (My translation.)

[4] Memorandum of the Bolivian Minister of Foreign Relations and Worship, August 4, 1946, Chile, *Memoria*, 1946, p. 54. (My translation.)

[5] "Declaration which the Undersecretary of Foreign Relations, Doctor Julio Alvarado, gave to the Press," November 2, 1946, Bolivia, *Boletín* (julio-diciembre, 1946), p. 98.

this time. No indication is given as to the members present at the meeting empowering the Venezuelan ambassador, as dean of the corps, to solicit the necessary guarantees. It is very likely, however, that the legations in which there were refugees approved the position taken here and in the subsequent communications in the name of the diplomatic corps. Refugees were sheltered in the legations of Venezuela, Paraguay, Peru, Argentina, Ecuador, Mexico, and the Holy See.[1]

In the case of at least one state, Venezuela, there can be no doubt that the charges were qualified as "political." Referring to the case in its report to the national congress, the Ministry of Foreign Relations noted that

> The embassy of Venezuela sheltered various persons pursued for political reasons [perseguidos políticos], who remained in the embassy until the safe-conduct necessary for leaving the country was issued to them.
> The exit of all the refugees from Bolivian territory was authorized after active measures by the diplomatic corps resident in La Paz, in which there was detached action on the part of Lieutenant Colonel Estaban Chalbaud Cardona, in his role of Ambassador from Venezuela and Dean of that Corps.[2]

Two Recent Cases. The *Colombian-Peruvian Asylum Case* and a case involving the Chilean embassy in Bogotá in 1952 provide a fitting close to this discussion. The first case shows the lack of any adequate body of precedents which could be used to establish the nature of a "political" offence. The whole Colombian thesis clearly *implied* that Haya de la Torre was a political refugee since it was agreed that asylum could only be granted to refugees of this class. First there seems to be an admission that the nature of a political offence is by no means well-established.

> Whatever opinion one may have concerning the elements which constitute a political offence, international jurisprudence admits the rule which accords the right to determine the nature of the offence to the state granting asylum . . .

Yet Colombia was reluctant to state *why* it had considered Haya de la Torre a political refugee. This is suggested in one of the notes exchanged before the case was presented to the Court.

> Passing now to the series of charges which in the note of Your Excellency are formulated against the American Popular Revolutionary Alliance for its political activities as well as against certain members of that party, I must limit myself to observing that the government of Colombia cannot analyze those

---

[1] Memorandum of the Diplomatic Corps, August 19, 1946, *ibid.*, p. 51.
[2] Venezuela, *Libro Amarillo*, 1947, pp. v–vi. (My translation.)
[3] Perú, *Proceso*, p. 113. (My translation.)

charges nor enter a discussion on this matter without interfering in the internal politics of Peru. But this same consideration, obvious for the rest, shows that the long historical-political exposition which the note of the Peruvian foreign office contains concerning the activities of APRA can only show that the case of Doctor Haya de la Torre, recognized leader of this party, is a typical case of political asylum.[1]

This same position was taken in the proceedings before the Court. No attempt was made to cite cases where similar circumstances might have set a precedent for holding that the offences charged here were "political." [2]

Peru insisted that crimes of terrorism, such as those charged against Haya de la Torre, were nothing more than common crimes even though they were connected with military rebellion and with political motives. But, again, no attempt was made to cite cases from diplomatic practice in order to show that a body of precedents were sufficiently similar in details to establish that such offences were customarily considered as "common" rather than "political" crimes.[3]

This point was of course not labored inasmuch as the Court was not asked to decide what was a political offence but, rather, which of the parties was competent to decide the question. In view of the cases discussed in this chapter one might well suspect that the latter question was submitted rather than the former simply because of the realization that precedents would offer nothing conclusive regarding the definition of a political offence.

The second and final case demonstrates most clearly the tendency to settle cases of asylum without regard to precise legal norms. In 1952 the Chilean embassy in Bogotá had granted asylum to a Colombian guerrilla who, according to the Colombian government, was guilty of, among other acts, "association to commit homicide in the form of assassination, robbery and incendiary activities." [4] It should be recalled that Chile and Colombia had both ratified the Montevideo Convention of 1933 and thus Colombia admitted that it would be up to Chile to qualify the nature of the offence. The Chilean attitude is best indicated by paraphrasing the published communique of its foreign office.

---

[1] Echeverri Cortés, Colombian Ambassador to Peru, to Díaz Dulanto, Peruvian Minister of Foreign Relations and Worship, March 4, 1949, Perú, *Proceso*, p. 18. (My translation.)

[2] Perú, *Proceso*, p. 120.

[3] *Ibid.*, pp. 191–192.

[4] Colombia, Ministerio de Relaciones Exteriores, *Noticias de Colombia*, 18 de abril de 1952, p. 2. (My translation.)

The Chilean ambassador had informed the foreign office that the refugee had been condemned *in absentia* by a council of war but had not shown any evidence that in Colombia there might have been a situation of fact that indicated the disappearance of individual guarantees. Traditional Chilean practice had held that four elements should be present in order to justify asylum: (1) urgency, (2) abnormal and violent situation, (3) manifest threat against the person and (4) gravity and imminence of the threat of danger. The Convention of Montevideo established that it is not lawful to grant asylum to those guilty of common crimes, condemned by ordinary tribunals. Even if it was clear that in the interior of Colombia there had been some acts of violence, at least in the city of Bogotá there was calm and absolute normalcy. Besides, the Chilean communique continued, the refugee had been tried and condemned for common crimes before legal Colombian tribunals. It has been established, according to the communique, that these were common crimes since assassination, even inspired by political motives, is still a common crime. Nevertheless, and with the object of safeguarding the humane principle, the foreign office initiated direct action with the Colombian government trying to obtain the greatest guarantees for the refugee. Colombia agreed to let him leave the embassy and granted him a period of 48 hours before any possible action would be taken by the authorities. The Chilean ambassador then resigned his post.[1]

The Chilean communique did not say *where* it had been established that assassination even inspired by political motives is still a common crime – a point certainly open to question. One thing is clear, however, and that is that the case certainly was not settled according to any legal rules and that both sides apparently recognized this.

SUMMARY

Latin American practice offers no precise list of offences which have been clearly regarded as "political." On the contrary, it appears that the nature of the charges has been given little consideration and that the diplomatic representative has been more concerned with whether or not the charges were only used as a means of gaining custody of the refugee. In some case the exact nature of the charges is not even

---

[1] *Ibid.*, pp. 2–3.

specified and in most cases they are given only in vague terms. Seldom (the Bolivian case of 1946 is an exception) is any evidence presented to the embassy or legation which has granted asylum beyond the vague statement of charges. Seldom is there any discussion as to whether this or that offence generally has been regarded as a political offence in Latin American practice. Instead the discussion centers around whether this or that individual is pursued for political reasons without indicating the exact nature of the charges against him. Where precedents are cited they show only that asylum has been granted in a number of cases without indicating whether the case or cases cited involved an individual charged with the same offence and under similar conditions.

Four general observations may be made concerning the cases discussed above.

(1) Earlier cases do not tell us much concerning the definition of a "political" offence. Where the territorial state has demanded the refugee it has not been clear whether it has done so because it did not regard the offence as "political" or whether it has held that asylum must offer no more than temporary protection in which case the refugee must be surrendered to the authorities of the territorial state regardless of the nature of the charges.

(2) States have granted refuge to members of deposed governments regardless of the nature of the charges against them. These charges have ranged all the way from mismanagement of public funds to governing unconstitutionally and committing crimes against humanity. But the cases discussed here also show that the territorial state has often denied that such cases were "political" or has at least insisted that the refugee be surrendered. Such cases occurred in Venezuela, 1858; Peru, 1865; Haiti, 1875; Chile, 1891; Peru, 1930; Cuba, 1932. In these cases the charges were issued *after* asylum had been granted. In the Bolivian case the diplomatic missions did not really declare whether or not they regarded the offences as "political" inasmuch as they insisted that this determination must be made *after* the refugee had left the country.

(3) Persons connected with revolutionary movements have been accorded refuge with little consideration of the charges against them. There is evidence that the nature of the charges against the refugee has not even been seriously considered so long as it appeared that they were in some way connected with a revolutionary movement. With the number of refugees amounting to thousands in the Spanish

Civil War cases and hundreds in the Argentine-Paraguayan case of 1911, there could have been no possibility of giving serious consideration to such charges. In the Bolivian case of 1946, the diplomatic representatives granting asylum refused even to consider the charges raised since they had been issued after refuge was granted. Military personnel who have been involved in such movements or who have in any way opposed the government in power and are being sought for such reason have been granted asylum even though treaties clearly prohibit the granting of asylum to military deserters.

(4) Although in most of the cases discussed in this chapter the refugee was permitted to leave the country or given other guarantees there is no evidence that this was done because both parties eventually concurred in the qualification of the offence or in the condition under which asylum was granted. In at least some cases there is evidence that this was not the case.

This certainly leaves an inconclusive picture. It cannot ignore the large number of cases of former office holders and persons, military and non-military, who, acting in opposition to the government in power, whether through open rebellion or various other forms of conspiracy, have received asylum in embassies and legations which has apparently been respected. A long list of such cases was cited by Colombia in the *Colombian-Peruvian Asylum Case*,[1] by Argentina in its 1937 *Project of Convention on the Right of Asylum*, and numerous other cases cited in the *Papers Relating to the Foreign Relations of the United States*. But we are given no information concerning specific charges, the circumstances surrounding the case or the attitudes of the governments involved. Furthermore, a considerable number of these cases involved asylum in consulates – in spite of bilateral and multilateral treaties to the contrary. In such cases we can hardly assume that asylum was granted and respected out of a feeling of legal right or obligation. Can it be assumed that, in these cases at least, legal considerations played a more important role in deciding upon the nature of the offence?

While there is no evidence that in each of these cases the territorial state concurred in the qualification of the offence as "political," one is tempted to assume that the state granting asylum undoubtedly considered them as such. Yet one must wonder, when the number of refugees amounts to hundreds and thousands, whether any consider-

[1] See Appendices, I, II.

ation can even be given to whether each refugee has in fact had any connection with a revolutionary movement.

It is significant that in the *Colombian-Peruvian Asylum Case* the Colombian government did not ask the Court to decide if the charges against Haya de la Torre were "political." It asked instead that it declare that the state granting asylum was competent to declare whether or not the charges were such. The former question would have served the Colombian purpose equally well assuming that Colombia could have proved that Haya de la Torre was a political refugee. The Court did in fact brush with the question but only in answer to the Peruvian contention that asylum had been improperly granted inasmuch as the charges against the refugee were for common crimes. All the court said in this case was that Peru had not proved its point.

It is the feeling of this writer that the data available as demonstrated by the cases discussed in this chapter are so lacking in details concerning the charges in each case, the circumstances surrounding it, and the attitudes of each government concerning the legality of their action as to make it impossible to apply them to any specific case. If Latin American practice shows anything, it shows that asylum has been granted whenever the diplomatic representative felt that the refugee was pursued for political reasons. If he has had any clear-cut criteria for determining whether or not this was the case, they have not been disclosed in the published diplomatic literature. Little regard has been had for the charges issued against the refugee and one simply does not find a careful presentation of precedents complete with a sufficient statement of all the facts and circumstances surrounding them in order to show that they correspond to the case under consideration. In short, it has been a highly intuitive process on the part of the diplomatic representative and, in the view of this writer, further emphasizes the extra-legal character of the whole institution.

CHAPTER X

QUALIFICATION OF THE OFFENCE: PRACTICE

It has already been suggested that in the absence of agreement as to what constitutes a political offence and what constitutes conditions that may be termed "urgent," a solution could be found in agreement upon which party to a controversy has the right to decide the question definitively. It has been insisted on more than one occasion that there is a customary rule of law in Latin America which provides that the state granting asylum may unilaterally qualify the nature of the offence. The clearest statement of this view was presented by the Colombian government in the oral proceedings before the International Court of Justice in connection with the *Colombian-Peruvian Asylum Case*. Referring to the principles laid down in the Montevideo Convention of 1933, and particularly to the right of the state granting asylum to qualify unilaterally the nature of the offence, Colombia presented the following argument.

But, in our opinion, the obligatory character of the principles codified in this convention is indisputable for Peru in her relations with Colombia. It is unnecessary to insist further upon the idea that the Convention of 1933 did no more than codify principles already recognized by Latin American custom and that, by that fact, those principles are imposed for that very reason without the necessity of a special convention. Even without the Convention of 1933, the principles which it contains would have obligatory force among the republics of Latin America. To sustain that the principles consecrated by the convention referred to are not valid for a State because the latter has not ratified it, is to eliminate arbitrarily the original source of all international law.[1]

At this point it is important to recall an observation made in chapter IV. It was stated there that the various conventions on asylum are often invoked with little consideration as to whether they have been ratified or even signed by the parties involved. This might in itself

---

[1] Perú, *Proceso*, p. 602. (My translation.)

suggest that the Latin American countries have regarded these treaties as merely declaratory of international law and have for this reason been less concerned with whether or not the party in question has signed and ratified. But the whole practice in invoking these conventions has shown so much inconsistency and has been applied in such ambiguous terms as to make it impossible to sustain such an interpretation. The following will provide some illustrations of this.

In 1944 the Peruvian legation in Panama asked for safe conduct for three refugees in the following words:

> I have the honor of informing Your Excellencies that today, at 7 PM, the Messrs. José B. Linares, Licenciate Humberto Solís Gallardo and Don Raúl Rodas M. appeared in this legation asking that they be granted, as refugees, the protection *which the conventions of Montevideo and of Havana* contract concerning the Right of Asylum.
>
> *Within the provisions of these conventions, I am soliciting, in turn,* from the government of the Junta of Your Excellencies; that it may be deigned to grant the guarantees there stipulated, arranging what is necessary in order that they may leave for Mexico, under the protection of this legation.[1]

In 1949, replying to a Colombian note which invoked the same conventions in asking safe conduct for Haya de la Torre, the Peruvian government offered the following:

> ... The note of January 14, 1949, could not but have caused painful surprise to the government of Peru, in which case Your Excellency, following the instructions of your Chancellery, qualified as a "political refugee" Victor Raúl Haya de la Torre, pointing out that it was done "in exercise of the right which article II of the Convention of Political Asylum signed at Montevideo, December 26, 1933 grants to you."
>
> Your Excellency should note that the Convention, although signed by the delegates from Peru, has not received the indispensable ratification of our Congress and, for that reason, does not constitute a law in force between Peru and Colombia.[2]

But in the exchange of notes with the Colombian government Peru was forced to qualify the latter position considerably. The Colombian government quoted a paragraph from an official brief of the Minister of Foreign Relations of Peru, published in *El Comercio* on October 26, 1948.

> In accordance with the international conventions in force, already referred to, it pertains to the state that grants asylum to qualify if the event which has

---

[1] De la Fuente Locker [First Secretary of the Peruvian Legation], for the Peruvian Minister to Panama, to the Members of the Revolutionary Junta of Panama, October 20, 1944, Perú, *Proceso*, p. 605. (My translation and italics.)

[2] Díaz Dulanto, Peruvian Minister of Foreign Relations, to Echeverri Cortés, Colombian Ambassador to Peru, February 22, 1949, *ibid.*, p. 6.

motivated it is a common offence or a political offence. Peru has sustained previous to this that in a case where a diplomatic representative does not surrender a refugee because he does not consider him a common criminal, it will proceed to concede extradition only after the refugee has left the territory of the country and according to the proceedings established in the international conventions which regulate the matter, a thesis which is accepted and recognized by all the countries of America.[1]

Peru answered that this was indeed its position but that this was qualified by another paragraph of the same note which the Colombian representative had not quoted.

It is understood that if previous to the event of asylum there might have been instituted a penal proceeding according to pre-established legal norms in which any person is held to be guilty of a common offence, the latter cannot be given asylum, and the diplomatic representative will have to take this circumstance into account, in order to define his line of conduct in cases where he is asked for asylum or where, without his previous consent, the criminal enters the mission.[2]

Thus the Peruvian note concluded:

1. Peru is not juridically obliged to accept the unilateral qualification of the refugee, made by Your Excellency ...
3. There exists, previous to the granting of asylum, a proceeding to examine the terroristic activities of APRA and the responsibilities of its chief, included since the first moment in said proceeding.[3]

It was for this very reason that the government of Peru had not ratified the Montevideo Convention of 1933. It lent itself to the dangerous interpretation that the state granting asylum might question the proceedings already instituted against the refugee.[4]

This certainly is an admission that the provisions of the Montevideo Convention of 1933, regarding the unilateral qualification of the offence by the state granting asylum, are evidence of a rule of law with the reservation that this is only so if proceedings against the refugee did not exist before the grant of asylum. But in the arguments before the Court even this position was further amended. Peru argued that the Montevideo Convention of 1933 contemplated only *provisional* qualification of the offence.[5] Presumably, then, it could be argued that the Montevideo Convention was declaratory of an existing rule of law insofar as it provided for unilateral *but only provisional qualification*

---

[1] Echeverri Cortés to Díaz Dulanto, March 4, 1949, *ibid.*, pp. 16–17. (My translation.)
[2] Díaz Dulanto to Echeverri Cortés, March 19, 1949, *ibid.*, p. 22. (My translation.)
[3] *Ibid.*, p. 30. (My translation.)
[4] Díaz Dulanto to Echeverri Cortés, April 6, 1949, *ibid.*, p. 50.
[5] *Supra*, p. 157.

of the offence by the state of refuge. This is precisely what the final Peruvian arguments asserted.

> The definitive and indeclinable [irrecusable] qualification of the offence is not included in the Convention of Havana and is incompatible with the universal right of asylum and with the spirit of the institution.[1]

This is quite a different interpretation than the one contained in the above quoted Peruvian note of October 26, 1948: It was asserted there that "Peru has previously taken the position that in a case where a diplomatic representative does not surrender a refugee because he does not consider him a common criminal, it [the state which grants asylum] will proceed to concede extradition only after the refugee has left the territory of the country and according to the proceedings established in international conventions which regulate this matter, a thesis which is accepted and recognized by all the countries of America." [2]

Thus it seems that about all that can be ascertained from the Peruvian interpretations of the Montevideo and Havana conventions is that the interpretation is largely dependent upon the needs of the moment.

The Chilean attitude toward the qualification of the offence during the Spanish Civil War shows the same opportunism on this point. This will be discussed in greater detail later in this chapter but a few general observations are in order here. It will be noted that Chile invoked the Montevideo Convention of 1933 as showing that the state granting asylum should unilaterally qualify the nature of the offence. Since Spain had neither signed nor ratified this convention it could be assumed that this was tantamount to asserting that said convention was evidence not only of a regional rule of law binding in America but of a rule of general international law. In view of the fact that no country outside Latin America has ever signed or ratified the Montevideo Convention of 1933, such extravagant claims seem to indicate that this convention was invoked more as a convenient argument than as a document genuinely felt to be evidence of international law. To this must be added the evidence against the existence of such a general rule of law discussed in chapter I.

But apart from references to conventional arrangements, can it be said that Latin American practice has shown a recognition of legal

---

[1] Perú, *Proceso*, p. 674. (My translation.)
[2] *Supra*, pp. 188–189.

obligation to respect the unilateral qualification of the offence by the state of refuge in cases where the territorial state has recognized a right of asylum for political offenders?

It has already been noted that, although Colombia cited a large number of cases where asylum had in fact been granted and respected, the Court rejected this because Colombia had "not shown that the alleged rule of unilateral and definitive qualification was invoked or – if in some cases it was in fact invoked – that it was, apart from conventional stipulations, exercised by the States granting asylum as a right appertaining to them and respected by the territorial States as a duty incumbent on them and not merely for reasons of political expediency." [1] Another reason for the unacceptability of such evidence was emphasized in an earlier Peruvian note to Colombia.

> The application of unilateral qualification has in many cases coincided with the criteria of the territorial government. We would go far to examine in each case if asylum was conceded because of the obligatory character of the rule or because of agreement in the qualification. [2]

Nor does a request for the refugee's safe conduct out of the country necessarily mean that the state of refuge is asserting a right of unilateral qualification. Peru pointed this out with reference to a case cited by Colombia before the Court. In this case Peru had granted asylum to a refugee in its embassy in Panama and had requested safe conduct for the refugee which was in turn granted. [3] To this Peru replied that "said republic [Panama] formulated no observation, granting safe conduct without discussing it, as an expression of its desire that the refugee might leave its territory, and for this reason we cannot understand why it is cited." [4] It will be the purpose of this chapter to investigate, through diplomatic exchanges and other official sources, the attitudes expressed on this question by Latin American governments.

In the earlier cases on asylum it is understandable that the practice had not crystallized to the point where a controversy revolved around the question of which party should rightfully qualify the nature of the offence. The previous chapter has shown that it is by no means clear that the nature of the offence was always regarded as being of particular importance and, even on recent cases, controversies have

---

[1] *Op. cit.*, p. 277.
[2] Díaz Dulanto to Echeverri Cortés, April 6, 1949, Perú, *Proceso*, p. 51. (My translation.)
[3] *Proceso*, p. 127.
[4] *Ibid.*, p. 184.

not always faced this question squarely. The question has often been whether or not a *particular* refugee was qualified for asylum without getting into the nature of a political offence generally or *who* has the right to decide the question.

The discussion in the previous chapter pointed out that Chile, in the controversy with the United States in 1851, admitted that, in certain cases and particularly when certain conditions prevail in a society, diplomatic asylum would be justified. Although Colonel Arteaga was permitted to leave the legation in safety, the evidence certainly does not indicate that Chile permitted this because it felt obliged to accept the American minister's qualification of the nature of the offence or of the circumstances which would permit asylum. This is suggested, first of all, in the American minister's note to Washington.

> Some days after the Minister's last note, in conversation with the Envoy Extraordinary from Brazil, . . . he very kindly offered his services and succeeded in arranging for the departure of Col. Arteaga from the Legation and from the country with the connivance of the Government . . .[1]

The expression "connivance of the Government" is of particular interest in view of the note which the American minister sent to the Chilean Minister of Foreign Relations *on the same day* that the above note was sent to Washington. After acknowledging receipt of the Chilean Minister's note regarding the question of asylum, it concluded with this paragraph:

> The Undersigned has to inform his Excellency, that Col. Arteaga has left his house, and is no longer within this Legation, which renders any reply to the very polite note of his Excellency unnecessary.[2]

In the Venezuelan case of 1858, the question as to who shall determine the nature of the offence was not directly discussed inasmuch as it does not appear that Venezuela felt that the nature of the offence would make any difference. No objection was raised to the original or provisional grant of asylum. The government asserted that it would "not judge the merits which might have moved Mr. Levraud to concede asylum to those individuals in the first moments of a transformation."[3]

---

[1] Peyton, U. S. Minister to Chile, to Webster, Secretary of State, May 23, 1851, extracts, Manning, *op. cit.*, V, p. 195.

[2] Peyton to Veras, Chilean Minister of Foreign Relations, May 23, 1851, *ibid.*

[3] "En los primeros momentos de una transformación," translated here as "in the first moments of a transformation," refers to a change of government. Toro, Venezuelan Secretary of Foreign Relations, to Bingham and Levraud, *Chargés d'Affaires* of Great Britain and

But when the refugee is demanded by the territorial state "in the ordinary course of the country's justice" he must be surrendered to its authorities.[1] Thus it is entirely up to the proper authorities of the territorial state to decide whether or not asylum shall be continued. The Diplomatic Guide of 1851 was quoted with approval:

> To wish to extend the privilege of exterritoriality to permit the foreign minister to detain the ordinary course of the country's justice, giving asylum in his house to nationals or foreigners pursued for an offence or crime, would be to undermine the independence of nations ... If it concerns an individual accused of a crime of state [crimen de estado] and it is ascertained that he has found protection in the house of the minister of a foreign power, not only may the government, by surrounding the house, prevent the escape of the culprit, but also remove him immediately and even by force, in case the minister, duly notified by the competent authorities, may refuse his extradition.[2]

Finally, it was asserted that "local justice and the interested parties have the incontestable right of doing what they may decide to the man sheltered in the house of the ambassador. This is not a special right, but common without distinction of country or legation.[3]

After a long controversy the British and French representatives were forced to concede Venezuela's right to jurisdiction over two of the refugees in the Convention Signed at La Guaira.[4] A third was given guarantees of security although this appears to have been done in deference to a previous promise which had been repudiated with the discharge of the official who had made the promise.[5]

The question was equally obscured in the 1865-66 case in Peru inasmuch as the Peruvian government insisted that it alone was competent to try the refugees whether for common or political offences and that "the right of asylum did not exist when the refugee was demanded by a judicial authority." [6] The legal force of the judicial action would not be altered even if the crimes for which the refugee was accused were political "because it is not certain, nor even admissible, that political crimes ought to remain unpunished, nor that it may be lawful for a diplomatic agent to remove from the action of justice

France, April 30, 1858, Venezuela, *Cuestión promovida a Venezuela por los agentes de Francia y de la Gran Bretaña*, pp. 28–43; Planas–Suárez, *op. cit.*, p. 464.

[1] *Ibid.*
[2] *Ibid.*
[3] *Ibid.*, p. 465.
[4] *Supra*, p. 161.
[5] *Ibid.*
[6] Pacheco, Peruvian Secretary of State for Foreign Relations, to the Representatives of Peru in Chile, Bolivia and Ecuador, May, 19, 1866, Perú, *Correspondencia diplomática relativa a la cuestión sobre asilo*, pp. 21–22. (My translation.)

delinquents of that kind when a tribunal formally demands them.[1]

As to the nature and legality of the proceedings, this was a matter to be judged solely by the territorial state. To the French envoy, the Peruvian minister said:

> You made some observations concerning the Central Tribunal, the status [condición] of the accused and of the character which, in your opinion, the judgment must have; to which I replied that such judgments were purely internal affairs and that they were not within the competence of the diplomatic agents.[2]

And once the court has decided a question, it is this judgment which must prevail. "To the *Corte Central* belongs exclusively the decision as to whether there be guilt or not on the part of the accused, but the duty of the Government is to adopt whatever measures are within its scope in order that the judgment and the decisions of the tribunals are not made illusory, and this is the reason why I am obliged to solicit the extradition of the refugees in the French legation." [3]

The case of General Lamothe in 1875 certainly offers no evidence that Haiti recognized an obligation to accept the British qualification of the offence as political.[4] On the contrary, Haiti seems to have gained its point that the charges were not political and that it had a right to try the refugee, a right which Britain in fact recognized while Haiti offered certain guarantees concerning the regularity of the proceedings. Furthermore, the interview recorded by the American minister suggests that the British and American representatives were more interested in reaching a practical solution without clearly insisting upon recognition of legal rights. Indeed, they clearly indicated that their legal position was open to question when they asserted that "once a person has been received as a refugee in a foreign legation, *the rule seemed to be* not to deliver him up on the requests or demands such as had been made for General Lamothe, without a guarantee for his personal security from irregular proceedings against him." [5] Intimations that they might be willing to give up the practice of asylum once this case had been settled and the securities to be posted by General Lamothe are a further indication that expediency played a greater role than recognized legal rights and obligations.[6]

---

[1] Pacheco, to Vion, French Envoy, January 2, 1866, *ibid.*, p. 10. (My translation.)

[2] Pacheco to Vion, December 29, 1865, *ibid.*, pp. 5–6. (My translation.)

[3] Pacheco to Vion, December 20, 1865, *ibid.*, p. 4. (My translation.)

[4] *Supra*, pp. 163–165.

[5] Bassett, U. S. Minister to Haiti, to Fish, Secretary of State, April 9, 1875, *For. Rel. of the U. S.*, 1875, II, p. 683. (My italics.)

[6] *Ibid.*

During the Civil War in Colombia in 1885, a Colombian citizen refusing to pay a levied war contribution was granted asylum by the Argentine minister. The Argentine minister did so by means of the unusual expedient of moving into the home of the person to whom he wished to grant asylum. His refusal to surrender the individual upon demand of the Colombian government was the immediate motive for a circular addressed to the foreign diplomatic missions by that government.[1] This carefully worded circular implied that the Colombian government was prepared to resort to any measures necessary in order to apprehend a refugee whom it properly demanded. The wording of the note requires a lengthy quotation in order to understand its full significance.

If, as I flatter myself, your excellency will acknowledge that the course of events has been and is such as I have described, I desire to invoke these antecedents, which of themselves command respect, in order next to make known to your excellency, according to instructions I have received from the citizen President of the Republic, the manner in which that magistrate and the Government over which he presides understand the immunities of foreign diplomatic ministers, in regard to the asylum they may possibly feel themselves called upon to grant to individuals hostile to the Government and *criminally engaged in the present civil conflict.*

The right of self-preservation and of the supreme defense of states is recognized by the most learned publicists as paramount to all other considerations, even to the immunities which are enjoyed by diplomatic agents.

The action of my Government will therefore be guided by that rule, if such occasion, truly and happily very remote, presents itself; but it naturally trusts that the respectable diplomatic body accredited to the Government of the Union, ... will not lay it under the *necessity of claiming the surrender of individuals who have taken refuge* in their residences, and of whom the *legitimate authority may, for any motive whatever, be in search* ...

For the rest, my Government *will recognize* to the fullest extent *the immunity of your excellency,* and that of your family and dependents, as likewise that of your residence, and as far as the abundant resources at its command, both material and moral, will allow, will cause that immunity to be respected at any cost, *provided that in doing so no damage or danger accrue to the nation* ...[2]

In the long controversy between Chile and the United States in 1891, Chile certainly admitted nothing more that a provisional right of qualification of the offence on the part of the state granting asylum. That government insisted that it must be the final judge of the offences charged against the individuals involved.[3] The Minister of Foreign

---

[1] Scruggs, U. S. Minister to Colombia, to Frelinghuysen, Secretary of State, February 23, 1885, extract, *For. Rel. of the U. S.,* 1885, p. 205.

[2] Restrepo, Colombian Minister of Foreign Relations, to Scruggs, February 16, 1885, (inclosures in Scruggs to Freylinghuysen, February 23, 1885), *ibid.,* p. 206. (My italics.)

[3] *Supra,* chapter IX.

Relations insisted that he did not recognize "that it is a legitimate right of the legation which gives the asylum to require a safe-conduct for the refugees, limiting therefore the penal jurisdiction of the country in which is its place of residence to the penalty of banishment ... nor could anyone recognize [it] in the post which he now actually occupies." [1] The next paragraph, far from suggesting any unilateral qualification by the diplomatic representative, suggests, on the contrary, that it is purely at the discretion of the territorial state.

Safe-conducts have been and may be given, but *in all cases*, not in virtue of sufficient rights on the part of the legation giving asylum to demand or receive them, but of the courtesy, convenience and will of the Government and of the country in which the legation resides, and in certain cases and under certain restrictions by which they are dictated, not by the prescription of certain laws and statutes, but by those of honor, discretion and delicacy. [2]

When the Minister of Foreign Relations finally agreed to permit the refugees to leave the country he took pains to point out that only personal or informal assurances had been given – he had acted with "*vista gorda.*" [3]

In the 1911–1912 case involving Argentina and Paraguay, the former government did *in fact* unilaterally qualify the refugees as "political" in the face of assertions to the contrary on the part of Paraguay. In asserting that it did not consider them in the category attributed to them by Paraguay (i.e., deserters) and flatly stating that they would leave the next day, Argentina certainly implied that the right of unilateral qualification belonged to the state of refuge. [4] On the other hand, the sharp note of protest from the government of Paraguay, following the reported *fait accompli*, indicates that it recognized no such right. [5]

The Peruvian government flatly denied any unilateral right to qualify the nature of the offence in the case of the former officials under the deposed Leguía regime who had taken refuge in the various embassies and legations in Lima in 1930. The United States minister

[1] Matta to Egan, October 20, 1891, M. A. Matta, *Cuestiones recientes con la legación i el Gobierno de los Estados Unidos de Norte-América* (Santiago de Chile: Imprenta Cervantes, 1892), p. 46. (My translation.) "Matta sometimes appears as "Mata."

[2] Matta to Egan, October 20, 1891 (inclosure in Egan to Blaine, October 26, 1891), *For. Rel. of the U. S.*, 1891, p. 199 (My italics.)

[3] *Supra*, chapter IX.

[4] Martínez Campos, Argentine Minister to Paraguay, to Irala, Paraguayan Minister of Foreign Relations, January 17, 1912, Argentine Republic, *Memoria*, 1911–1912, pp. 94–95.

[5] Irala to Martínez Campos, December 22, 1911, *ibid.*, pp. 90–92. See also *supra*, chapter IX.

to Peru reported that at a meeting of the diplomatic corps, convened to discuss the replies which the various representatives had received in response to their solicitations of safe conduct, "it appeared that in every case, though in varying phraseology, the Junta declined to recognize the letter or practice of the Treaty of Montevideo, setting itself up to all appearances as the arbitrator of whether the asylees were political refugees or to be classed as criminals." [1]

Bolivia in this case invoked article 23 of the Montevideo Treaty of 1889, and article 16 of the Bolivarian Agreement of 1911. Article 23 of the former treaty appears under Title III of the treaty which deals with extradition [2] and the latter treaty is called an "Agreement on Extradition." [3] Thus the Bolivian government's report on the case noted that Peru had pointed to this fact:

> In the opinion of Chancellor Montagne [Peru], Minister Ostra [Bolivia] confounded diplomatic asylum with extradition, arguing as follows: " the common criminal who takes refuge in a legation must be surrendered by its chief to the local authorities after action by the Minister of Foreign Relations when it does not take place spontaneously" and that for that reason, in such cases, no previous qualification of foreign tribunals or requirable judicial security was necessary.[4]

Bolivia based her case upon article 15 of the 1889 treaty which provided that "no delinquent given asylum in the territory of a state can be surrendered to the authorities of the other, except in conformity with the rules regulating extradition." [5] From this point it was argued that "through the principle of exterritoriality the premises of the legation are compared to the territory of the respective state" and that "the refugee in a legation is in the same situation as the refugee in the State which the former represents." [6] Thus "it was the Supreme Tribunal of Justice of Bolivia which would have the right to determine whether the crimes of which Dr. Salomon is accused are of a political or common character." [7] It noted, finally, that Dr. Salomon was willing to offer guarantees of all his property.

Apparently the Peruvian government accepted the guarantees

[1] Mayer, U. S. *Chargé d'Affaires* in Peru, to the Secretary of State, September 5, 1930, *For. Rel. of the U. S.*, 1930, III, p. 746.

[2] Perú, Ministerio de Relaciones Exteriores, *Congresos y conferencias internacionales en que ha tomado parte el Perú*, coleccionados sus trabajos por Ricardo Aranda (Lima: Oficina Tipográfica de "La Opinión Nacional," 1910), p. 296.

[3] *Ibid.*, V, pp. 267, 633.

[4] Bolivia, *Boletín*, (abril-diciembre, 1930), p. 39. (My translation.)

[5] *Ibid.*

[6] *Ibid.*

[7] *Ibid.*, p. 38.

without necessarily accepting Bolivia's qualification of the offence. It pointed out in its arguments in the *Colombian-Peruvian Asylum case* that "Peru accepted it [qualification by the state of refuge] in consideration of the fact that the refugee had given guarantees to the *Tribunal de Sanción* which demanded it for obligations of an economic character." [1]

Peru took the same position with regard to Dr. Salazar. The latter came under the protection of the Cuban legation after Uruguay (who had first given him asylum) broke relations with Peru. The Cuban Secretary of State in reporting on this case in 1937 said:

> The special circumstances which surrounded the case of Salazar made accession to the Cuban demands very painful, demands which consisted of obtaining absolute guarantees for the departure of the refugee from Peruvian territory, the government of Cuba in turn committing itself to keep Salazar, against whom public opinion was most inflamed, removed from all political interference in the affairs of his country. The certain fact is that rancor was destroyed through generosity and that Salazar, even if he was unable to leave the country, was respected in his asylum in the Cuban legation, *dying many months later in the same legation.* [2]

This certainly sounds more like respect for the inviolability of the legation than respect for asylum. At most Peru was willing to admit provisional qualification of the offence by the state of refuge, but reserved the right to decide for itself whether he was a political refugee or one accused of common crime.

From the report in the Brazilian government's *Relatorio* for that year it appears that the break in diplomatic relations between Peru and Uruguay was the result of the fact that Peru had taken an equally dim view of Uruguay's action in granting asylum in the first place.

> During the revolutionary movement in Peru, in September of 1930, the legation of Uruguay in Lima having granted asylum to Sr. Jesús M. Salazar, ex-minister of the deposed government, the Junta Revolucionaria declared Sr. Fozalla, the minister from Uruguay in said capital, *persona non grata.* [3]

In 1932 the Brazilian embassy in Cuba granted asylum to ex-President Menocal. In this case the usual disagreement as to who should qualify the nature of the offence was clearly settled outside

---

[1] Perú, *Proceso*, p. 22. (My translation.)

[2] Remos, Cuban Secretary of State, to Saavedra Lamas, Argentine Minister of Foreign Relations, August 18, 1937, Cuba, Secretaría de Estado, *Documentos diplomáticos relativos a la guerra civil de España* (La Havana, 1939), pp. 125–126. (My translation and italics.)

[3] Brazil, *Relatorio*, 1930, I, p. 25. (My translation.)

the scope of any legal rules.[1] A note from the United States ambassador to Cuba further emphasizes this.

On June 30, the Foreign Office issued what was, in effect, a joint declaration, stating that in the conversations sustained between the Cuban Secretary of State and the Minister of Brazil, it had not been possible to arrive at an interpretative agreement of the convention of asylum in force between Cuba and Brazil, but that an effective solution of the matter had been found: for its part, the Government of Cuba was assured that General Menocal would not be in the future an obstacle to the maintenance of public peace and would go to Europe to reside for one year, whlle the Government of Brazil was satisfied that the necessary guarantee would be given General Menocal for his unmolested departure from Cuban territory.[2]

During the Spanish Civil War the government of Chile maintained in deed, if not in word, the right of the state granting asylum to qualify the nature of the offence. It not only insisted that the persons in the legations were innocent of crimes but insisted also that "there is no obligation on the part of the diplomatic corps to submit their names to the government."[3] If safe conduct was to be granted by Spain without knowledge of the names of the persons to whom granted, as Chile demanded, this could only mean that the state of refuge would be the sole judge of the type of individual to whom it would be granted. Later, however, the Chilean position was established beyond all doubt. When the Franco government had established its authority there were 17 Republican Spaniards in the Chilean embassy in Madrid.[4] The Franco government asserted that, although some of these refugees were writers and intellectuals against whom there were no charges, there were others who "were accused of criminal acts" and should be submitted to trial in Spanish courts.[5] The Chilean position was pointed out in a memorandum of the Ministry of Foreign Relations which was distributed at a meeting of chiefs of mission called by the Chilean Foreign Ministry on June 15.

The government of Chile considers, for its part that the solution of the problem is in the concession, by the Spanish government, of the corresponding safe

[1] Remos, Cuban Secretary of State, to Saavedra Lamas, Argentine Minister of Foreign Relations, August 18, 1937, Cuba, Secretaría de Estado, *Documentos diplomáticos relativos a la guerra civil de España* (La Havana, 1939), p. 126.

[2] Guggenheim, U. S. Ambassador to Cuba, to the Secretary of State, July 6, 1932, *For. Rel. of the U. S.*, 1932, V, pp. 551–552.

[3] *Supra*, p. 177.

[4] Trueblood, U. S. *Chargé d'Affaires* in Chile, to the Secretary of State, June 15, 1939, tel., *For. Rel. of the U. S.*, 1939, II, p. 779.

[5] "Memorandum of Conversation, by the Undersecretary of State (Wells)," August 7, 1939, *ibid.*, pp. 783–784.

conduct for the departure of the refugees from the country, considering that, according to Article 2 of the Convention of Montevideo, the qualification of the political offence corresponds to the state which gives asylum . . .[1]

Inasmuch as Spain was not a party to this treaty it can only be assumed that the government of Chile regarded it as evidence of an already existing customary rule of law. But even this position seems rather absurd in this case since the convention had never been signed by any country outside of Latin America.

The government of Venezuela, while not dealing *explicitly* with the question of qualification of the offence, seems to have implied, that if anything, this right would belong to the territorial state. The lengthy extract taken from one of its notes shows first that it was unwilling to support fully the sweeping claims made by Chile. Secondly, the portions italicized by this writer suggest that asylum would be only temporary and that the nature of the offence would be determined by the territorial state in the absence of conventions to the contrary.

Consistent with this doctrine, the government of Venezuela considers that asylum can only be respected in the countries which have expressly admitted it and are parties to international instruments formulated in order to recognize and regulate such right. Venezuela is not a party to such agreements and does not admit that the foreign missions accredited here can accord asylum nor invoke it or demand it as an admitted and recognized juridical principle. For that reason our government would not be able to collaborate in any collective action which has as an object a claim of such principles before a third power.

The government holds that in cases in which it is not established by convention, asylum is a humanitarian practice derived from traditional custom, and whose *efficacy and extension depend entirely on the sovereign appraisal of the state in whose territory the mission functions which claims to accord it, and it does not correspond to the latter but to the government to which the latter is accredited to appraise the origin and extension of the privilege invoked.*

In the case where, founded on humanitarian principle, American diplomatic representatives in Spain might have to take steps to attain from the Spanish government a measure of exception in favor of the refugees in the Chilean embassy and to call attention to the sympathy with which the act would be received in America, the government of Venezuela would contribute amply to such action tending to save life and protect the life of the refugees, in cooperation with other American governments who are inspired by the same humanitarian sentiments.[2]

---

[1] Perú, *Boletín*, año XXXVI (2° trimestre de 1939), pp. 93–94. (My translation.) That this Memorandum originated in the meeting referred to is apparent from Trueblood, U. S. *Chargé d'Affaires* in Chile, to the Secretary of State, June 15, 1939, tel., *For. Rel. of the U. S.*, 1939, II, p. 779.

[2] Borges, Venezuelan Minister of Foreign Relations, to Carnivali, Venezuelan Minister to Chile, August 23, 1939, *ibid.*, p. 131. For a similar statement in the "Position of Venezuela on the Problems of the Conference," prepared for the Eighth Inter-American Conference at Lima, 1938, see *Libro Amarillo* (1939), I, pp. 81–83. For a similar statement by the Minister of Foreign Relations printed in the *Memoria* for 1880 (now superseded by *Libro Amarillo*), see Planas-Suárez, *op. cit.*, p. 505.

Peru nowhere explicitly asserted a right of unilateral qualification of the offence although her conduct in this case certainly amounted to just that. Repeated assertions by the Spanish government that it would decide in each individual case whether to grant safe conduct out of the country were answered with vague statements that Peru insisted upon upholding the "juridical and moral fundamentals" of asylum.[1] But the fact remains that the latter was unwilling to accept anything less than the granting of safe conduct for all its refugees and this Spain finally agreed to.[2]

The position is best demonstrated in the case of the refugees in the Peruvian consulate in Madrid. Certainly it cannot be argued that *greater* rights would be claimed in the case of a consulate than in the case of a legation so we may consider this case applicable here. Spain insisted that many of these refugees were accused of offences which must be tried in Spanish courts. Without indicating precisely what these charges were she insisted that Spain alone must decide whether they could be granted safe conduct out of the country.[3] That Peru took the opposite view is obvious from the fact that the government of Spain resorted to the extreme measure of invading the Peruvian consulate in order to remove the refugees.[4] The fact that Peru broke relations with Spain when the latter refused to return the refugees certainly indicates that Peru was *in fact* insisting upon the right to qualify unilaterally the nature of the offence. Nor does it appear that Peru did this merely to vindicate the violation of the consulate and apart from the question of asylum. This is evident from the government's report on its attitude toward a later Chilean solicitation for support in its efforts to secure grants of safe conduct from the Franco government. The *Memoria* for the period from April 20 to December 8, 1939, reported that "the foreign office, after studying the diverse aspects of this incident, instructed the ambassador of the Republic in Spain to express to the Minister of Foreign Affairs the sympathy with which Peru – who had always defended and respected the right of asylum, to the point of breaking diplomatic relations with the deposed Republi-

---

[1] Ulloa, Peruvian Minister of Foreign Relations, to the Spanish Minister of Foreign Relations [state], September 2, 1936, Perú, *Memoria*, 13 abril–22 octubre, 1936, pp. LXXII–LXXIII; pp. 94–95; Ulloa to the Spanish Minister of State, October 22, 1936, Perú, *Boletín*, año XXXIII (4° trimestre de 1936), p. 105.

[2] Perú, *Memoria*, 13 abril–22 octubre, 1936, pp. LXXII–LXXIII.

[3] Reyes, *Chargé d'Affaires* of Mexico in Peru serving as representative of Spain, to the Peruvian Minister of Foreign Relations, May 16, 1937, Perú, *Boletín*, año XXXIII (4° trimestre de 1936), p. 105.

[4] *Ibid.*

can Government, among other causes, for having disregarded that right and violated the consulate of Peru in Madrid – would receive a favorable solution to the incident with Chile." [1]

It is true, of course, that Peru supported her demands partly upon the fact that other states had been accorded favorable treatment for their refugees. "To deny to the government of Peru the same favorable treatment for its refugees conceded to other states, amounts to an unequal treatment out of accord with the desire to maintain cordial relations," the Peruvian government argued.[2] But to support strongly the demands of other states, as Peru did, and then insist that it be awarded similar treatment would be the equivalent of demanding it as a right in itself.

Little evidence is available concerning a number of cases in the Dominican Republic in 1945. Yet such evidence as is available when considered in connection with other evidence suggests that this government did not feel bound to recognize anything more than provisional qualification of the offence by the state granting asylum. Manuel Arturo Peña Batlle, who was Dominican Secretary of Foreign Relations at the time (1945), gave the following interpretation in 1951 (when he was no longer in office).

> In 1945 the Dominican Foreign Office laid down a definitive criterion on the matter in the face of various cases of asylum which then occupied its attention. The conventions of Montevideo do not admit of qualification by the granting state [Estado asilante] except provisionally and as a point of departure for study of the case by the interested governments. Anything else would openly abandon the most elementary attributes of national sovereignty ...[3]

The reader's attention is called to the official denunciation of the conventions of Havana and Montevideo by the Dominican government in 1954. This denunciation was discussed in chapter V but two paragraphs are worth repeating here.

> CONSIDERING: That diplomatic asylum permitted by the conventions of Havana (1928) and Montevideo (1933) is an obstacle to the domestic defense of States, inasmuch as it permits the most dangerous individuals to frustrate the course of justice and to pursue their dissolvent and subversive activity;
> CONSIDERING: That said conventions give rise to real interventions among

---

[1] Pp. XI–XII.

[2] De la Fuente, Peruvian Minister of Foreign Relations, to the Spanish Minister of State, June 22, 1937, Perú, *Boletín*, año XXXIV (2° trimestre de 1937), pp. 216–217. (My translation.)

[3] "Una sentencia de la Corte Internacional de Justicia," *El Caribe* (Ciudad Trujillo), 8 de abril de 1951. (My translation.)

States, through the obscurity and uncertainty of the concepts which they lay down and the frequent contradictions in interpretation; ...[1]

This should be considered in connection with an article appearing in the *Revista juridica dominicana*, official publication of the Dominican Department of Justice. After noting the denunciation above, it stated that "in view of that denunciation, some organs of the national press have brought up-to-date the editorial commentary which was published by the periodical *El Nacional* of the Capital of the Republic, April 15, 1876, which says:

> If it is said that international congresses dictate a code for the people it is in vain, because the nations who are strongest on land and sea do not wish to put into exact words that which must bow to the impulse of their guns.
>
> Thus we continue, and in the meantime, with tolerance, we dig an abyss which each time is opened, each step threatening us in the middle of the road which is undertaken to arrive at stability and consolidation of peace on our soil.
>
> The immunity [inviolabilidad] of those domiciles, that is, the exterritoriality which is conceded to them through tolerance, is the anchor of the conspirators against all constitutional government. That immunity does not exist and we ought not to tolerate it. The right of exterritoriality has been recognized only in the domicile of diplomatic representatives of the first class, far from which are the greater part of the consuls or agents which are in the Republic ...[2]

While this editorial appears to have been directed primarily against the practice of granting asylum in consulates it can hardly be assumed that this is what the Dominican government had in mind in reprinting the article inasmuch as the conventions referrred to in the denunciation specifically refer to asylum granted in embassies, legations, and warships.

The editorial quoted is of course not an official publication and it is not suggested here that this is the kind of thing an international tribunal would give much weight. For one interested in knowing the attitude of the Dominican government at the time, however, this writer would suggest that it is a very good indication.

In the 1946 case involving the foreign legation in Bolivia, it was noted in the previous chapter that the diplomatic corps emphasized that, regardless of the nature of the charges against any of the refugees, if these charges were instituted *after* the grant of asylum, the refugees could not be surrendered to the Bolivian authorities except through extradition proceedings after they had left the country.[3] Although it

---

[1] *Gaceta oficial*, (Ciudad Trujillo, 27 de septiembre de 1954), pp. 9–11. (My translation.)
[2] *Revista juridica dominicana*, año XVII (julio-diciembre, 1955), p. 24. (My translation.)
[3] *Supra*, pp. 179–181.

would seem unnecessary under these circumstances, the diplomatic corps by unanimous agreement did invoked the right of unilateral qualification of the offence.

> In accord with Article 23 of the Treaty of International Penal Law signed at Montevideo in 1889 and ratified by Bolivia, the qualification of the offence pertains to the nation which grants asylum.This concept was reaffirmed when plenipotentiaries ... subscribed to the Treaty on Asylum and Political Refuge concluded August 4, 1939, in which Article 3 establishes: "the qualification of the causes which motivate asylum concerns the state that concedes it." In consequence, only the Tribunals of Justice of the nations which grant asylum, are those named to establish if any of the present refugees, once they leave Bolivian Territory, have engaged in the commission of common crime, political crime or common crime connected with political crime.[1]

Primary emphasis is placed upon the Montevideo Treaty of 1889. Article 23 of this treaty appears under the title dealing with extradition.[2] It is interesting to note that Peru argued in the *Colombian-Peruvian Asylum Case* that this part of the treaty was not applicable to diplomatic asylum,[3] a view which was affirmed by the Judgment of the Court in that case.[4] In view of the fact that Peru was one of the states with refugees in its legation it must have been aware of this memorandum submitted with the unanimous agreement of the diplomatic corps.

In spite of rather flimsy grounds for invoking the 1889 treaty,[5] the right of unilateral qualification of the offence by the state granting asylum seems to be based squarely upon this agreement. There are two reasons for this assumption.

1. The references to "the principles of international law" and "Customary Latin American Law" appeared only in connection with general requests for safe conduct and the assertion that charges instituted after asylum had been granted were not grounds for the surrender of the refugee until he had left the country. When a right of unilateral qualification was asserted only the above treaty was

---

[1] Memorandum of the Diplomatic Corps, August 6, 1946, Chile, *Memoria*, 1946, pp. 54–55. (My translation.)

[2] G. Fr. de Martens, *Nouveau recueil général de traités et autres actes relatifs aux rapports de droit international* (2me série par Stoerb; Goettingue: Librairie Dieterich, 1893), p. 436.

[3] Perú, *Proceso*, pp. 168–169.

[4] *Op. cit.*, p. 277.

[5] According to the Memorandum of the Diplomatic Corps of August 19, 1946, Bolivia, *Boletín*, n° 13 (julio-diciembre, 1946), p. 51, the "complete list of the refugees in the different embassies and legations" listed Venezuela, Paraguay, Peru, Argentina, Ecuador, Mexico, and the Holy See as countries whose embassies and legations were sheltering refugees. Of these countries, only three – Paraguay, Peru, and Argentine – had ratified the 1889 treaty (as had Bolivia), *supra*, p. 64.

invoked without any reference to "the principles of international law" or "Customary Latin American Law." This plus the fact that it was found expedient to resort to a convention legally binding on only four of the eight parties to the controversy and to give it an interpretation which the International Court of Justice and one of the parties to the controversy would flatly reject only four years later suggests that unilateral qualification was not felt to be defensible as a customary rule of law.

2. If the above treaty had been regarded as merely declaratory of a rule of law, certainly the Montevideo Convention of 1933 would have offered stronger evidence of this. The Montevideo Convention of 1933 had certainly received much wider support *in Latin America generally* than had the 1889 treaty. As of 1946, no less than 17 Latin American states had signed, and 9 had ratified the former as compared with but 7 signatures and 5 ratifications for the latter.[1] But only one of the parties *to this particular case* (Mexico) had ratified the 1933 convention and Bolivia and Venezuela, the two principals in the case, had not even signed it.[2] At least four of the eight parties to the case (including Bolivia) had ratified the 1889 treaty.[3] Thus there were stronger grounds for invoking the 1889 treaty *as a binding agreement* but there were stronger grounds for invoking the 1933 convention *as evidence of a customary rule of law*. The fact that the former treaty was chosen suggests that it was felt necessary to base this claim upon a treaty obligation.

It is also worth noting that Paraguay, one of the parties to the case, did invoke the Montevideo Convention of 1933, but did so in a separate Memorandum. The second of the "Points of View" listed there asserted that:

The qualification of the political offence corresponds to the requesting nation, or, the one which has granted asylum (Art. 3 of the Convention on Political Asylum, Montevideo, December 26, 1933, VII International American Conference).[4]

---

[1] Pan American Union, Division of Law and Treaties, *Inter-American Treaties and Conventions: Signatures, Ratifications, and Deposits with Explanatory Notes* (Washington, 1954), p. 42; Pan American Union, Division of Law and Treaties, *Status of Pan American Treaties and Conventions* (revised to September 1, 1955, Washington: Pan American Union, 1955), p. 7.

[2] Pan American Union, Division of Law and Treaties, *Inter-American Treaties and Conventions: Signatures, Ratifications, and Deposits with Explanatory Notes* (Washington, 1954), p. 42.

[3] *Supra*, p. 64.

[4] September 24, 1946, Bolivia, *Boletín*, n.° 13 (julio-diciembre, 1946), p. 62.

Since, as has been noted above, neither Paraguay nor Bolivia had ratified this convention, this would suggest that the convention was considered as evidence of a rule of law – but apparently by Paraguay only. But in the same memorandum Paraguay seemed to emphasize that the *obligation* was based upon treaty rather than custom.

> The Bolivian government should concede the exit from the country of all the refugees. Thus, the fulfillment of obligations clearly established in treaties in force and uniformly observed in practice .. loudly and imperatively demands it.[1]

Thus the obligations are "established" in treaties and "observed" in practice.

The Bolivian government also based its action upon the 1889 convention but, at first, indicated that this did not require unilateral qualification of the offence by the state granting asylum. It asserted that "the Ministry of Foreign Relations of Bolivia will comply with the conventional obligation of conceding safe conduct to the refugees of a purely political character, but reserves the right of not granting it to those included within the penal sanctions applicable to the perpetration of common crimes." [2] It was two days later that the dean of the diplomatic corps invoked the right of unilateral qualification under the 1889 convention. In reply to this the Bolivian government indicated at least partial agreement:

> In the exercise of the right that treaties in force and international practice confer on it, the government of Bolivia makes a reservation in the case of refugees who have committed common crimes. Those treaties and that international practice recognize the right of presenting the judicial instruments which according to Bolivian laws, establish the character of common delinquencies of several of the refugees. The complete documentation issued by the ordinary tribunals will be opportunely remitted in order that the Honorable Diplomatic Missions may transmit it to their respective governments so that the latter after study of the antecedents may determine if it deals with common or political crime.[3]

Then, in the same memorandum, Bolivia herself invoked the Montevideo Convention of 1933:

> It is by virtue of this that the Bolivian government declares its firm decision to execute all the stipulations relating to the right of asylum, one of them being the obligation of the government whose diplomatic mission accords it, to pro-

---

[1] *Ibid.*

[2] Memorandum of the Bolivian Minister of Foreign Relations and Worship, August 4, 1946, Chile, *Memoria*, 1946, p. 54. (My translation.)

[3] Memorandum of the Bolivian Ministry of Foreign Relations and Worship, August 19, 1946, *ibid.*, p. 60. (My translation.)

nounce upon the righteousness or unrighteousness of the surrender of the refugees, after a study of the antecedents in conformity with Article 2 of the convention signed at the Seventh American Conference at Montevideo in 1933.[1]

It should be recalled that the above mentioned article 2 provides that "the judgment of political delinquency concerns the State which offers asylum."

Safe conduct was finally granted for all the refugees and in its press release the government of Bolivia clearly based its action upon conventional obligations. It asserted that "at the very moment of its constitution, the *Junta Institucional de Gobierno* affirmed that it would respect treaties and international agreements, emphasizing on repeated occasions that this respect included the right of asylum." [2] It then noted that some parties had ignored these statements and then implied that the most it had ever intended was a temporary delay in the granting of safe conduct. Thus "the Honorable Diplomatic Corps was informed that the intense popular exaltation against some of the refugees would make it necessary to defer, for a reasonable period of time, the concession of safe conduct." [3] That safe conduct had been granted in deference to the unilateral qualification of the offence by the states granting asylum rather than as a result of its own determination that the refugees were political is obvious from this same press release. It noted that there remained "the proceedings of extradition, provided by the conventions of Havana and Montevideo, exclusively in the hands of the tribunals of justice." [4]

It appears, then, that while both the diplomatic corps and the Bolivian government based their action upon international agreements there are important differences arising from the particular conventions invoked by each party. The diplomatic corps seems to have invoked the 1889 treaty as an agreement binding by the very fact that it is an agreement *among the parties involved*. It was at least binding for Bolivia and three of the states granting asylum. Bolivia, however, in invoking article 2 of the Montevideo Convention of 1933 could only have invoked it as a convention which was binding in the sense that it was evidence of a customary rule of law inasmuch as it

---

[1] *Ibid.*
[2] "Declaration which the Undersecretary of Foreign Relations, Doctor Julio Alvarado gave to the Press, November 2, 1946," Bolivia, *Boletín*, n.° 13 (julio-diciembre, 1946), p. 98. (My translation.)
[3] *Ibid.*
[4] *Ibid.*

had not itself even signed the convention and only one of the other parties had ever ratified it.

In 1948 the Cuban embassy in Lima granted asylum to two refugees whom it qualified as "political." [1] The Peruvian government took the same position that it took in the Haya de la Torre case, i.e., that it had not ratified the Montevideo Convention of 1933 and thus was not bound by its provisions concerning the unilateral qualification of the offence.[2] Cuba, at first invoking only the Havana Convention, declared that the state granting asylum was qualified to determine the nature of the offence.[3] In response to the Peruvian assertion that it had not signed the Montevideo Convention of 1933 and that the Havana Convention made no such a provision, however, the Cuban government took a rather curious position:

> Previous reference to the unilateral qualification of the offence by the state granting asylum did not claim to establish a presumption that the government of Peru or that of Cuba had ratified the Convention of Montevideo, but that it established a general rule of law, which Peru as much as Cuba has indicated that it considered morally binding [moralmente vigente].[4]

Exactly what the phrase "morally binding" means in this case would be difficult to say but it is not inconceivable that it was good diplomatic language intended not to commit the Cuban government on this point.

In January of 1949, the Chilean and Guatemalan governments asked the Council of the Organization of American States to take note of the fact that Venezuela had refused to grant a safe conduct to ex-President Betancourt who had taken refuge in the Colombian embassy in Caracas.[5] The Venezuelan reply to these communications pointed out that safe conduct had already been granted. But the grounds upon which it accepted the obligation to grant a safe conduct are of significance for two reasons. (1) It based this obligation squarely on the Montevideo Treaty of 1933. (2) It certainly implied that the

---

[1] See "Notes Exchanged between the Minister of Foreign Relations of Peru and the Embassy of Cuba, Concerning the Asylum of Fernando León de Vivero and Pedro Muñiz," *Revista peruana de derecho internacional*, Tomo IX (mayo-agosto, 1949), pp. 142–185. (Title, my translation.)

[2] Díaz Dulanto, Peruvian Minister of Foreign Relations, to Espinoza, Cuban *Chargé d'Affaires* in Peru, March 9, 1949, ibid., pp. 152–160.

[3] Espinoza to Díaz Dulanto, February 21, 1949, *ibid.*, pp. 150–152.

[4] Espinoza to Díaz Dulanto, March 31, 1949, *ibid.*, p. 165. (My translation.)

[5] Del Rio, Chilean Ambassador to the United States, to Corominas, Chairman of the Council of the O. A. S., January 20, 1949 and González Arévalo, Guatemalan Ambassador to the United States, to Corominas, January 21, 1949, *Annals of the Organization of American States*, I (1949), p. 216.

obligations laid down in this treaty were *not* applicable to Venezuela in the absence of *specific action on the part of the latter indicating that it would be so bound.*

The Foreign Ministry of Venezuela notes for the record also that the question of granting the safe-conduct in reference was handled at all times in the greatest harmony and in strict conformity with the Treaty of Montevideo, *applicable to the case by virtue of the agreement concluded by an exchange of notes in June 1948 between the Republics of Venezuela and Colombia.*[1]

The full text of the notes referred to in the above communication apparently has not been published,[2] but the important points seem clear from a Colombian note of June 10, 1948, which was a response to an earlier Venezuelan note.

My government understands that the Venezuelan government, as concerns the cases of asylum which may arise in the Colombian embassy in Caracas as well as in the Venezuelan embassy in Bogotá, accepts in advance the rules laid down in the cited Convention of Montevideo, so that it is established that the norms of the Montevideo Convention on Political Asylum will regulate the matter reciprocally for Colombia and Venezuela.[3]

Venezuela agreed that "the rules laid down in the cited convention will regulate reciprocally the diplomatic relations of both countries."[4]

In a note to the government of Chile, Venezuela again emphasized that obligations in this case were entirely dependent upon conventions.

The problem of asylum in its entirety presents two aspects: one is the acceptance of rule of asylum, that which is manifested as a right, by the signing of the pertinent conventions and *de facto*, when the existence of asylees in the diplomatic representations is tolerated.

The country which refuses to become a party to treaties on this matter would reject the principle of asylum; the country which, having contracted such agreements, refuses to permit the access by refugees to such representations would violate its international agreements on asylum.[5]

In addition to the evidence connected with specific cases of asylum there are scattered bits of evidence which indicate that there has been no general agreement on this question and that Latin American states have been reluctant to declare unequivocally that they recognize the

---

[1] "Communication of the Ministry of Foreign Affairs of the United States of Venezuela," January 22, 1949, *ibid.*, p. 217. (My italics.)

[2] The note quoted below appears in an annex to Planas-Suárez, *op. cit.*, which apparently was added after the main text was ready for publication, where he indicated that the note had never been made public, see pp. 576–577. He does not give his source for the notes quoted and whether or not additional notes were exchanged is not clear.

[3] Planas-Suárez, *op. cit.*, p. 673. (My translation.)

[4] Note of June 11, 1948, *ibid.* (My translation.)

[5] January 28, 1949, quoted in Planas-Suárez, *op. cit.*, p. 610.

existence of a customary rule of law sanctioning the unilateral qualification of the offence by the state granting asylum.

In the discussion of the project relating to diplomatic representatives
at the 1927 meeting of the International Commission of American
Jurists, the Haitian delegate observed that "the obligation to give up
to local authorities the individuals who have taken refuge in Legations
or Consulates, or to give them asylum, has been a never ending source
of troble [sic] ... and believed that it is a question of American mo-
rality to have the suppression of diplomatic asylum for political
delinquents figure in an international Public Law Code drawn up by
American Jurists." [1]

The report on political asylum by the Fourth Sub-Committee at the
Seventh International Conference of American States indicates that,
at least up until this time, there had been considerable controversy on
this point.

Since the signing of the Havana Convention in 1928 differences of interpretation have arisen, causing painful controversies which have menaced cordi-
ality ... The one receiving asylum has been indefinitely held in the Legation
in an embarrassing situation and converting it into a veritable prison ..
The Havana Convention did not clearly specify who should judge the political
character of the delinquency, which omission has given rise to lamentable incidents. It imposes a categorical declaration which omits those causes of ill-being
and difficult elucidation in heated moments which provoke conditions pre-
carious for the refugee and dangerous for the one granting asylum. [2]

The Guatemalan *Memoria* for that year recognized the same situation.

Many incidents have caused a coolness, if not a divisiveness, in the international relations of American states after the Convention on Asylum, signed at
Havana, February 20, 1928. There were the antecedents of concrete cases
which caused the rupture of diplomatic relations as was the case of Cuba with
Brazil and of Peru with Mexico. The cases were of world notoriety and demanded
the attention of the conference in order to define who has the right of qualification of the political nature of the refugee ... [3]

In connection with the *Colombian-Peruvian Asylum Case* the
Colombian government published a document in which it attempted
to show that American opinion supported its position with regard to

---

[1] Brazil, Minister of State for Foreign Affairs, *International Commission of Jurists:* 1927
Meeting, Vol II (Rio de Janeiro: Imprensa Nacional, 1929), Minutes of the 16th Session,
May 12, 1927, p. 83.
[2] International Conference of American States, Seventh, *Minutes and Antecedents with
General Index* (Montevideo: 1933), pp. 171–172.
[3] Guatemala, *Memoria*, 1933, pp. 149–150. (My translation.)

the qualification of the offence.[1] It is significant that it was able to muster the opinions of only five foreign offices, and of these only three could be said to have supported the Colombian thesis. The governments of Ecuador, El Salvador and Guatemala clearly supported the thesis that the right of unilateral qualification of the offence by a state granting asylum was inherent in the right of asylum and should apply even in cases where no specific treat provisions existed.[2]

The Cuban reply really said nothing as to the existence of any customary rule of law on the matter.

> The legation of Cuba in Bern, acting in conformity with instructions of its Minister of Foreign Relations (Ministry of State); and in connection with the right of asylum, has the honor of informing the International Court of Justice at the Hague that the Government of the Republic of Cuba "regulates" its conduct by the principles established by the Convention of Havana (1928) and the Convention of Montevideo (1933), especially as concerns the qualification of the offence which corresponds to the government granting asylum.[3]

Inasmuch as Cuba had signed and ratified both of these conventions it was really not declaring much in saying that it "regulates" its conduct by these treaties, unless it meant that it so regulates its conduct even in relation to states which have not ratified the conventions. In the latter case it might or might not represent nothing more than a "practice."

As for the government of Costa Rica, it expressed the opinion that

---

[1] Colombia, Ministerio de Relaciones Exteriores, *La opinión americana y el derecho de asilo* (Bogotá: 1951). R. B. Greenburgh and Sir Harold Duncan, "Recent Developments in the Law of Diplomatic Asylum," *The Grotius Society: Transactions for the Year 1955* (London: The Grotius Society, 1956), p. 114, assert that "in 1951 the Colombian Government dispatched a questionnaire; and in their replies to it seventeen ministries of foreign affairs supported the Colombian thesis on qualification." The authors cite *La opinión americana y el derecho internacional, Ministerio de Relaciones Exteriores de Colombia*, Bogotá, 1951. *Noticias de Colombia*, No. 152, December, 1953, p. 1, notes the publication of a pamphlet on the Second Meeting of the Inter-American Council of Jurists, April-May, 1953 (the pamphlet was never published, however). The article notes that 17 countries supported the Colombian thesis but the conclusion is drawn from the fact, pointed out by Colombia at the above mentioned meeting, that 17 countries had shown their support *through ratification of conventions* and *treaties* which provide for unilateral qualification of the offence by the state granting asylum. Letter from Janet Hohmann de Tobon, Bogotá, Colombia, February 12, 1958. It may be noted also that it seems most unlikely that the Colombian government should have failed to present such strong evidence as that cited by Mr. Greenburgh in support of the draft convention under discussion two years later and that it should have been content to rest its case upon the seemingly weaker evidence provided by treaty ratification. See Inter-American Commission of Jurists, Second Meeting, *Actas y Documentos*, II, (Washington: Pan American Union, 1953), pp. 41–43.

[2] Colombia, Ministerio de Relaciones Exteriores, *La opinión americana y el derecho de asilo* (Bogotá: 1951), pp. 8–13.

[3] Valdes Roig, Cuban Minister to Switzerland, to the International Court of Justice, November 20, 1950, *ibid.*, p. 8. (My translation.)

"in the case under consideration [*the Colombian-Peruvian Asylum Case*] the right to determine the nature of the crime be attributed preferably to Colombia." [1] It then went on to propose a plan whereby the Supreme Court of each of the parties would declare their opinion on the nature of the offence and if the respective Supreme Courts reached conflicting decisions the matter would be submitted to the International Court of Justice.[2]

We also find evidence of disagreement in the preparation of a draft convention on diplomatic asylum by the Inter-American Council of Jurists at their 1953 meeting in Buenos Aires.

The Brazilian member of the Council sought to secure a middle position by which the decision of the asylum-granting state could, if protested by the territorial state, be referred to an arbitral tribunal. But this proposal being unacceptable to a majority, the draft, as revised by the Council, was approved and forwarded to the Council of the Organization. The United States refrained from signing on ground of its traditional position in regard to diplomatic asylum. Brazil abstained on ground of the absence of any limitations upon the discretion of the asylum-granting state. The delegations of the Dominican Republic and Peru entered reservations, the latter explaining its position at length and expressing its preference for the Brazilian proposal of arbitration in the event of differences between the territorial state and the state granting asylum.[3]

The Dominican objections can be ascertained from references to the Tenth Inter-American Conference and Honduran reservations might well nullify its application to that country.

The same conflicting views were in evidence when the draft convention approved by the Council of Jurists came before the Tenth Conference at Caracas ... the Dominican Republic objecting to the unilateral determination of the urgency; and Honduras making *reservation of articles in violation of the Constitution and laws of Honduras.*[4]

All this cannot ignore the fact that nineteen states eventually signed the Convention on Diplomatic Asylum (although two added reservations which would seem to be capable of nullifying much of what the convention was intended to accomplish).[5] More important, however, is the number of ratifications – at present only eleven.

---

[1] Toledo, Costa Rican Undersecretary of Foreign Relations, to Kerno, Legal Department of the United Nations, April 3, 1950, *ibid.*, p. 7. (My translation.)

[2] *Ibid.*, pp. 7–8.

[3] *Inter-American Juridical Yearbook:* 1952–1954 (Washington: Pan American Union, 1955), 57–58.

[4] *Ibid.*, p. 58. (My italics.)

[5] Pan American Union, Legal Division, Department of International Law, *Inter-American Treaties and Conventions: Signatures, Ratifications and Deposits with Explanatory Notes* (2d ed.; Washington, 1957), p. 47.

1. In cases where it can be shown that there has been a disagreement as to the nature of the offence with which the refugee is charged (or in some cases where there is simply disagreement as to whether or not the refugee can rightly be given asylum) there is no indication that, apart from cases regulated by treaty, they were settled out of recognition that the state granting asylum should make the qualification. While in most of the cases discussed the refugee was in fact permitted to leave the country there is often no indication that the state granting asylum felt that it was exercising a legal right in qualifying the offence as political and certainly no indication that the territorial state felt that it was legally obligated to accept this qualification.

2. Where a right of unilateral qualification of the offence has been explicitly claimed as a legal right by the state granting asylum, it has generally been claimed on the basis of treaty obligations rather than on the basis of a customary rule of law. Thus in connection with specific cases as well as in statements of policy not connected with specific cases, states have been reluctant to claim that such a right exists apart from treaty obligations.

3. Recognizing that the evidence presented offers by no means a clear-cut case, this writer must, nevertheless, conclude that it cannot sustain the contention that there is a customary rule of law in Latin America sanctioning the unilateral qualification of the offence by the state granting asylum. This position is taken in the full realization that in most of the cases discussed it can no more be proved that the states did *not* regard themselves as bound by such a rule than it can be proved that they *did*. Nevertheless, one of the basic assumptions upon which this thesis rests is that rules in derogation of recognized rules of international law (of which territorial jurisdiction is one) must be clearly established. This would seem to be particularly applicable in the case where a distinct regional rule of law is claimed. It is also recognized that an approach such as this is clearly open to the charge that it makes the development of a body of international law extremely difficult. This matter will be discussed in the summary and conclusions.

CHAPTER XI

LEGAL NORMS AND POLITICAL REALITY

The practice of diplomatic asylum in Latin America seems to have been more the result of that area's own conditions and antecedents than the result of conscious application of European practices. We see repeated here much the same pattern of development that appeared in European practice. Churches first served as places of sanctuary and were replaced by foreign embassies, legations and even consulates with the coming of independence. There can be no doubt, of course, that the foreign diplomatic representatives were familiar with the practice which had existed in Europe at an earlier date and it is impossible to tell exactly what influence this might have had upon their decisions to grant asylum. The earliest cases which give us any idea of attitudes on the part of the governments involved appear about the middle of the nineteenth century. In these cases there is evidence that the diplomatic agents recognized that the practice was no longer sanctioned in Europe but justified their action in terms of Latin American experience. It is not known whether the practice referred to, which obviously took place in the first twenty-five years of the independence period, originated as an extension of European experience but in view of the antecedents of the colonial period it is more likely that it was a local development growing out of turbulent conditions, familiarity with the earlier practice of religious asylum and the fact that the newly established governments, anxious for recognition by the major powers, were not inclined to violate the immunity of diplomatic premises.

A basic assumption throughout this discussion has been that proof of a customary rule of law must not only show the existence of a practice but must also show the existence of the psychological element of *opinio juris sive necessitatis*. While it is felt that the rulings of international tribunals support this position this discussion has also attempted to show that a careful investigation of the details concerning a great many asylum cases shows that the requirement is particularly applicable here. Such an investigation shows that very often the practice is tolerated by the territorial state because it is not particularly interested in gaining custody over the refugee. Indeed, it often happens that the state may welcome the cooperation of a foreign embassy or legation in getting an unpopular individual safely out of the country. In some cases it is doubtful if, in the confusion surrounding political upheavals, the territorial state was even aware of the fact that asylum had been granted in a particular embassy or legation.

Furthermore, it does not appear that the state granting asylum has always felt that it was *legally* justified in doing so. There is at least some evidence that the diplomatic representative has at times gone beyond what his government would claim and that his government has been more interested in removing itself from a difficult situation than in strict legal considerations. This has been most obvious in the case of United States practice.

To insist that a practice which has grown up in this manner should become legally obligatory would seem to be as harmful to the development of a set of rules of international conduct as it would to the extension of international comity.

Further investigation into treaties and practice has suggested that Latin American states have not consistently recognized the existence of a legal obligation to respect such a practice or a legal right to engage in it. Bilateral treaties apparently have been of no significance but multilateral treaties have shown a reluctance to declare unequivocally that a right of asylum would be respected. In the two conventions which have received the widest ratification, (Havana, 1928 and Montevideo, 1933) the right was made dependent upon pre-existing custom, treaties, or legislation. International agreements which flatly declare that the institution will be recognized have received much less support. A great deal of inconsistency can be noted within the practice of particular states and, while some states have shown a greater consistency, there is evidence that in doing so they have insisted that the practice of asylum *is not* sanctioned by any customary rule of law.

Nowhere is this extra-legal basis more evident than in the practice of consular asylum. A considerable number of treaties, multilateral and bilateral, have been signed which explicitly or implicitly forbid the granting of asylum in consular establishments. In spite of this the practice has been widespread and Latin American states have cited these cases, when convenient, without distinction from the practice of diplomatic asylum. This is another indication that the practice has been largely an extra-legal matter depending primarily upon considerations of expediency and comity.

A second basic assumption throughout this discussion has been that rules in derogation of established rules of international law must be clearly established. This has led to the conclusion that a practice which has shown so much inconsistency and expediency cannot be said to have reached the stage where it can be considered as a rule recognized as law when, as in this case, it would be a limitation on the well recognized rule of territorial jurisdiction. The controversy over the existence of a *particular* international law (in this case an "American international law") has been noted. This is just another reason for demanding indisputable evidence of the existence of such a rule growing out of a practice which has been limited to a given region and a clear departure from an established rule of general international law.

The fact remains, however, that a large number of Latin American states have, through treaties, bound themselves to recognize the practice of asylum although it is not always clear from the treaties exactly what this obligation involves or upon what it depends – i.e., pre-existing custom, recognition by the state granting asylum, etc. In all cases, however, it is only in the case of "political refugees" that this obligation exists. But *what* is a "political refugee" and *who* determines whether an individual can be qualified as such?

No treaty on the subject even attempts to define a political refugee" or a "political offence." A study of Latin American practice offers little assistance. Evidence suggests that in most cases the details and circumstances surrounding any given case were not carefully weighed and discussed. Indeed, it is difficult to see how a diplomatic representative could do this without getting involved in domestic affairs and casting reflections upon the machinery of justice in the country to which he is accredited. In short, there are not sufficient details available to build up a body of precedents which could be applied to particular cases in defining a "political offence." The best that can be said is that states have granted asylum when they have felt that an individual was in some way connected with a revolutionary movement or some political activity which would mean that he might not receive a fair hearing. When such circumstances have existed they have generally refused to surrender the refugee even though there were charges against him for what would otherwise appear to be common crimes. This seems to have been largely an intuitive process on the part of the diplomatic representative. In any event, if he had any clearly defined rules for determining when such circumstances exist they have not been revealed in the diplomatic exchanges relating to the case.

A number of Latin American states have signed and ratified treaties and conventions which provide that the state granting asylum shall determine the nature of the offence. The usefulness of the Montevideo Convention of 1933 is somewhat reduced by the fact that it makes no such provision for the determination of a situation of "urgency." Since the International Court of Justice pointed out that this was one of the two prerequisites to a proper grant of asylum under the Havana convention (which only provided that asylum would be respected for political refugees in cases of urgency) this may well open new controversies in the future. The Caracas Convention of 1954 provides that the State granting asylum shall determine both of these points but only eleven states have ratified this convention to date.

In the *Colombian-Peruvian Asylum Case* the International Court of Justice ruled that Colombia had not proved the existence of a customary rule of law which permitted the granting state to qualify the nature of the offence unilaterally. The Court took note of a large number of cases cited by Colombia where the refugee had been permitted to leave the country. But the Court asserted that this proved very little inasmuch as it had not been shown whether this had been done out of a recognition of any legal right on the part of the granting state or legal obligation on the part of the territorial state.

This discussion has attempted to examine the available details on these and other cases of asylum in an effort to determine whether or not the element which the Court demanded might have been present. Such evidence has not been found. On the contrary, most of the cases discussed *suggest*, although they do not prove conclusively, that one or both of the parties to the controversy felt that no such legal right or obligation existed.

It is recognized that by requiring that proof of a customary rule of law must show that states, in following a given practice, did so out of a feeling of right or obligation, one makes proof of such a rule extremely difficult. It is also recognized that the body of law which may be built up as a result of this will be considerably smaller than many would like to see. Yet in a system of law which must depend primarily upon the will of the sovereign state for its enforcement it is questionable how useful any body of law would be that is not at least built upon the basic requirement of *opinio juris sive necessitatis*. Likewise an international tribunal which attempts to apply law that does not rest squarely on this foundation may well find itself with a great deal of law but no cases in which to use it so long as that tribunal must also depend upon the voluntary acceptance of its jurisdiction. Finally, the liberal application of rules not meeting these standards can only assure that the jurisdiction of international tribunals will remain entirely dependent upon voluntary acceptance by the sovereign state in each case.

But an even more important consideration must be emphasized here. To say that an examination of practice does not establish a legal obligation with regard to the institution of diplomatic asylum is *not* to deprecate the importance of the institution nor its effectiveness in bringing order and predictability into the relations among Latin American states. Professor Charles de Visscher has wisely admonished us that he who would understand the international legal order must not see in the process by which norms are formed only the special procedure that constitutes the last phase and marks its full achievement.[1] The normative function of well established practices that are not necessarily regarded as "law" should not be underestimated. Here is a practice which has responded to the unstable and often violent political climate of Latin America for more than a century and has fulfilled a social need.

One thing that must by now be clear to the reader is that, in spite of vague and often contradictory official statements, the institution of diplomatic asylum is *in fact* respected. Not only has the refugee been allowed to remain unharmed within his place of asylum; in most cases safe conduct out of the country has eventually been granted. The fact that the practice has been able to survive the impact of social revolution and Cold War is proof of its viability. Although, in 1954, the Trujillo regime denounced the conventions of 1928 and 1933, it continued to grant safe conduct out of the country until the eve of the dictator's assassination. On August 10, 1960 it was reported that the Dominican President, Balaguer, promised safe conduct passes and passports for some seventy-one refugees in the Argentine, Brazilian and Mexican embassies. In the course of the controversy, however, two refugees were killed and two others were wounded in the garden of the Brazilian embassy.[2]

[1] Charles de Visscher, *Theory and Reality in Public International Law*, trans., P. E. Corbett (Princeton: Princeton University Press, 1957) p. XII.
[2] *New York Times*, July 10, August 1, 2, 10, 1960.

The practice has also survived the bitterness and violence of the Cuban revolution. There are arguments, threats and delays, to be sure, but, with very few exceptions, the refugee has eventually been permitted to leave the country in safety. On September 1, 1961 the Venezuelan Consul General in Havana reported that the Cuban government had granted safe conduct passes to 800 persons who had received asylum in various embassies and legations there. Some 250 refugees in the Venezuelan embassy had already arrived in Venezuela.[1] A year later, the Uruguayan government announced that it was dispatching air force planes to remove about 400 refugees who had been given asylum in Uruguay's embassy in Havana.[2]

Why, then, the reluctance to make an unqualified and unambiguous commitment? First of all, it must be noted that this is an institution very susceptible to abuse and, if abused, an open invitation to plotting and insurrection against a government. It creates especially delicate problems because it is so closely linked with the most vital of all rules of international law – the immunity of diplomatic officers and the inviolability of embassies and legations. These rules can be violated only at the risk of interrupting vital international intercourse. The present somewhat nebulous legal status of the institution at least allows the territorial state a measure of regulation and control. It is *not* likely that states that have refused to commit themselves more explicitly on this are contemplating at some future date the possibility of forcing the surrender of a refugee from a diplomatic establishment. Rather, they are reserving for future use the weapon of indefinite delay in granting safe conduct and of inflicting other inconveniences upon the embassy or legation that might abuse the privilege. This provides some protection against too extravagant an application of the practice. The more precise the commitment to respect the practice, the more difficult it becomes to apply measures of delay and inconvenience.

The decision of the International Court of Justice on the *Colombian-Peruvian Asylum Case* was greeted with considerable dismay, especially among a number of Latin American Jurists. But would it have made the practice into a more effective institution had the Court decided that unilateral qualification of the offense by the state granting asylum was sanctioned by *law*? Or is it possible that such a ruling would

---

[1] *Ibid.*, Sept. 10, 1961.
[2] *Ibid.*, Aug. 17, 1962.

have made the practice less viable? There is at least some reason to believe the second a more probable development.

Clearly this left the case as unsettled as it had been before the endless learned arguments and counter-arguments had been offered to the Court. But this is precisely the wisdom of the decision. The Court refused to apply rules for which it could not find definitive evidence and left the matter to be settled the way thousands of asylum cases have been settled in the past. An amicable solution is eventually worked out which may or may not be the result of legal considerations, but the refugee is, almost without exception, permitted to leave the country. This is precisely what happened with Haya de la Torre.

Had the Court insisted on putting this practice into a legal mold, it is by no means clear that it would have had a beneficial effect upon the institution of asylum. How many states would then have announced that they would not in the future tolerate the practice (as the Dominican Republic did in 1954)? Would the diplomatic representative continue to use the same caution when the law was more clearly on his side? [1]

The increased use of terrorism in Latin American politics makes it more essential than ever before that the diplomatic representative use the utmost caution in granting asylum and that the territorial state retain the means by which it can protect itself against abuses without provoking major diplomatic crises. The Venezuelan government recently tried to head off such a crisis when, following an attempt on the life of President Betancourt, it announced that it would not recognize a right of asylum for persons guilty of assassination.[2] If the use of terrorism continues to increase, the continuation of the practice of asylum will require that the informal regulating mechanisms which have served reasonably well in the past not be weakened.

The fact that the United States has been able to extricate itself from the practice has at least removed one complicating element. Should the United States again become involved the problem would become infinitely more complex. The granting of asylum to political offenders can easily be a means of intervention in the domestic politics of another state. It is probably more than mere coincidence that the United States ended the practice in the very years when complaints against Yankee

---

[1] For a development of this view in the context of a number of legal questions in inter-American relations, see C. Neale Ronning, *Law and Politics in Inter-American Diplomacy* (New York: John Wiley & Sons, 1963).

[2] *Hispanic American Report* (August, 1960), p. 391.

intervention were the bitterest and when the new non-intervention policy was emerging.

Given the continued "disengagement" of the United States, the flexible nature of the institution of diplomatic asylum holds out the hope that it will be able to survive contemporary social upheavals. That it is a product of Latin American traditions, responding to the peculiar needs of these societies explains its survival when so many of the traditional rules of international law are challenged or ignored.

APPENDICES

I. CONVENTION ON ASYLUM [1]

Signed at La Habana, February 20, 1928, at the Sixth International Conference of American States

Signatory Countries	Date of Instrument of Ratification	Date of Deposit of the Instrument of Ratification
Argentina		
Bolivia		
Brazil	July 30 1929	September 3, 1929
Colombia	August 25, 1936	February 20, 1937
Costa Rica	May 8, 1933	June 7, 1933
Cuba	January 12, 1931	May 4, 1931
Chile		
Dominican Republic [d]	March 22, 1932 [d]	April 8, 1932 [d]
Ecuador	June 15, 1936	September 4, 1936
El Salvador	July 26, 1936	January 9, 1937
Guatemala	May 20, 1931	September 25, 1931
Haiti	January 3, 1951	March 13, 1952
Honduras	August 24, 1956	September 10, 1956
Mexico	January 11, 1929	February 6, 1929
Nicaragua	December 22, 1929	March 20, 1930
Panama	March 20, 1929	May 21, 1929
Paraguay	September 20, 1948	October 28, 1948
Peru	April 9, 1945	June 21, 1945
United States *		
Uruguay	July 21, 1933	September 16, 1933
Venezuela		

* With a reservation.

The original instrument is deposited with the Ministry of State of Cuba. The Pan American Union is the depository of the instruments of ratification.

[d] The Dominican Republic denounced the above Convention on October 6, 1954. It has also denounced the Convention on Political Asylum signed at the Seventh Conference of Montevideo in 1933.

[1] Reproduced from: Pan American Union, Legal Division, Department of International Law, *Inter-American Treaties and Conventions: Signatures, Ratifications, and Deposits with Explanatory Notes* (2d ed.; Washington, 1957), p. 24. (Irrelevant details have been omitted.)

II. CONVENTION ON POLITICAL ASYLUM[1]

Signed at Montevideo, December 26, 1933, at the Seventh International Conference of American States

Signatory Countries	Date of Instrument of Ratification	Date of Deposit of the Instrument of Ratification
Argentina		
Brazil	September 1, 1936	February 23, 1937
Colombia	June 22, 1936	July 22, 1936
Costa Rica *	June 2, 1954	June 10, 1954
Cuba	December 20, 1950	January 17, 1951
Chile	February 2, 1935	March 28, 1935
Dominican Republic d	November 22, 1934 d	December 26, 1934d
Ecuador	March 20, 1955	August 11, 1955
El Salvador	July 26, 1936	January 9, 1937
Guatemala	April 28, 1935	July 3, 1935
Haiti	June 29, 1951	March 13, 1952
Honduras	December 10, 1935	February 15, 1936
Mexico	August 13, 1935	January 27, 1936
Nicaragua	December 25, 1952	February 4, 1953
Panama	November 11, 1938	December 13, 1938
Paraguay	September 20, 1948	October 28, 1948
Peru		
Uruguay		

* Adherence.

d The Dominican Republic denounced the above Convention on October 6, 1954. It has also denounced the Convention on Asylum signed at the Sixth Conference of Havana in 1928 ....

The original instrument is deposited with the Ministry of Foreign Affairs of Uruguay. The Pan American Union is the depository of the instruments of ratification.

[1] Reproduced from: Pan American Union, Legal Division, Department of International Law, *Inter-American Treaties and Conventions: Signatures, Ratifications, and Deposits with Explanatory Notes* (2d ed.; Washington, 1957), p. 38. (Irrelevant details have been omitted.)

III. CONVENTION ON DIPLOMATIC ASYLUM[1]

Signed at Caracas, March 28, 1954, at the Tenth Inter-American Conference

Signatory Countries	Date of Instrument of Ratification	Date of Deposit of the Instrument of Ratification
Argentina		
Bolivia		
Brazil		
Colombia		
Costa Rica (s)	January 13, 1955	February 24, 1955
Cuba		
Chile		
Dominican Republic *		
Ecuador	March 20, 1955	August 11, 1955
El Salvador	September 6, 1954	September 28, 1954
Guatemala *		
Haiti	January 18, 1955	February 18, 1955
Honduras *		
Mexico	January 25, 1957	February 6, 1957
Nicaragua		
Panama		
Paraguay	October 4, 1956	January 25, 1957
Uruguay *		
Venezuela	December 15, 1954	December 29, 1954

* With reservations.

(s) Costa Rica signed on June 16, 1954, at the Pan American Union.

The original instrument is deposited with the Pan American Union, which is also the depository of the instruments of ratification.

[1] Reproduced from: Pan American Union, Legal Division, Department of International Law, *Inter-American Treaties and Conventions: Signatures, Ratifications, and Deposits with Explanatory Notes* (2d ed.; Washington, 1957), p. 47. (Irrelevant details have been omitted.)

IV. SUMMARY OF CASES CITED BY COLOMBIA IN THE
COLOMBIAN-PERUVIAN ASYLUM CASE[1]

Date	Territorial State	State and Place of Refuge	Disposition of Case
1840	Ecuador	Peruvian warship	Left the country
1850	Ecuador	Colombian and U.S. consulates	Not indicated
1859	Ecuador	Peruvian ship	Not indicated
1865	Peru	U.S. legation	Not indicated
1865	Peru	French legation and various ships	Safe conduct granted
1870	Haiti	U.S. legation	Left the country
1870	Guatemala	British legation	Obtained permission to leave country
1874	Bolivia	U.S. embassy	Not indicated
1875	Haiti	British legation U.S. legation	Not indicated
1876	Haiti	French legation	Permitted to leave country
1878	Haiti	U.S., British and Liberian legations	Safe conduct granted
1879	Haiti	British and French legations	Left the country
1885	Ecuador	Colombian legation	Not indicated
1891	Chile	U.S., Spanish and other legations	Permitted to leave country
1894	El Salvador	U.S. warship	Not indicated
1904	Dominican Republic	Italian and U.S. consulates	Not indicated
1906	Ecuador	Colombian legation	Not indicated
1908	Paraguay	Argentine legation	Not incidated
1909	Nicaragua	Mexican warship	Left the country
1911	Ecuador	Chilean legation	Not indicated
1911	Mexico	U.S. warship	Left the country
1911	Paraguay	Argentine warships	Not indicated
1914	Peru	Bolivian legation	Not indicated
1920	Bolivia	U.S. and all missions accredited to La Paz except Chile and France	Not indicated
1920	Guatemala	Spain [legation?]	Not indicated
1922	Paraguay	Foreign diplomatic missions	Not indicated
1922	El Salvador	Spanish legation	Not indicated
1930	Brazil	Nearly all foreign missions	"Right of asylum respected"
1930	Peru	Bolivian legation	Not indicated
1931	Argentina	Spanish embassy	"Full guarantees given"
1933	Brazil	Spain [legation?]	Not indicated
1933	Chile	Argentine embassy	Not indicated

[1] Compiled from: Perú, Ministerio de Relaciones Exteriores, *Proceso sobre asilo entre el Perú y Colombia ante la Corte Internacional de Justicia* (Lima: 1951), pp. 377-382.

Date	Territorial State	State and Place of Refuge	Disposition of Case
1933	El Salvador	Paraguay [legation?]	Safe conduct granted
1935	Venezuela	Spanish legation	Authorized to leave
1936	Spain	Peruvian consulate	Not indicated
1941	Guatemala	El Salvador [legation?]	Safe conduct granted
1944	Guatemala	Peruvian legation and other legations and embassies	Safe conduct granted
1945	Dominican Republic	Venezuelan legation	Safe conduct granted
1945	Guatemala	Nicaraguan and Salvadoran embassies	Safe conduct granted
1946	Bolivia	Peruvian, Argentine, Venezuelan embassies	Safe conduct and "necessary guarantees to leave Bolivia"
1946	Ecuador	Venezuelan embassy	Permitted to leave country
1948	Guatemala	Brazilian and Ecuadoran embassies	Left the country
1948	Panama	Peruvian embassy	"Peru solicited the necessary" safe conduct
1948	Peru	Brazilian, Colombian, Chilean, Paraguayan, Mexican and Venezuelan embassies	Safe conduct granted
1948	Colombia	Venezuelan embassies	Safe conduct granted
1948	Venezuela	Colombian embassy	Authorized to leave
1949	Guatemala	Embassies of Argentina, Brazil, Costa Rica, Chile, Honduras, Mexico, Panama, Apostolic Nuncio and legation of Colombia	Safe conduct granted
1949	Argentina	Uruguayan embassy	Safe conduct granted

V. SUMMARY OF ASYLUM CASES TO WHICH THE UNITED STATES HAS BEEN A PARTY AS CITED BY COLOMBIA IN THE *COLOMBIAN-PERUVIAN ASYLUM CASE*[1]

Date	Territorial State	Place of Refuge (when indicated)
1843	Ecuador	–
1843	Argentina	–
1849	Peru	legation
1850	Ecuador	–
1874	Argentina	legation
1875	Haiti	–
1877	Mexico	consulate
1878	Haiti	–
1889	Haiti	–
1891	Chile	–
1895	Chile	ship
1895	Ecuador	legation
1904	Dominican Republic	–
1920	Bolivia	–
1922	Paraguay	–

[1] Compiled from: Perú, Ministerio de Relaciones Exteriores, *Proceso sobre asilo entre el Perú y Colombia ante la Corte Internacional de Justicia* (Lima: 1951), pp. 383–384.

BIBLIOGRAPHY

TREATISES

Accioly, Hildebrando. *Tratado de derecho internacional público*. 3 vols. Rio de Janeiro: Imprensa Nacional, 1945–1946.

Almanza Rosales, Alfredo. *Algunas anotaciones sobre la evolución del concepto de asilo*. Tesis (licenciatura en derecho) Universidad Nacional Autónoma de México. México: 1947.

Alvarez, Alejandro. *Le droit international américain*. Paris: A. Pedone, 1910.

Antokoletz, Daniel. *Tratado de derecho internacional público en tiempo de paz*. 2 vols. Buenos Aires: J. Roldán y cía., 1924–1925.

Briggs, Herbert W. *The Law of Nations: Cases, Documents, and Notes*. 2d. ed. New York: Appleton-Century-Crofts, 1952.

Cabral de Moncada, Hugo. *O asilo interno em direito internacional público*. Coimbra: Edição do autor, 1946.

Castillo y Bahena, Raphael V. *El asilo diplomático*. Tesis. Universidad Nacional Autónoma de Mexico. Mexico: 1951.

Corbett, P. E. *Law and Society in the Relations of States*. New York: Harcourt, Brace and Company, 1951.

— *The Study of International Law*. Short Studies in Political Science. Garden City, New York: Doubleday, 1955.

Depetre, José Lion. *Derecho diplomático*. México, D. F.: Librería de Manuel Porrua, 1952.

Evans, Lawrence B. *Leading Cases on International Law*. 2d. ed. Chicago: Callaghan and Co., 1922.

Fenwick, Charles G. *The Inter-American Regional System*. New York: The Declan X. McMullen Company, 1949.

— *International Law*. 3rd. ed. New York: Appleton-Century-Crofts. 1948.

Flassan, M. de. *Histoire générale et raisonnée de la diplomatie française ou de la politique de la France*. II, IV. Paris: Treuttel et Würtz, Libraires, 1811.

Foster, John W. *The Practice of Diplomacy as Illustrated in the Foreign Relations of the United States*. New York: Houghton, Mifflin and Co., 1906.

Galdámes, Luis. *A History of Chile*. Translated and edited by I. J. Cox. Chapel Hill: The University of North Carolina Press, 1941.

García Mora, Manuel R. *International Law and Asylum as a Human Right*. Washington: Public Affairs Press [1956].

Genet, Raoul. *Traité de diplomatie et de droit diplomatique*. I. Paris: Libraire de la Cour d'Appel et de l'Ordre des Avocats, 1931.

Gonzalez Uzcategul, J. R. *El derecho internacional en Venezuela*. Caracas: Empresa Gutenberg, 1930.

Hall, William Edward. *A Treatise on International Law.* 8th ed. Edited by Pearce Higgins. Oxford: The Clarendon Press, 1924.

Haring, C. H. *The Spanish Empire in America.* New York: Oxford University Press, 1947.

Helfant, Henry. *The Trujillo Doctrine of Humanitarian Diplomatic Asylum.* [Mexico, D. F., 1947].

Hershey, Amos S. *The Essentials of Public Law and Organization.* Rev. ed. New York: The Macmillan Co., 1927.

Holland, Thomas Erskine. *Studies on International Law.* Edited by T. A. Walker. London: Sweet and Maxwell, 1933.

Hudson, Manley O. *The Permanent Court of International Justice, 1920–1942.* New York: The Macmillan Co., 1943.

Jacobini, H. B. *A Study of the Philosophy of international Law as seen in Works of Latin American Writers.* The Hague: Nijhoff, 1954.

Luque Angel, Eduardo. *El derecho de asilo.* Bogotá: Temis 1959.

McNair, Lord [Arnold Duncan]. *International Law Opinions: Selected and Annotated.* II. Cambridge: Cambridge University Press, 1956.

Markham, Clements R. *A History of Peru.* Chicago: Sergel and Company, 1892.

Martens, Charles de. *Causes célèbres du droit des gens.* I. 2d ed. Leipzig: F. A. Brockhaus, 1858.

Martens, Georg Friedrich. *The Law of Nations, Being the Science of National Law, Covenants, Power, etc., Founded Upon the Treaties and Customs of Modern Nations in Europe* ... Translated from the French by Wm. Cobbett. 4th ed. London: W. Cobbett, 1892.

Mecham, J. Lloyd. *Church and State in Latin America: A History of Politico-Ecclesiastical Relations.* Chapel Hill: The University of North Carolina Press, 1934.

Moreno Quintana, Lucio M. *Derecho de asilo.* Buenos Aires: Imprenta de la Universidad, 1952.

Núñez Morgado, Aurelio. *Los sucesos de España vistos por un diplomático.* Buenos Aires: Talleres Gráficos Argentinos, L. J. Rosso, 1941.

Ogdon, Montell. *Bases of Diplomatic Immunity.* Washington: John Byrne and Co., 1936.

Oppenheim, Lassa Francis L. *International Law; A Treatise.* 8th ed. Edited by H. Lauterpacht. I. London, New York: Longmans, Green, 1955.

Padelford, Norman J. *International Law and Diplomacy in the Spanish Civil Strife.* New York: Macmillan Co., 1939.

Parra, Francisco J. *El derecho de asilo; a los estudiantes universitarios del Perú.* Lima: Librería e Imprenta Gil, 1936.

Phillimore, Robert. *Commentaries on International Law.* II. 2d ed. London: Butterworths, 1871.

Planas-Suárez, Simón. *El asilo diplomático. Estudio jurídico y político sobre este execrable uso latinoamericano, distructor de la soberanea nacional y de la cordialidad internacional.* Buenos Aires: 1953.

Plaza Martínez, J. Juan. *El asilo diplomático.* Tesis. Universidad Nacional Autónoma de Mexico: 1952.

Pradier-Fodéré, P. *Cours de droit diplomatique.* II. Paris: Libraire de la Cour d'Appel et de l'Ordre des Avocats, 1899.

Redlich, Marcellus Donald A. R. *The Law of Nations.* 2d ed. [Phoenix, Ariz.]: World League for Permanent Peace, 1937.

Rouzier, Raoul. *Le droit d'asile en Haiti.* Port-au-Prince, Haiti: Éditions "La Nation," 1943.

Satow, Sir Ernest. *A Guide to Diplomatic Practice.* I. 2d ed., revised. New York: Longmans, Green and Co., 1922.

Schwarzenberger, Georg. *International Law*. I. 2d ed. London: Stevens and Sons, 1949.
Starke, Joseph Gabriel. *An Introduction to International Law*. 3d ed. Butterworths, 1954.
Stuart, Graham H. *American Diplomatic and Consular Practice* 2d ed. New York: Appleton-Century-Crofts, 1952.
Stewart, Irvin. *Consular Privileges and Immunities*. New York: Columbia University Press, 1926.
Tobar y Borgono, C. M. *L'asile interne devant le droit international*. Barcelona: Impr. de Carbonell y Esteva, 1911.
Urrutia-Aparicio, Carolos. *Opúsculo sobre derecho de asilo diplomático, con anotaciones históricas, doctrinas y judiciales*. Guatemala: 1952.
Ursua, Francisco A. *El asilo diplomático*. México, D. F.: Editorial Cultura, 1952.
Valle Muñoz, Mario del. *El derecho de asilo eclesiástico en el reino de Chile*. Publicaciones de los Seminarios de la Facultad de Ciencias Jurídicas y Sociales de la Universidad Católica de Chile. Santiago: [1952?].
Vattel, Emmerich de. *The Law of Nations or Principles of the Law of Nature, Applied to the Conduct and Affairs of Nations and Sovereigns*. Translated by Joseph Chitty. Philadelphia: T. & J. W. Johnson and Co., 1861.
Westlake, John. *International Law*. I. 2d ed. Cambridge: The University Press. 1910.
Wicquefort, Abraham de. *L'Ambassadeur et ses fonctions*. Amsterdam: Janssons a Waesberger, 1730.

ARTICLES

Alfonsin, Quintín. "El asilo diplomático." *Revista de derecho público y privado* (Montevideo), XXXIII (noviembre, 1954), pp. 259–271.
Alvarez, Alejandro. "Latin America and International Law," *American Journal of International Law*, III (April, 1909), pp. 269–353.
Anze Martienzo, Eduardo. "Acotaciones sobre el derecho de asilo," *Pan América: revista de derecho internacional americano*, II (febrero, 1957), pp. 19–24.
Arévalo Correal, Edilberto. "El derecho de asilo," *Revista de la Academia Colombiana de Jurisprudencia*, XX (1950), pp. 391–419.
Asua, Luis Jiménez. "El asilo diplomático," *Revista jurídica argentina: "La Ley,"* LIII (enero, febrero, marzo, 1949), pp. 906–918.
Barcia Trelles, Camilo. "El derecho de asilo diplomático," *Revista de derecho internacional*, (Habana), LIX (1951), pp. 161–180.
— "El derecho de asilo diplomático y el caso Haya de la Torre; glosas a una sentencia," *Revista española de derecho internacional*, IV (1951), pp. 59–66.
Briggs, Herbert W. "The Colombian-Peruvian Asylum Case and Proof of Customary International Law," *The American Journal of International Law*, XLV, (October, 1951), pp. 728–731.
Corbett, P. E. "The Consent of States and the Sources of the Law of Nations," *The British Year Book of International Law*, VI (1925), pp. 20–30.
"El derecho de asilo en el caso de Managua," *Diario de Centro-américa* (Guatemala), 25 mayo, 1954.
Deusta A., Alejandro, "Derecho de asilo," *Revista peruana de derecho internacional*, VII (1947), pp. 23–81; 178–201; VIII (1948), pp. 13–32; 109–127.
Evans, Lawrence B. "The Primary Sources of International Obligations," *Proceedings of the American Society of International Law at its Fifth Annual Meeting held in Washington, D.C., April, 27–29, 1911*, pp. 257–274.

Fenwick, Charles G. "The Law of the Organization of American States," *Cursos monográficos*, IV (Habana, 1954), pp. 255–290.

García Mora, Manuel R. "The Colombian-Peruvian Asylum Case and the Doctrine of Human Rights." *Virginia Law Review*, XXXVII (November, 1951), pp. 927–965.

Gilbert, Barry. "The Practice of Asylum in Legations and Consulates of the United States." *The American Journal of International Law*, III (July, 1909), pp. 562–595.

Greenburgh, R. B. and Duncan, Sir Harold. "Recent Developments in the Law of Diplomatic Asylum," *The Grotius Society: Transactions for the Year 1955*. London: The Grotius Society, 1956, pp. 103–122.

Jiménez de Asua, Luis. "Direito de asilo," *Revista forense* (Rio de Janeiro), CXXIV (julho, 1949), pp. 40–44.

Kopelmanas, Lazare. "Custom as a Means of the Creation of International Law," *The British Year Book of International Law*, XVIII (1937), pp. 127–151.

Molina Orantes, Adolfo. "Aspectos históricos de derecho de asilo en Guatemala," *Revista de la Asociación Guatemalteca de Derecho Internacional* (enero, 1954), pp. 106–119.

Morgenstern, Felice. "Extra-Territorial Asylum," *The British Year Book of International Law*, XXV (1948), pp. 236–261.

Nys, Ernest. "The Codification of International Law," Translated by Courtesy of Mr. Clement L. Bouve, of the District of Columbia Bar. *The American Journal of International Law*, V (October, 1911), pp. 871–900.

Ralston, Jackson H. "The Value of Authorities in International Law," *Proceedings of the American Society of International Law at its Fifth Annual Meeting held in Washington, D. C., April 27–29, 1911*, pp. 257–274.

Soriano, Aviles. "El derecho de asilo, institución religiosa," *Información jurídica* (Madrid), (julio-agosto, 1948), pp. 31–55.

Stowell, Ellery C. "Diplomatic Privileges and Immunities," *The American Journal of International Law*, XX (October, 1926), pp. 735–738.

— "Humanitarian Intervention," *The American Journal of International Law*, XXXIII(October, 1939), pp. 733–736.

Vargas, José María, P. "El punto de derecho en el caso del asilo diplomático de Haya de la Torre," *Revista del Colegio de Abogados*, VI (octubre, 1950), pp. 347–348.

JUDGMENTS AND OPINIONS OF INTERNATIONAL COURTS

The Case of the S.S. "Lotus," Judgment of September 7, 1927: Publications of the Permanent Court of International Justice. *Series A, No. 10, 1927*.

Colombian-Peruvian Asylum Case, Judgment of November 20th, 1950: International Court of Justice *Reports 1950*, p. 266.

Hambro, Edvard. *The Case Law of the International Court: A Repositoire of the Judgments,Advisory Opinions and Orders of the Permanent Court of International Justice and of the International Court of Justice*. Leyden: A. W. Sijthoff's Publishing Company, 1952.

Haya de la Torre Case, Judgment of June 13th, 1951: International Court of Justice *Reports 1951*, p. 71.

Jurisdiction of the European Commission of the Danube between Galatz and Braila, Advisory Opinion of December 8th, 1927: Publications of the Permanent Court of International Justice, *Series B, No. 4, 1927*.

Scott, James Brown (ed.). *The Hague Court Reports*. New York: Oxford University Press, 1916, pp. 141–225.

DIGESTS AND TREATY COLLECTIONS

Cuba. [Secretario de Estado.] *Tratados, convenios y convenciones celebrados por la república de Cuba desde 1916.* La Habana: Imprenta y Papelería de Rambia, Bouza y Cía, 1929.

Ecuador. [Ministerio de Relaciones Exteriores.] *Colección de tratados, convenciones, capitulaciones, armisticios y otros actos diplomáticos y políticos celebrados desde la independencia hasta nuestros días.* II, por el Doctor Aurelio Noboa. Guayaquil: Imprenta Noboa, 1902.

Feller, A. H. and Hudson, Manley (eds.). *A Collection of the Diplomatic and Consular Laws and Regulations of Various Countries.* 2 vols. Washington: Carnegie Endowment for International Peace, 1933.

Guatemala. [Ministerio de Relaciones Exteriores.] *Derecho internacional guatemalteco.* II, III. Guatemala: Tipografía y Encuadernación Nacional, 1894, 1919.

Hackworth, Green Haywood. *Digest of International Law,* II. Washington: U.S. Government Printing Office, 1941.

Hudson, Manley O. (ed.). *International Legislation: A Collection of the Texts of Multipartite International Instruments of General Interest.* IV, VI, VII. Washington: Carnegie Endowment for International Peace, 1931, 1937, 1949.

League of Nations. *Treaty Series: Publication of Treaties and International Engagements Registered with the Secretariat of the League.* Vols. 1–205, September 1920–July 31, 1946.

Martens, Georg Friedrich. *The Law of Nations: Being the Science of National Law, Covenants, Power, etc. Founded Upon the Treaties and Customs of Modern Nations in Europe.* Translated from the French by Wm. Cobbett. 4th ed. London: W. Cobbett, 1829.

Martens, G. Fr. de. *Nouveau recueil général de traités et autres actes relatifs aux rapports de droit international.* Continuation du grand recueil de G. Fr. de Martens. X. 2me série par Hopf. Goettingue: Dieterich, 1885.

— *Nouveau recueil général de traités et autres actes relatifs aux rapports de droit international.* Continuation du grand recueil de G. Fr. de Martens. XIV, XVI–XVIII. 2me série par Stoerb. Goettingue: Dieterich, 1888, 1893.

— *Nouveau recueil général de traités et autres actes relatifs aux rapports de droit international.* Continuation du grand recueil de G. Fr. de Martens. XII–XIV, XVI, XX, XXI, XL. 3e série par Triepel. Leipzig: Weicher, 1924–1926, 1929–1930, 1940.

Mexico. [Secretaría de Relaciones Exteriores.] *Tratados y convenciones vigentes entre los Estados Unidos Mexicanos y otros Paises.* 6 vols. México: Secretaría de Relaciones Exteriores, 1930–1938.

Miller, Hunter (ed.). *Treaties and Other International Acts of the United States of America.* 6 vols. Washington: U. S. Government Printing Office.

Moore, John Basset. *A Digest of International Law as Embodied in Diplomatic Discussions, Treaties, and other International Agreements, International Awards, the Decisions of Municipal Courts and the Writings of Jurists.* II. Washington: U. S. Government Printing Office, 1906.

Pan American Union. *Convention on Diplomatic Asylum Signed at the Tenth Inter-American Conference, Caracas, March 1–28, 1954.* Law and Treaty Series. Washington: Pan American Union, 1954.

Pan American Union. Division of Law and Treaties. Department of International Law. *Documents and Notes on Privileges and Immunities.* Washington: Pan American Union, 1953.

— *Inter-American Treaties and Conventions: Signatures, Ratifications and Deposits with Explanatory Notes.* 2d ed. Washington: Pan American Union, 1957.

— *Status of the Pan American Treaties and Conventions.* Revised to September 1, 1955. Washington: Pan American Union, [1955].

Paraguay. Ministro de Relaciones Exteriores. *Colección de tratados: históricos y vigentes.* I. Asunción: Imprenta Nacional, 1934.

Parra, Francisco J. *Doctrinas de la cancillería venezolana; digesto.* New York: Las Américas Publishing Co., [1952].

— *Estudios de derecho venezolano.* New York: Las Américas Publishing Co., [1955].

Perú. Ministerio de Relaciones Exteriores. *Colección de los tratados, armisticios y otros actos diplomáticos y politicos.* II, IV. Lima: Imprenta del Estado, 1890, 1892.

United Nations. *Treaty Series: Treaties and International Agreements Registered or Filed and Recorded with the Secretariat of the United Nations.* Vols. 1–197. December, 1946–1954.

U. S. Department of State. *Treaties and Other International Acts Series 2045.* Washington: U. S. Government Printing Office, 1950.

U. S. Department of State. Treaty Division. *Treaties in Force: A List of Treaties and Other International Acts of the United States in Force on December 31, 1941.* Washington: U. S. Government Printing Office, 1944.

U. S. Senate. *Treaties, Conventions, International Acts, Protocols, and Agreements between the United States of America and Other Powers: 1923–1927.* IV. Washhington: U. S. Government Printing Office, 1938.

Uribe, Antonio José. *Anales diplomáticos y consulares de Colombia.* 6 vols. Edición oficial. Bogotá: Imprenta Nacional, 1914, 1920

Wheaton, Henry. *Elements of International Law.* 8th ed. Edited, with notes, by Richard Henry Dana, Jr. Boston: Little, Brown and Co., 1866.

DOCUMENTS AND OFFICIAL PUBLICATIONS

American Institute of International Law. "Diplomatic Agents" and "Consuls," *American Journal of International Law,* XX, Special Number (October, 1926), pp. 350–357. (Projects of Conventions, Numbers 22 and 23, Prepared at the Request of the Governing Board of the Pan American Union for Consideration of the International Commission of Jurists, and submitted by the American Institute of International Law to the Governing Board of the Pan American Union, March 2, 1925.)

Annals of the Organization of American States, (1949), pp. 216–217; III (1951), pp. 118–119; IV (1952), pp. 19, 42.

Argentine Republic. Ministerio de Relaciones Exteriores. *Memoria de relaciones exteriores y culto presentado al honorable Congreso Nacional correspondiente al año 1911–1912.* Buenos Aires: Talleres Gráficos de Selin Suárez, 1912.

— *Memoria presentada al honorable Congreso Nacional correspondiente al período 1936–1937.* I. Buenos Aires: Talleres Gráficos, J. Rosseli y Cía., 1938.

— *Memoria presentado al honorable Congreso Nacional correspondiente al período 1937–1938.* I. Buenos Aires: Talleres S. A., Casa Jacobo Peuser, 1938.

Argentine Republic. Ministry of Foreign Affairs and Worship. *Project of Convention on the Right of Asylum.* Buenos Aires, 1937.

Bolivia. Ministerio de Relaciones Exteriores. *Boletín del Ministerio de Relaciones Exteriores.* III abril-diciembre, 1930.)

— *Boletín del Ministerio de Relaciones Exteriores.* (Julio-diciembre, 1946.)

Brazil. Ministério das Relações Exteriores. *Indice analytico e systemático dos relatórios do Ministério das Relações Exteriores do ano de 1831 a 1951,* por Fernando Saboia de Madeiros. 2 vols. Rio de Janeiro, Imprensa Nacional, 1938.

— *Precedentes diplomáticos de 1889 a 1932,* por Fernando Saboia de Medeiros. Rio de Janeiro: Imprensa Nacional, 1940.

— *Relatório apresentado ao Ministro de Estado das Relações Exteriores pelo Presidente do delegação do Brasil a 6ª Conferencia Internacional Americana, realizada em Havana, em 1928.* Rio de Janeiro: Imprensa Nacional, 1929.

— *Relatório apresentado ao Chefe do Governo Provisório da República dos Estados Unidos do Brasil pelo Ministro de Estado das Relações Exteriores, ano de 1930.* I, II. Rio de Janeiro: Imprensa Nacional, 1934.

— *Relatório apresentado ao Dr. Getulio Vargas, Presidente da Republica do Brasil pelo Dr. Afranio de Mello Franco, Ministro de Estado das Relações Exteriores, ano de 1933.* III. Rio de Janeiro: Imprensa Nacional, 1939.

— *Relatório apresentado ao Chefe do Governo Provisório da República dos Estados Unidos do Brasil pelo Ministro de Estado das Relações Exteriores, ano de 1933.* II, pt. 1. Rio de Janeiro: Imprensa Nacional, 1937.

— *Relatório, ano de 1938.* I. Rio de Janeiro: Imprensa Nacional, 1942.

Brazil. Ministry of State for Foreign Affairs. *International Commission of American Jurists, 1927 Meeting.* I, II, IV. English Edition. Rio de Janeiro: Imprensa Nacional, 1929.

[Carnegie Endowment for International Peace, Division of International Law.] *Conferencias internacionales americanas: 1889–1936.* Washington: Dotación Carnegie para la Paz Internacional, 1938.

Chile. Ministerio de Relaciones Exteriores. *Estados Unidos i Chile.* Notas cambiadas entre la legación de los Estados Unidos de Norte-América i el Ministerio de Relaciones Exteriores de Chile, a propósito de las cuestiones suscitadas entre ambos paises. Santiago de Chile: Imprenta Ercilla, 1891.

— *Jurisprudencia de la cancillería chilena hasta 1865, año de la muerte de Don Andrés Bello,* por Alberto Cruchaga Ossa. Santiago de Chile: Imprenta Chile, 1935.

Chile. Ministerio de Relaciones Exteriores y Comercio. *Memoria correspondiente al año 1930.* Santiago de Chile: Imprenta Chile, 1931.

— *Memoria de relaciones exteriores y comercio correspondiente al año 1934.* Santiage de Chile: Imprenta Chile, 1936.

— *Memoria del Ministerio de Relaciones Exteriores y Comercio correspondiente al año 1936.* Santiago de Chile: Imprenta Chile, 1937.

— *Memoria del Ministerio de Relaciones Exteriores y Comercio correspondiente al año 1937.* Santiago de Chile: Imprenta Chile, 1938.

— *Memoria del Ministerio de Relaciones Exteriores y Comercio correspondiente al año 1938.* Santiago de Chile: Imprenta Chile, 1941.

— *Memoria correspondiente al año 1940.* Santiago de Chile: Imprenta Chile, 1943.

— *Memoria del Ministerio de Relaciones Exteriores correspondiente al año 1944.* Santiago de Chile: Imprenta Chile, 1947.

— *Memoria del Ministerio de Relaciones Exteriores correspondiente al año 1946.* Santiago de Chile: Imprenta Chile, 1949.

Colombia. Ministerio de Relaciones Exteriores. *Circular de la Secretaría de Relaciones Exteriores de Colombia al cuerpo diplomático en Bogotá.* Bogotá: Imprenta de "La Luz," 1885.

— *El derecho de asilo ante la Corte Internacional de Justicia.* Suplemento a "Noticias de Colombia." Bogotá Imprenta Nacional, 1951.

— *Historia de la Cancillería de San Carlos*. I. Bogotá Imprenta del Estado Mayor General, 1942.

— *Informe que el Ministro de Relaciones Exteriores de la República de Colombia dirige al Congreso Constitucional de 1888*. Bogotá: Cas Editorial de J. J. Pérez, 1888.

— *Informe del Ministerio de Relaciones Exteriores al Congreso de 1929*. Bogotá: Imprenta Nacional, 1929.

— *Memoria presentada al Congreso Nacional, 1940*. Bogotá: Imprenta Nacional, 1940.

— *Noticias de Colombia*. Boletín semenal. 8 junio, 1951; 18 abril, 1952; 25 julio, 1952; 3 octubre, 1952.

— *La opinión americana y el derecho de asilo*. Suplemento a "Noticias de Colombia." Bogotá: Imprenta Nacional, 1951.

Cuba. Secretario de Estado. *Documentos diplomáticos relativos a la guerra civil de España*. La Habana [imprenta "El Siglo XX,"]1939.

"Documentos importantes: Notas cambiadas entre el Ministro de Relaciones Exteriores del Perú y la embajada de Cuba, referentes al asilo de Fernando de Vivero y Pedro Muñiz," *Revista peruana de derecho internacional*, IX (1949), pp. 148–185.

"Documentos importantes: Notas cambiadas entre el Ministro de Relaciones Exteriores del Perú y el Embajador de Colombia en Lima, referentes al asilo de Victor Raúl Haya de la Torre," *Revista peruana de derecho internacional*, IX (1949), pp. 56–110.

Dominican Republic. Archivo General de la Nación. *Correspondencia del consul de Francia en Santo Domingo*. Ciudad Trujillo: Editoria, 1944.

Dominican Republic. Secretaría de Justicia y Trabajo. Departamento de Justicia. *Revista jurídica dominicana*. Año XVII (julio-diciembre, 1955).

— *Gaceta oficial*. Año LXXV (27 septiembre, 1954).

Great Britain. 11 *Parliamentary Debates*. CXCIII (1908).

Harvard Law School. *Research in International Law*. "Diplomatic Privileges and Immunities," *American Journal of International law*, Supplement, XXVI, (1932.)

Honduras. [Ministerio de Relaciones Exteriores.] *Informe general de la delegación de Honduras a la Séptima Conferencia Internacional Americana de Montevideo, diciembre de 1933*. Tegucigalpa: Talleres Tipográficas Nacionales [1944].

Institute of International Law. "Asylum in Public International Law (Excluding Neutral Asylum)," *American Journal of International Law*, Supplement, XLV (1951), 15–23. (Resolutions Adopted at its Bath Session, September, 1950: Translation by Sir Arnold D. McNair.)

Inter-American Council of Jurists. Second Meeting. *Actas y Documentos*. II. Washington: Pan American Union, 1953.

— *Regime dos asilados, exilados e refugiados políticos: parecer y projectos de convenção preparados pela Comissão Juridica Interamericano de Jurisconsultos em sua 2. reunião, Buenos Aires Argentina, 1953*. Washington: Pan American Union, 1952.

— *Report of the Executive Secretary of the Inter-American Council of Jurists: Buenos Aires, Argentina, 20 April–9 May, 1953*. Washington: Pan American Union, 1953.

Inter-American Juridical Yearbook, 1952–1954. Washington: Pan American Union, 1955.

International Conferences of American States. *Bibliografía de las Conferencias Americanas*. Prepared by the Columbus Memorial Library of the Pan American Union. Bibliographic Series No. 41. Washington, 1954.

International Conference of American States. Sixth. *Diario de la VI Conferencia Internacional Americana*. Habana, 1928.
— *Final Act. Motions, Agreements, Resolutions and Conventions*. Habana: Imprenta de Rambla Boza y Cía., 1928.
— *Report of the Delegates of the United States of America to the Sixth International Conference of American States*. Washington: U. S. Government Printing Office, 1928.
— *Sixth International Conference of American States, 1928: Minutes and Reports of Committees*. Binder's Title. Havana, 1928.
International Conference of American States. Seventh. *Minutes and Antecedents with General Index*. Montevideo, 1933.
— *Projects on Certain Topics of the Program Submitted by the Executive Committee of the American Institute of International Law, Pursuant to a Resolution of the Governing Board of the Pan American Union*. No. 4. Washington Pan American Union, 1933.
International Conference of American States. Ninth. *Actas y documentos*. III, IV, VI, VII. Bogotá: Ministerio de Relaciones Exteriores de Colombia, 1953.
— *Final Act of the Ninth International Conference of American States*. Washington: Pan American Union, 1948.
International Conference of American States. Tenth. *Colección Cronológica de documentos de la Décima Conferencia Inter-americana*. Caracas, 1954.
— *Final Act*. Washington: Pan American Union, 1954.
— *Report of the Delegation of the United States of America to the Tenth Inter-American Conference*. Washington: U. S. Government Printing Office, 1955.
— *Report of the Pan American Union on the Conference*. Conference and Organization Series No. 36. Washington: Pan American Union, 1955.
League of Nations. Assembly. *Official Records of the Eighteenth Ordinary Session of the Assembly*. Plenary Meetings. Geneva, 1937.
League of Nations. Committee of Experts for the Progressive Codification of International Law. *Reports of the Council of the League of Nations on the Questions which Appear Ripe for International Regulation* (C. 196. M. 70. 1927. V.). Geneva, 1927.
League of Nations. Council. *Official Journal*. Minutes of the Ninety-fifth (Extraordinary) Session of the Council. Geneva, 1937.
Manning, William R., ed. *Diplomatic Correspondence of the United States: Inter-American Affairs, 1831-1860*. 12 vols. Washington: Carnegie Endowment for International Peace, 1932-1939.
Matta, M. A. *Cuestiones recientes con la legación i el gobierno de los Estados Unidos de Norte-America*. Santiago de Chile: Imprenta Cervantes, 1892.
Mexico. Secretaría de Relaciones Exteriores. *Memoria de la Secretaría de Relaciones Exteriores de agosto de 1927 a julio de 1928, presentado al H. Congreso de la union por Gevaro Estrada, Subsecretario de Relaciones Exteriores Encargado del Despacho*. Imprenta de la Secretaría de Relaciones Exteriores, 1928.
— *Memoria general y actuación de la delegación de México: Séptima Conferencia Internacional Americana*. Apendice A. México, D. F.: Imprenta de la Secretaría de Relaciones Exteriores, 1934.
— *La participación de México en la Sexta Conferencia Internacional Americana*. Informe general de la delegación de Mexico. México: Imprenta de la Secretariá de Relaciones Exteriores, 1928.
Organization of American States. Council. *Decisions Taken at Meetings of the Council of the Organization of American States*. IV. Washington: Pan American Union, 1952.
[Organization of American States. Council.] *Regulations of the Council of the*

Organization of American States. Approved by the Council of the Organization of American States at the Special Meeting of July 16, 1952. Washington: Pan American Union, 1953.

Paraguay. Ministerio de Relaciones Exteriores y Culto. *El Paraguay en la VII Conferencìa Internacional Americana en Montevideo.* Asunción: Imprenta Nacional, 1934.

Perú. *El Peruano.* Diario oficial. 7 diciembre, 1950.

Perú. Ministerio de Relaciones Exteriores. *Boletín del Ministerio de Relaciones Exteriores.* Año XXXII (1935).

— *Congresos y conferencias internacionales en que ha tomado parte el Perú,* coleccionados sus trabajos por Ricardo Aranda. II, V. Lima: Oficina tipográfica de "La Opinión Nacional," 1910; Imprenta Americana, 1920.

— *Correspondencia diplomática relativa a la cuestión sobre asilo, publicado por orden de S. E. el Jefe Supremo Provisorio para ser presentada al Congreso Constituyente.* Lima: Imprenta del Estado por J. Enrique del Campo, 1867.

— *Boletín del Ministerio de Relaciones Exteriores.* Año XXXIV (2º. trimestre de 1937).

— *Boletín del Ministerio de Relaciones Exteriores.* Año XXXIV (3er. trimestre de 1937).

— *Boletín del Ministerio de Relaciones Exteriores.* Año XXXIV (4º. trimestre de 1937).

— *Boletín del Ministerio de Relaciones Exteriores.* Año XXXV (1 trimestre de 1938).

— *Boletín del Ministerio de Relaciones Exteriores.* Año XXXVI (2º. trimestre de 1939).

— *Boletín del Ministerio de Relaciones Exteriores.* Año XXXVI (3er. trimestre de 1939).

— *Boletín del Ministerio de Relaciones Exteriores.* Año XXXVI (4º. trimestre de 1939).

— *Boletín del Ministerio de Relaciones Exteriores.* Año XXXVII (3er. trimestre de 1940).

— *Memoria del Ministerio de Relaciones Exteriores, 1914.* Lima: Imprenta Americana, 1914.

— *Memoria del Ministerio de Relaciones Exteriores, Don Alberto Ulloa, 13 de abril a 22 octubre de 1936.* Lima Imprenta Torres Aguirre, 1938.

— *Memoria del Ministerio de Relaciones Exteriores, Don Carlos Concha, 20 de noviembre de 1937–20 de abril de 1939.* Lima: Imprenta Torres Aguirre, 1939.

— *Memoria del Ministerio de Relaciones Exteriores, Don Enrique Goytisolo B., 20 de abril a 8 de diciembre de 1939.* Lima: Imprenta Torres Aguirre, 1940.

— *Proceso sobre asilo entre el Perú y Colombia ante la Corte Internacional de Justicia: documentación pertinente al desarrollo del juicio sentencia del 20 de noviembre de 1950.* Lima: 1951.

— *Proceso sobre asilo entre el Perú y Colombia ante la Corte Internacional de Justicia.* Segunda parte (Juicio relativo a la ejecución de la sentencia del 20 de noviembre de 1950: sentencia del 13 de junio de 1951). Lima: 1952.

El Salvador. Ministerio de Relaciones Exteriores. *Informe de la delegación de El Salvador a la VII Conferencia Panamericana celebrada en Montevideo, Uruguay, del 3 al 26 de diciembre, 1933.* San Salvador: Imprenta Nacional [1934].

Scott, James Brown. *The International Conference of American States: 1889–1928.* New York: Oxford University Press, 1931.

U. S. *Federal Register.* XI (1946).

— *Federal Register.* XIII (1948).

U. S. Department of State. *Instructions to the Diplomatic Officers of the United States.* Washington: U. S. Department of State, 1897.

— *Papers Relating to Foreign Affairs, Accompanying the Annual Message of the President.* Diplomatic Correspondence. Washington: U. S. Government Printing Office, 1861–1869.

— *Papers Relating to the Foreign Relations of the United States.* Washington: U. S. Government Printing Office, 1870–.

— *Regulations of the Consular Service of the United States.* Washington: U. S. Government Printing Office, 1896.

Venezuela. Ministerio de Relaciones Exteriores. *Boletín del Ministerio de Relaciones Exteriores de los Estados Unidos de Venezuela.* Año IV (abril-julio 1928).

— *Cuestión promovida a Venezuela por los agentes de Francia y de la Gran Bretaña.* Caracas: Imprenta de J. M. Soriano, 1858.

— *Libro Amarillo de los Estados Unidos de Venezuela, presentado al Congreso Nacional en sus sesiones de 1929 por el Ministro de Relaciones Exteriores.* Caracas: Tipografía Americana, 1929.

— *Libro Amarillo de los Estados Unidos de Venezuela, presentado al Congreso Nacional en sus sesiones ordinarias de 1939 por el Ministro de Relaciones Exteriores.* I. Caracas: Tipografía Americana, 1939.

— *Libro Amarillo de los Estados Unidos de Venezuela, presentado al Congreso Nacional en sus sesiones ordinarias de 1940 por el Ministro de Relaciones Exteriores.* I. Caracas: Tipografía Americana, 1940.

— *Libro Amarillo de los Estados Unidos de Venezuela que presenta a la Asemblea Nacional Constituyente el titular del Ministerio de Relaciones Exteriores, 1947.* Caracas: Tipografía Americana, 1947.

— *Tratados públicos y acuerdos internacionales de Venezuela (incluyéndose los de Antigua Colombia), 1820–1900.* I, II. Caracas: Tipografía Americana, 1924.

INDEX

Accioly, H., 37, 77
Alessandri, Don A., 48–49
Alvarez, A., 36, 39
American Declaration of Rights and Duties of Man endorsed, 91; results of, 93; significance of, 93–94
American Institute of International Law, 150
American International Law, 28–37, 51, 84, 90–91, 216
Ancillary Offense, 147
Antokoletz, Daniel, 37–38
Argentina
  as state of refuge, 169; invocation of Treaty of Montevideo (1889), 174–176
Asylum
  and degree of consensus in practice, 125; and common crimes, 8–9, 20–23, 145–147; and consulates granting asylum, 125; and International Law, 15–16, 21, 30, 35, 108, 122–124; and multilateral agreements, 52, 90–91; and political offenses, 8–9, 145–147
  definitions:
    Definitive asylum, 8
    Diplomatic asylum, 5, 218
    Temporary asylum, 8
    Territorial asylum, 5
  grounds for granting diplomatic asylum convention and custom, 70, 74, 92; expediency, 61, 66, 95; good will, 71; humanitarian reasons, 68, 74–75; 77–82, 108, 123–124, 215; immunity, 7, 22–23, 139; indifference, 66; right of asylum, 77, 80, 98, 125; toleration, 66, 74, 77, 102–105, 123–124
  legal status of, 3, 14–15, 35, 52–67, 71, 75–76, 95–96, 108, 125
  regional patterns of existence, 21–22, 33, 35
  religious asylum

decline of in Latin America, 27–28
  in Chile, 26
  in Guatemala, 25
  in early period of development, 24
  practice in Latin America, 27–28, 214
  see also entries for specific countries
  Soviet Union's viewpoint on, 7

Balaguer, 218
Balmaceda, 119
Baron del Asilo, 14
Betancourt, Rómulo, 69, 80–81, 208, 220
Bolivia
  and right of asylum, 30, 33, 90–91; definition of political offense, 179–181; invocation of treaty obligation, 206–208
Brazil
  and right of asylum, 30, 77; and Havana Convention, 58–59; and Sixth International Conference of American States, 77
Brierly report on extradition, 146
Briggs, H. W., 6

Canal, Boisrand, 71, 73, 115, 165
Caracas Convention, 55, 154–157
  obligations, 63–65
  results of, 63–65
  state of "urgency", 147, 156
Caicedo Castilla, M., 90
Chile
  and right of asylum, 5–6, 30, 78–80, 134–135; as territorial state, 48–49, 119; asylum in Spain, 60, 80; qualification of offense during Spanish Civil War, 190, 199–202; religious asylum in, 26
Cleveland, Grover, 120
Colombia
  and diplomatic asylum, 89; and asylum during Spanish Civil War, 90; consu-